Why Men Don't Iron

Why Men Don't Iron

The Real Science of Gender Studies

ANNE AND BILL MOIR

HarperCollins*Publishers*

HarperCollins*Publishers*
77–85 Fulham Palace Road,
Hammersmith, London W6 8JB

Published by HarperCollins*Publishers* 1998

1 3 5 7 9 8 6 4 2

A catalogue record for this book
is available from the British Library

ISBN 0 00 257035-1 (tpb)
ISBN 0 00 257048-3 (hb)

Set in Meridien

Printed in England by Clays Ltd, St Ives plc

To Bernard Cornwell

Contents

Acknowledgements

The basis of this book is the research work carried out by scientists all over the world. There are now thousands of studies that illustrate the many biologically based sex or gender differences. It is these many scientists that we have most to thank, for without their painstaking and thorough research we would still be in the dark as to why men can't be like women. A detailed list of references appears at the back of the book. One scientist deserves our special thanks: Katherine Hoyenga, formerly Professor of Psychology at Western Illinois University and author, along with her husband Kermit, of the seminal scientific books on sex differences. She went through our manuscript and corrected and advised on our interpretation of the science. One research organization, Mintel, was very generous in providing survey data. MEDLINE's database was an invaluable tool, ensuring a comprehensive coverage of the research.

The title of the book was the inspiration of Sara Ramsden of Channel Four, who also commissioned a three-part televison series based on some of the areas covered here.

Thanks to Trish Rushen, who runs the local library for the village of Aldbourne, Wiltshire, and who efficiently supplied many hundreds of requests for academic papers and books that formed the backbone of our research. Also in the same village, our friends who listened to the ideas, discussed and argued, inadvertently adding their own contributions. Also to friends from afar like Judy Wiggins, who travels in frequently and added much. To Bill's mother, Bunny Moir, who also came often and made work possible for both of us.

Special thanks go to our GP, Ros Symon, and the team of district nurses at the Ramsbury Surgery. Also to Philip Burgess, David Cole and the staff of Princess Margaret Hospital, Swindon. This book would not have been completed without their medical care for Bill.

To Susan Watt, Publishing Director of HarperCollins, special thanks too. She is just the best editor any author could hope to have and we have been privileged to receive her guidance.

In the end, however, the book is ours, and only we can be held responsible for any flaws it may have.

Introduction

This is a book about men.

About what makes them different. So inevitably it is a book about women too.

A small box sits on Anne's desk. The top reads: 'All that men know about women'. Open it and there is nothing inside. Funny? Sad? Humbling? An innocent admission that men have tried to follow women's pattern of thought and failed? Or is it an insult? The box could imply that a man is incapable of understanding a woman because her complexities are beyond his simplicities. That is to define him in her terms. Or perhaps it reflects the traditional male view that she is beyond understanding because she is silly – irrational? Which is to define her in relation to himself. We tend to see in the other sex a lesser version of our own. Yet the manner in which we describe another's mind shows the limits of our own.

'Why keep the box?' asks Bill.
'To turn it over,' says Anne. 'To puzzle out what it means.'
'Isn't it insulting?'
'Didn't you say that we often hide behind clichés?'
'Did I?'
'When you gave me the box.'

It is a cliché that men cannot fathom women. But what of her image of him?

Roseanne Barr, the weighty sitcom actress, summed up her view on men in the television programme *Hollywood Men: Boys Will Be Boys*: 'The real Hollywood man,' she said, 'is a terrified little boy and wants his mommy.'[1] Hers is the classic female caricature of the male. 'Yes they can have control, but only in two areas,' says Barr. 'Starting barbecues is one; the other is walking around in packs and peeing on things.'[2] Such expertise was rewarded when Barr was appointed editorial adviser to a special issue of the *New Yorker* devoted to the subject of women.

> Men are nothing but overgrown children, really.
> They need to be told what to do.
> The only difference between men and boys is the price of their toys.
> Boys will be boys: they have to watch football.
> Wars are little boys fighting.[3]

In Alison MacLeod's postmodern novel *The Changeling*,[4] the big themes of boys' history – war, political intrigue and empires – are represented as comic and trivial.

It is common for women to describe men as 'boys'. To her way of thinking he never grows up, while she does. This attitude is as matronizing as his is patronizing. He puts her down by claiming not to understand her, that she is indeed beyond understanding, and she keeps her self-respect by claiming the opposite. Men and women are seldom more equal than in their lack of understanding of one another. Why else would women enjoin men to 'get in touch with their feminine side'? But where does he find it? How does he look for it? Does it even exist? Perhaps, as Gertrude Stein said of Oakland, California, 'there is no there there'. To ask men to improve themselves by relating to their feminine side is to ask them to become like women, but men are distinct: they are possessed of the differences that make for a real difference.

So why, some women ask, must his differences make him so brutally dominant? For too long, she feels, he has forced her into his social frame, into the role of *the wife* or *the little woman*, excluding her from his privileged world. As a result women feel anger and resentment, which are not unjustified. There is a need to strike a better balance between the traditional male view that he must manage her world (protect her; give her what he wants) and the hardline feminist view that she should gain power over his world (to protect both her and him from himself).

One way out of the conflict between his view of her and hers of him is to claim that there is essentially no difference between men and women. Anything he can do, she can do. Underpinning that conviction is the idea that, when we look beyond the obvious physical attributes, men's and women's brains are the same. But they are not. Science has upset the egalitarian applecart by conclusively showing that the sexes are distinct in how they act and think.

Some people will argue against the science, while others will accept that while there are differences between the sexes, those differences are socially engendered (they even claim that the brain differences are socially engendered) – and what society can construct, society can also destroy. In other words, by a conscious act of will, we can create the egalitarian ideal. This is the message of most university-based 'Gender Studies'.

Gender refers to sex differences, both social and biological, but most who teach gender studies today choose to define 'gender' to mean only those differences that are the results of cultural pressures. 'Gender is constructed and social,' (neither more nor less) says a contributor to *Feminist Approaches to Science*. It is 'the politics of the socialisation of sex'.[5] Note the finality of the claim. Of course biological differences can be socially created; anything that socialization does to behaviour it achieves by affecting the brain. But in the usual course on gender studies, the differences between men and women are ascribed not to biology but to society, and thus an academic course on gender can exclude any reference to the hard science that demonstrates substantial biological differences between the sexes; differences that are not, and cannot be, culturally engendered. 'Gender studies' is too often an academic course on sex differences that excludes the real study of sex differences – which must include biology.

It is insulting to the reader to qualify everything to death. This is a book about the biological science of gender differences, and science is about the probable. There is no need to keep saying this. So when we write 'Science finds such and such' it plainly means that this is the best bet: no more, no less. Similarly, a word like 'men' is used as a general term for most men – men in general. In the use of such a general term there will plainly be exceptions. Thus, when we write: 'Men run 8% faster than women', we leave it to the fourth-rate mind to point out that some women run faster then most men.

Our aim is to explain, not to campaign.

Today's man is under pressure to change. He is told to get in touch with his feelings, to be more considerate, to be more communicative and open to his emotions. Yet this new, softer, more caring male, just like the old-fashioned patriarchal man, is a one-dimensional caricature of what it is to be masculine. It is a form of sexism, a masculine stereotype as extreme and as crudely reductionist as its predecessor, the traditional male.

The traditional male is a dominating bully, a misogynist who stamps his views on women. He believes the female is merely a pale and inferior copy of himself, an adumbration of the superior male. This male sets the standard: he is normal, she is deficient. He sees only one side, his.

Any man who matches this stereotype is indefensible, for he reduces women to an inferior status by denying her essential and valuable feminine qualities. But equally, those with a gender agenda deny the essential male qualities.

The new, caring male has recognized his shortcomings and corrected them. He sees that the old sex boundaries had nothing to do with biology, but were the results of social pressures (perhaps he was given toy guns instead of dolls). This is the male who has got in touch with his 'female side', and the defining quality of his masculinity has become the denial of his masculinity. She is the new standard, and he can only aspire to be more like her.

The reader may find one or both of these views a farrago of nonsense. But both viewpoints, if only because they are widespread, must be taken seriously. Each highlights a set of social aspirations and both lead to false expectations. Past and present views of the male – traditional and postmodern – are equally poor measures of the masculine.

The traditional male is well known; the postmodern version is less so (at least outside the academic world). The 'new' man is predicated on the understanding that all significant differences in gender are socially conditioned, constructed or learned. This is crucial. A man is not born a man, but is made into one by the assumptions of the culture in which he grows up. Take away the assumptions and he would grow up – what? A woman? There is an ambivalence here, but we need to recognize that there is a ritual obeisance in postmodern studies to all things complex and ambivalent. Postmodernism is a rejection of hitherto accepted certainties. Uncertainties are therefore good. The ambiguous is good, the clear-cut is bad. Seeing things as good or bad is also bad; right or wrong is wrong, and clarity is out.

When ambiguity becomes the answer then the clear distinctions between male and female disappear. Differences are there to be *ironed* out. Conventional gender boundaries are there to be erased. The war between the sexes can be ended by the realization that there are no sexes ('we are all the same'). This belief rests on the perception that gender differences are a social construct (on the same grounds, this perception might appear no more than a social construct of the academy). The dispersal of our identities offers the hope of social and sexual reconciliation and thus an end to confrontation.

'Do the postmodern academics really believe all that?' asks Anne.

'Worse,' says Bill.

Postmodernists assert that all knowledge is constructed. Therefore there is no scientific truth or facts; only several versions of 'facts', constructed out of every individual's cultural conditions. No one person's version of the 'facts' can take precedence over any other's. However, they often go on to say that, in the interests of 'diversity', the version of the 'facts' held by minority groups is to be given precedence. Somehow, postmodern women consider themselves a minority group.

'No scientific truths –?' asks Anne.
'Maybe they give equal weight to the theory that the earth is
    flat,' suggests Bill.

In an article entitled 'How Feminism is Now Alienating Women from Science', Noretta Koertge says: 'Feminists add a new twist to this old litany of repudiations of analytical reasoning by claiming that the standard norms and methods of scientific inquiring are sexist because they are incompatible with women's ways of knowing.'[6] These 'subjectivist' women see the methods of logic, analysis and abstraction as 'alien territory belonging to men' and they 'value intuition as a safer and more fruitful approach to truth'.

Paul Gross and Norman Levitt note in an abstract of their book *Higher Superstition* that: 'if they [the recruits to the cause of feminist science] attempt to hold fast to the most emphatic tenets of feminist dogma – for instance, the stylish assertion that "women" can't be "scientists" under the present order, because society constructs these as mutually exclusive categories, and therefore that scientific practice must be reconstituted along radical-feminist lines before women can participate – they will quickly find themselves effectively excluded from serious scientific work.'[7]

Listen to Rosi Braidotti, Professor of Women's Studies at the University of Utrecht, describe her postmodern version of science:

It is because of this dynamic, life-giving element that I have chosen the term *nomadic* to describe this feminist style. Nomadic subjects are capable of freeing the activity of thinking from the hold of phallocentric dogmatism, returning thought to its freedom, its liveliness, its beauty. There is a strong aesthetic dimension in the quest for alternative nomadic figurations and feminist theory such as I practice that is informed by this joyful nomadic force … I think it is extremely important for feminists to break away from the patterns of masculine identification that high theory demands, to step out of the paralyzing structures of an exclusive [read, 'scientific'] academic style.[8]

The shift is from the modern to the postmodern world: to a world without graven rules or certitudes (except for the law against laws). The overriding cliché is that there is as much variance within a sex as exists between the sexes. The postmodern, deconstructed intellectual cannot say simply, 'Women are like this' or 'Men are like that', because such statements acknowledge a biological difference; there can be no such difference if sexual identities are constructed and, consequently, capable of being deconstructed. This view, which became popular in the 1980s, was labelled 'deconstructive feminism'. 'This form of academic feminist thinking,' wrote Lynne Segal, a feminist theoretician, 'was increasingly sceptical of *any* generalisations about "women" or women's "distinctive perspective". Some feminist theoreticians were now questioning all types of fixed categories, identities and relationships, stressing what they saw as the complex, shifting and plural nature of the social meanings.'[9]

Plainly the traditional male, the deeply unreconstructed brute himself, is a sad anachronism in this shifting, boundary-free world, and so the attempt is being made to change him. This can only be done, of course, if we accept that masculinity is a social, cultural, political or historical construct in the first place. At Hobart College in New York State there is a men's study programme, Course 245: Men and Masculinity, and the course summary offers the underlying assumption that 'masculinity is problematic – for men and for women – but also socially conditioned and historically variable, and therefore subject to change.'[10] 'Male and female created he them', but the academy is at hand to undo the damage. The academy holds to a common subtheme that the world was first *constructed* by men and the female's role in the world was also made by him; that being the case, women can now return the compliment by reconstructing the world and his role. Call it revenge, if you like, but there is a conscious attempt to undermine masculine identity.

'In the social sciences,' says Bill, 'there is too often a presumption against things that are not socially conctructed.'

'But,' says Anne, 'there are other, harder sciences that show real sex differences.'

'Hmm …' says Bill. 'Then in exploring the new science of gender differences we also explore the limits of social theory and its capacity to transform the sexes.'

If (and it is a big IF) gender is socially conditioned, then it must be true that it can be socially unconditioned and that sexual roles can be unlearned. In part this is true, inasmuch as the male who stamps his views on women can learn to recognize the existence of another mind (and vice versa). What then of the view that the sexes are alike, but the male can never be wholly deconstructed because he lacks the female experience? He cannot experience the menses, birthing or lactation. Trivialities, says the feminist. Failure to experience such physical processes does not affect the male's ability to embrace and adopt feminine virtues: peace, co-operation, holistic dreams. The time when the lion will lie down with the lamb or, even better, the lioness. How much the world would be improved if only they, men, were more like women.

When the communicators of our society (the academy and the media) fail to get a grip on a subject – fail, that is, to understand what they are supposed to be explaining – the failure is often depicted as a deeper form of understanding. It is presented as a kind of wry humility, summed up by the adage 'the more we know the less we know'. Lack of understanding is taken as a virtue instead of a failing. It seems that one cannot be sure about anything except the advantages of not knowing. It is the postmodern understanding; and, perhaps, the foxhole for the spooked and lost in every generation.

Postmodernists have no answers (answers are unambiguous, and unambiguity is bad), and that is the problem. They confront certainty with the question, 'How can you be so sure?' It is a useful logic for unsettling coherence (and is used not only by postmodern academics but also by neo-Nazis in their rejection of the existence of the Holocaust). It also advances all the frontiers of ignorance.

This postmodern 'understanding' rides in tandem with a common female approach to the world in general, an approach that is non-confrontational, non-judgemental, unaligned and multi-cultural. The past is seen as having been defined by male certainties, summed up in the dismissive acronym DWEM, which defines and rejects the philosophy, art, literature and cultural assumptions bequeathed to us by Dead White European Males. The old canon – that body of knowledge which was thought essential to an understanding of our culture – has been dismissed by many parts of the academy. To claim that Shakespeare is a greater writer than, say, some previously unknown woman is to be elitist. Thus we witness the feminization of the academy.

What is fixed is decreed authoritarian. What is authoritarian is male. What is male is bad.

We move from a time of sharply drawn lines to a time where the line drawn is against the drawing of lines. Fifty years ago a man was expected to play the dominant role; expected, if successful, to provide for his wife and children. Today the great expectation is of a sexual parity at home and at work, in the ways we relax and in the games we play, in our learning and in our parenting. Lines of demarcation, present for millennia, are being blurred.

The traditional male draws lines too tight, with himself as the norm. Postmodernism denies the existence of any lines, yet to deny the existence of the major sexual differences (always done, of course, in the name of toleration) is to play the most dangerous gender game. Those who believe that our differences are all culturally caused wish to eradicate those differences. Their burning ideology is to eliminate the distinct in society. There are historical antecedents, rooted in the conviction that we are all one; if you disagreed you were placed beyond the pale, and beyond the pale lay the cleansing fire with its waiting stake.

'Failing to draw the line,' says Anne, 'they give equal voice to the absurd.'
'Which is to say themselves,' says Bill.

The new orthodoxy claims that there is no distinctive male mind – nor, indeed, a distinctive female mind. The old demarcation between *him* and *her* has been replaced with a muddling whirl of complex and shifting social assumptions.[11] A reverence for equity in all things has dulled the critical faculties. 'You can't generalize about people.' 'You mustn't stereotype people.' 'All generalizations are misleading [except, of course, this one].' 'We are all different' [a safely vacuous remark to which is often added] 'but not *that* different' – which is to collapse meaning. Such claims are good ways to paper over cracks; but they hardly lead to understanding.

Return, for a moment, to the postmodern ideal of a man. He rejects the old traditional male assumptions, preferring to recognize the existence within himself of female virtues: co-operation, tolerance, non-judgementalism and an instinctive acceptance of equality (meaning sameness). O brave new world, that has such creatures in it. Get rid of the artificial lines and how the barriers will fall! There will be no more 'glass ceiling' (the barrier traditional males erect against female success), no more 'homophobia' (the barrier which encourages heterosexual males to treat gays as lesser beings). The lion, lioness and lamb are all one.

But suppose this postmodern ideal is wrong. Not morally wrong, but scientifically wrong. Suppose, perish the thought, that there *are* lines, not drawn by society but etched by blind, uncontrollable nature. Lines as ineradicable as the leopard's spots. Lines drawn by biological forces.

That is the subject of this book, which attempts to explain the findings of current scientific research into gender differences. The assumption of the book is not that 'we are all the same', but rather that we are distinctly different. That to be a man is not to be an inferior version of a woman, nor a better version, but to be what nature intended. This is not to say that a man (or woman) cannot change, but it is to claim that there are constant masculine values. The postmodernists want men to change, to become, indeed, more like women; when men constantly fail to live up to their expectations it should be allowed that the expectations themselves might be false, and here science can be of assistance.

Science can help because it sets certain limits to the probable. Like an accurate record of the past (postmodernists, of course, claim that no such thing is possible), science is a benchmark as to what is improbable. Science offers a large measure of explanatory power. The probabilities of science, like the events of the past, are impervious to the human will. You might wish the earth were the centre of the universe, but blowing out every last birthday candle will not make the sun revolve about the earth. You might wish men and women to be the same, but the scientific evidence suggests your wishes are fantasies. Men and women possess different neural nets, hormonal systems and neurotransmitters – splendid differences that make the sexes distinct.

A discrete body of knowledge is building up. Evidence is being brought together from mainstream science – from psychology, psychiatry, neurophysiology, endocrinology – and the sum of the evidence suggests that men and women are different. It does not suggest that one is better than the other, it makes no claims for 'equality', it simply describes the differences. To understand those differences is to understand each other. Mutual respect can only be based on a clear-eyed acceptance of sexual difference; not on their denial. To insist on sexual sameness – to be blind to male, female or homosexual characteristics – is the sexism of the late 20th-century intellectual. Victorian prudes would be delighted with the postmodern refusal to face up to the physical basis of sexual difference.

Those who look forward to the social transformation of human nature often reject science when it suggests certain things are unchangeable. If something, say a biological finding, does not square with an aspiration, then the science must be rejected, or its findings must be vigorously (though unscientifically) rebutted. Thus those who believe that gender differences are socially caused damn the science that finds otherwise. Yet science moves on and those left behind are voluntarily removing themselves from the real debate.

There is more to life than the social and biological. Awe, love, virtue ... so much more. We do not hold, as many do, that the beast lies at the root of humanity. We can all learn to tell right from wrong, learn when not to yield to the primal urge to care only for the family, and learn when not to go along with the social norm. Humans can rise above mob and mafia. We tell of the biology which swims within us and, equally, of the social environment in which we swim, so that men and women might rise above both.

CHAPTER ONE

He's Not Part One, Part Another
The bisexual fallacy

We hear a lot these days about the 'new man'. He is more sensitive than the older model, more ready to help about the house or to spend time with his children. He is civilized, de-clawed and gentle. He can still be strong, of course, but his strength is manifested by patience and emotional warmth. This paragon sounds suspiciously like a female; indeed, it is often said that the new man is 'in touch with his feminine side'. The supposed compliment betrays a *fin de millnium* unisex ideal. It is RuPaul, supertransvestite, advertising M.A.C.'s Viva Glam lipstick (all profits to an AIDS charity). It is Generation X – with a splash of Calvin Klein's CKOne – cruising the line between sexual identities and possessing the best traits of both with none of the old male's inconvenient faults.

Today New Man is updated by another: Postmodern Man, the new man dressed to the hilt in academic theory. He is also a sharing, softer sort of guy, less competitive than the traditional male, and at home with his amorphous sexuality. He too is meant to be in touch with *his female side*. It might seem, then, that there is a biological component to his makeup. But no, he is entirely moulded by social forces. He is a human object of whom no part is given by nature. Postmodern man is a boy-child of intellectuals who teach gender studies. New man is a creation of popular feminism, media hype and out-of-touch copywriters. What is common to both postmodern man and new man is that they are aspirational figures: neither exists outside the academic mind or Gucci perfume ads. There is one big obstacle to the whole theoretical caboodle: a realistic account of sex differences will close the door on the intellectual postmodern republic.

'My squeeze, what do you call a guy who irons a blouse?'
'I don't know,' says Anne. 'I've never met one. But this sounds like a bar-room joke, a hostage to fortune if ever I –'
'He's a postmodern man.'
'Eyes glaze at the word.'
'*Mañana* man, then,' says Bill. 'Like tomorrow, he never comes.'
'But how can he be postmodern? Post-all-that's-present. Post today? Post now?'
'Post the present era. Us male humans are to be transformed. We're all to be part one and part another: the world of both. It's a world in which the dividing lines of opposition – oppression or competition – are no more. It's a land of blur, of ambiguity. Little wonder the eyes cloud over.'
'I get it,' says Anne. 'Postmodern means post men.'

Some cynics may doubt whether this gender-bending new postmodern man truly exists outside advertisements, women's magazines and a few urban enclaves, but the ideal persists. It is based on the assumption of bisexuality: that within each of us lies both a male and a female nature, and that the male can be tamed by getting in touch with his feminine side. A man who succeeds in doing so will be less threatening, especially to women and gays, and it is hardly surprising that most of the strident headline pressure for men to cast off their old macho image and become sensitive, caring, new-model males stems from the women's and homosexuals' lobbies. Women and gays, after all, have most to fear from the old, unreconstructed male who can be intolerant, crude and show a frightening capacity for violence; the new man, if he can be fetched into existence, will be a much pleasanter creature. We have turned Professor Higgins's question on its head. Now we ask why a man can't be more like a woman?

The straight answer would be that it is not in most men's nature to be like a woman, nor in hers to be like him. That assertion, however, ignores another fashionable belief which insists that our sexuality is not natural at all, but a social construct. This belief, which goes hand in hand with claims about bisexuality, insists that we all have the capacity to be heterosexual, homosexual or bisexual, and the only thing which determines our sexual orientation is social pressure. At first glance this might seem an odd assertion, but increasingly the western world is being driven by the belief, often enshrined in law, that the only differences between men and women, other than their obvious physical attributes, are those caused by privilege, opportunity and influence.

Social reformers, with their aim of eliminating oppression, now think they have found a way to eliminate male aggression. The male is to be socially transformed. He is to be turned into a non-hostile, uncompetitive type. There is an obstacle: any realistic account of gender differences which denies the male competitive world denies the nature of men. Does that bother the social reformers? Not at all. What cannot be changed can be swept under the carpet. It is to this end that the male is found by the liberal arts academics to be a social, cultural construct – open to deep transformation. Only sexual orientation does not wash away in the communal bath; human nature is not biodissolvable.

'Nothing is transmitted but the social?' asks Anne.

'It's in the vested interest of the social sciences to find all things socially transmitted,' Bill answers.

'You mean,' Anne asks, 'that if we transform man's social world then we transform him?'

'Those who believe in the perfectibility of man do not want to know about the masculine as natural.'

'There's evidence to support the social hypothesis …'

'… but only if you don't look beyond the external.'

Scholars are no longer allowed to imply that heterosexuality is the norm for sexual attraction. In the standard US handbook for avoiding bias in language (*Guidelines for Bias-Free Writing* by Marilyn Schwartz and the Task Force on Bias-Free Language of the Association of American University Presses, 1995) we are not to talk of *husband, wife, spouse* or *marriage*. We are asked to substitute gender neutral terms like *domestic companion, longtime partner* or *primary relationship*. Language is freighted with splendid deceits, and to impose rules of thumb as to what can (cannot) be said is to put one's finger on the point of a tack. To the average male the language of the thought police is disparaging, offensive and prejudicial. There is fear and loathing in the new sexism: it is both anti-sex and anti-male.

The male is pre-judged – as prejudiced. Here is the belief that all should conform to the bisexual ideal: a social idyll in which sexual differences are eliminated. He is wrong-footed at the starting line. He is accused of homophobia. But what of heterophobia? What if it is not the average male who is prejudiced but all those who assume that straight is potentially bent – unisexual, bisexual, part-one-part-another, desexed, androgynous, queer, both/and, homosexual, crossing over, in between.

'The word police will get you.'

'The charge?' asks Anne.

'Heterosexism.'

'Because we say that the heterosexual male is normal? Or the norm?'

'To be born Chinese is the norm in China.'

'A gay might stand out as abnormal.'

'My green eyes might stand out in Mongolia,' says Bill. 'Would that be queer? You know I'm no more likely to change my sexual orientation than the colour of my eyes.'

'Lots of people think everyone's a bit unisex.'

'Like being a bit pregnant?

"'DELETE, DELETE, DELETE,'' say the word police. We are all potentially bisexual.'

'One in a hundred, more like,' says Anne. 'Those who include speak only for themselves.'

If women, the argument goes, are given the same opportunities as men, and are not restrained by the dead hand of 'old boy networks', then they can achieve all that a man can achieve. It is hard to argue against that well-meaning assertion, even though a dangerous and unscientific assumption lies behind it: that men and women are the same.

Perhaps the most extreme and obvious example of this assumption is seen in America where, in the last few years, lawyers have forced the hitherto male-dominated military to open all its doors to women. The result has been legal equality and constant trouble. The men are consistently accused of insensitivity or, worse, of sexual harassment – and it does not take much for a serviceman to be accused of that most heinous crime. Indeed, according to guidelines laid down by the Pentagon, if a soldier merely looks at one of his female colleagues for more than three seconds then he is harassing her. The US Navy even closed itself down for a whole day so that its men could be lectured on the evils of sexual harassment. The whole experiment, which rushes on with the inevitability of the Gadarene swine nearing the precipice, can be simply summarized: women demand equal opportunity, gain it, then complain that the men behave badly. 'Sensitivity training', or even disciplinary action, then follows to change the men's behaviour to make them gentler; in fact, to make them more like women. It would be easier, surely, to recruit only women?

The homosexual lobby is as eager as some women to blur gender identities. It is axiomatic among many gay lobbyists that everyone's sexuality is a mix of male and female, and that where any one person ends up on the sliding scale depends solely on social pressures and influences. Homosexuality, they tell us, is a convenient social label, no more 'real' than heterosexuality. Ten years ago a conference devoted its entire agenda to just that assertion. One of the conference's published conclusions was that 'homosexuality is not inherent in an individual but constructed'.[1] No wonder such people believe that a little social pressure will shift all the old, crude, uncomfortably macho males along the continuum to a place where they will be subtly feminized and so become less threatening. Violence against women and gays would drop dramatically, and no one will deny that this would be a desirable outcome. Men's violence against women is well documented; perhaps less well known is the growing intolerance shown by heterosexual males for gays, an intolerance that has certainly led to a dramatic increase in assaults on homosexuals by 'straight' men.[2]

The growing incidence of anti-gay violence is even adduced as further evidence for our bisexuality. A Dutch study of anti-gay violence noted that the victims were usually 'the least manly' in appearance.[3] Without citing evidence (no questions were directed to the attackers) the study solemnly reported that 'it was presumed that [the attackers] victimised this group of men ... because they themselves were homosexual and could stamp out the fire within them by the use of violence against "obvious gays".' So straight men attack gays because they are really gay themselves? Freud and his followers have much to answer for in this tortuous reasoning. Not one to cling to a single fallacy when he could hold two, Freud asserted that men were partly women (they have nipples, don't they?) and that they repressed their 'natural bisexuality'. That notion has given intellectual respectability to the claim that we all have the ever-present possibility of being gay or straight.

To be anti-gay is thus explained as a reaction to the male's fear of his own latent homosexuality, an explanation that is supported by the word used to describe such prejudice, homophobia, which means 'fear of sameness'. 'People are homophobic because they fear their own latent homosexuality, or because they are insecure in their own masculinity. This answer represents one of the most popular "common sense" explanations for homophobia. It is a theory that guides our practice.'[4] Homophobia, another learned journal says, 'reflects three assumptions; that anti-gay prejudice is primarily a fear response; that it is irrational and dysfunctional for individuals that manifest it; that it is primarily an "individual aberration" rather than a reflection of cultural values.'[5] This is now received wisdom. In every straight man there is a gay screaming to be let out.

> 'The heterosexual norm is taken as Enemy Number One,' says Anne.
> 'Mere heterophobia,' says Bill.

Collins' dictionary defines homophobia as: 'intense hatred or fear of homosexuals or homosexuality'. Thus to use the word 'homophobia' is to imply that the aversion that most straight males feel towards gays is a psychological disorder. The word is a description of the extreme – 'intense fear' and 'hatred' – and to employ it as a description of the average male's reaction to homosexuality is absurd. His feelings are not of hatred, but of aversion. The aversion might include an element of disgust, but never of fear. Nor is it a psychological disorder, rather it is the normal straight male's instinctive revulsion from the idea of same-sex relations. That reaction is innate, natural, so prejudice it is not.

You will note that this 'latent homosexual' explanation is described as *common sense*, not as a scientific finding – hardly surprising, for there has been too little research into the aversion that most men feel for homosexuality. But what research does exist suggests that straight men do not fear gays, nor do they fear the possibility of gayness within themselves. 'Common sense', indeed, suggests the very opposite: gays, as a group, are not perceived as threatening, and since most men are oblivious of any homosexual urges within themselves, why should they fear such urges? Fear, or phobia, does not seem to play any part in the average man's dislike of gays. The bisexual explanation of homophobia might be 'common sense' to the gay lobby, but it also might be plain wrong.

Heterosexuality is the norm for sexual attraction. This is not to assume or imply that homosexuality is deviant. It too is natural. Although most Americans still believe that our sexual orientation is a matter of choice,[6] it is not. But that is a society in which you are meant to be free to become what you want – not least when that want implies a moral choice. And where there's a choice, one should choose to be upright: straight. There is a confusion here. Gayness is no more a matter of choice than being born American or Mexican, black or white.

A new explanation is required for the average man's anti-gay attitude. And the word 'average' is used deliberately, for research reveals that a majority of heterosexuals do have negative attitudes towards homosexuals. Those attitudes range from mild distaste to the extremes described in the dictionary definition, but their widespread existence suggests that 'homophobia', far from being an 'individual aberration', is in fact a reflection of something more than cultural and biological values. But what values?

One study correlated the masculinity profiles of male college students with their attitudes towards homosexuals and discovered, unsurprisingly, that the most masculine students were the most anti-gay. This might suggest that those who argue that 'macho' men fear their feminine side are right, but the survey did not uncover that fear. Instead the 'homophobic' subjects complained of gay harassment. Gays were 'getting too close' or 'brushing against my body'. Another complained he was being 'checked out'. Such homosexual behaviour made 42% of heterosexuals move away.[7] A common heterosexual aversion to overt homosexuality is captured in these studies, but never commented on. Instead the 'common-sense' explanation is advanced; that the most masculine heterosexuals are really gays in flight-denial.

Another study reports that 47% of men have *a purely negative reaction* to gays. 'I don't like them'; 'I want nothing to do with them'; 'I hope Aids wipes them out'.[8] At least 47% is a minority, but the same study discovered that a further 45% of men were mildly anti-gay; their attitude was summed up as, '[Gays] generally don't bother me so long as they don't try and press their beliefs on me.' So if this study is right, then an astonishing 92% of heterosexual males will experience anti-gay feelings if homosexuality is overtly pressed on them. Again, this hardly suggests an 'individual aberration': it begins to look more and more like a common feeling. And once again 'fear' does not come into it. These heterosexual males show no fear of homosexuals, but merely feel distaste or revulsion at a homosexual approach.

And it is not men alone who experience this aversion. Alan Wolfe, a professor at Boston University, interviewed two hundred suburban Americans for a book on the state of American society and discovered that his slice of middle America was happily unprejudiced, open-minded and tolerant. 'Yet,' he reported, 'there is one exception to America's persistent and ubiquitous nonjudgmentalism. However much they are willing to accept almost anything, most of the middle class Americans I spoke to were not prepared to accept homosexuality.'[9] Wolfe's interviewees used words like 'abnormal', 'immoral', 'sinful', 'unacceptable', 'sick' or 'unhealthy' to describe the gay lifestyle, and other American studies show a similar widespread aversion. One such study reported that no less than 66% of American adults, male and female, condemned 'homosexual behaviour as morally wrong or as a sin'.[10] A similar result was yielded by another American study which reported that 60% of adults (male and female) thought that homosexuality in and of itself was no great problem, but it was still 'obscene and vulgar'.[11] The same survey suggested that these negative attitudes to homosexuality were associated with 'sexual conservatism, anti-feminist attitudes, and with strong beliefs in male sex-appropriate behaviour'. For the gay or feminist lobbies this is a litany of horrors, but try putting it another way: so-called 'homophobia' is associated with men and women who lead decent lives, respect sexual fidelity and consider the male–female relationship to be natural. These same socially conservative people supported the right of homosexuals to attend church (80%) and their right to consensual sex in private (70%).

The broad conclusion to be drawn from these studies is that something under half of all straight men harbour strong anti-gay attitudes, and that about the same proportion possess a milder antipathy. Women share these attitudes, but perhaps the important thing to remark on is that the majority, despite their reservations about the morality of homosexual behaviour, are on the side of toleration: if the gays leave us alone, they seem to be saying, we will leave them alone. And yet the average person is condemned for feeling a dislike of homosexuality. Homophobia, the extreme manifestation of the aversion, is obviously reprehensible, but instead of trying to understand it the gay lobby attempts to eradicate it with the message that homophobia is mere denial. Once we all recognize our bisexuality, the argument claims, we will lose our irrational and sometimes violent prejudices, but the research suggests a much simpler reason for the straight's aversion to the gay, and a reason which really is rooted in common sense.

The attraction of gay to gay, or of lesbian to lesbian, is natural. The gay or lesbian is attracted to members of the same sex. The gay does not want sex with women, nor does the lesbian want sex with men. There is a corollary. A heterosexual male is attracted to a heterosexual female. He does not want sex with men. That too is normal.

It is a consequence that gays (or lesbians) may cruise on a crash course. Gays are naturally attracted to those of the same sex, which means they are attracted to men in general. A problem arises in that the majority of men are not sexually attracted to gays nor, indeed, to any other men. Again, that is natural. What to the normal gay is natural and desirable is to most men unnatural and they recoil from it. No one accuses a woman of a 'phobia' if she repels an unwanted sexual advance, yet men are apparently phobic if they dislike being 'checked out' by a gay. The intolerance of straights is not of gays as such, but rather of the assumption by gays that others are like, or have the capacity to be like, themselves. The conventional male can be unsettled by those who are not plainly heterosexual. The thought of a homosexual act is unenjoyable to him in the obvious sense that it is not what he enjoys. Nor does he feel mere indifference towards it: it troubles him. The gay man desires what he finds undesirable and so the gay advance is unwelcome. It is a foray across conventional boundaries, an invasion of the Eros and private space that is part of the self, and it is seen as gay harassment. Any gay reviewing the results of the studies might decide that the best way to reduce society's antipathy towards homosexuality is for the gay to be more aware of the heterosexual's need for a private space; in other words, to practice more restraint.

'What I don't understand,' Anne asks, 'is why you men are so rude about gays, calling them bloody shirt-lifters, fairies, queers.'

'We can call them much worse than that,' Bill says.

'But why? They aren't a threat to you. They're not competing.'

'Perhaps it's because what they desire of us,' Bill says, 'is abhorrent to us. I can't stand the idea of having sex with another man.'

'You fear it?'

'What's to fear? I might as well be frightened of becoming a vegetarian.'

'No chance of that!'

'I suspect most men shun gays,' Bill says, 'and maybe even despise them, because they don't compete in the great male race.'

'In which women are the prizes?'

'Thank God, yes.'

'But why be repelled by homosexuals? Surely what they do with each other is their own business, and they have the right to privacy.'

'Privacy, yes, but I don't want them anywhere near my private space. My private space is you and I, and I don't want a third person in there telling me that with a little gender-bending I could enjoy lifting his shirt.'

'Bill!'

'Do what they want – unto themselves – but to camp on my
   ground is to test the limits of tolerance.'

To tolerate something is to put up with what you do not like and
gays, of course, want more than toleration: they want acceptance,
and believe that the rest of us must give that acceptance. They
think we will do so more easily once we recognize that we are all
gay – or at least, that all of us are bisexual and so have the capacity
for gayness within us. But are we bisexual? Freud certainly
believed as much, but it was Alfred Kinsey's studies in the 1940s
and 1950s that seemed to set the seal of academic approval on the
bisexual theory. When Kinsey's famous study was first published
it caused shock, for he claimed that 37% of all males had
experienced (or were experiencing) homosexual relationships,
and that a further 13% had homosexual urges even though they
did nothing to satisfy those desires.[12] Here was startling proof that
fully 50% of males were actively or potentially gay, and Kinsey did
not conclude that the other 50% were free of homosexual urges.
He postulated a scale of male sexuality which ranged from wholly
heterosexual to exclusively gay, and he concluded:

> Males do not represent two distinct populations, heterosexual
> and homosexual. The world is not to be divided into sheep and
> goats. Not all things are black nor all things white. It is a
> fundamental of taxonomy that nature rarely deals with discrete
> categories. Only the human mind invents categories and tries to
> force facts into separate pigeon-holes. The living world is a
> continuum of each and every one of its aspects. The sooner we
> learn this regarding human sexual behaviour the sooner we
> shall reach a sound understanding of the realities of sex.[13]

Kinsey's influence was tremendous. His survey was the first to
offer an estimate of gayness as a proportion of the population and
his estimate shocked, but so it should for Kinsey used a very odd

group of people to arrive at his figures. Instead of finding a representative sample from the general population, he essentially used a self-selected sample. Not only that, but his concerns about his own sexuality – although married he was probably homosexual – biased his choice of subject.[14] No modern academic would recognize Kinsey's survey as reliable, yet its influence persists, mainly because his results reinforce the fashionable bisexual theory. So Kinsey keeps his place in the pantheon despite the fact that study after study has demonstrated how utterly wrong his results were.[15] Later research, as we shall see, demonstrates again and again that the incidence of homosexuality is much lower than Kinsey stated.

The gay lobby ignores the new research, preferring to claim that homosexuality is widespread. There is, after all, strength in numbers, so the more gays, the more clout the gay lobby wields. The usual figure quoted in the newspapers is that 10% of all men are exclusively homosexual and up to 33% have experienced some homosexual activity. The gay lobby publicizes these figures despite the fact that survey after survey has shown them to be wild exaggerations. The truth appears to be that between 1% and 4% of men are homosexual, and even fewer women are lesbians. An examination of the many post-Kinsey studies concludes that 'it is unreasonable to consider the often-used figure of 10% of the male population as more or less regularly engaging in same-sex activities. The figure is closer to half that. And the figure for the lesbian population is even smaller. Further, routinely exclusive or predominantly exclusive homosexual activities are more common than bisexual activities.'[16] Milton Diamond, the author of the survey, goes on to say that 10% is a political figure. In fact not one post-Kinsey survey has ever yielded an estimate as high as that. An NOP poll in America in 1989 suggested that homosexuals were 3.3% of the male population. A 1988 survey by America's National Opinion Research Center (NORC) yielded a figure of 2.4%.[17] A survey conducted for the USA's Centers for Disease Control in 1989 suggested that the total number of men who had ever experienced male to male sexual conduct, as either exclusively or occasional homosexuals, was 7.3%.[18] A survey of several polls, published in 1991, derived a figure of 5–7% for men who had had homosexual experience,[19] while Milton Diamond's own study in Hawaii suggests that only 3% of males ever engage in same-sex activity. Another extensive review concluded that exclusive homosexuality was practised by no more than 5%.[20] Even a telephone survey conducted in San Francisco, surely the gay capital of the world, did not reach the oft-quoted figure of 33% of males as exclusively homosexual. Only 10% of respondents admitted to some homosexual experiences.[21]

The most comprehensive study to date surveyed 34,000 high school students in America and reported that, by the age of 18, 99.2% of males were exclusively heterosexual.[22] Just 2.8% of the 18-year-olds had experienced homosexual acts, but less than 1% were exclusively gay. That low figure is reinforced by the findings of the National Survey of Men, considered to be the most representative study of American males, which suggested that only 1.1% of all men were exclusively homosexual and only 2.3% (which includes the previous 1.1%) had ever experienced homosexuality.[23]

So survey after survey suggests that the real figure of exclusively homosexual men is in the region of 1–4%. The percentage of bisexuals is so small as to count in that range. Which means that 96–99% of men are heterosexual, and almost certainly exclusively heterosexual, for the surveys also indicate that sexual preferences are overwhelmingly one way or the other. Very few men are bisexual. The vast majority of men are either gay or straight, and most men are straight.[24] It is time to forget Kinsey's extraordinary figures and time to abandon the much touted 10%.

The gay lobby's response to that low figure is either to quote old surveys that used unreliable samples, or else to allege that the more recent results are misleading because most men are unwilling to admit to homosexual experience. 'Homophobia', in other words, makes men lie to researchers and thus all the surveys are flawed because people won't be honest about their sex lives. So it is reassuring to hear about the work of Kurt Freud who investigated male sexual orientation with a machine which measured the smallest changes of penile engorgement. Erections, as any man will testify, are hard to fake and if a man has no homosexual feelings then lubricious pictures of naked boys will leave him limp, just as the most luscious centrefold will fail to arouse a gay man. Kurt Freud's findings demonstrated almost beyond doubt that the vast majority of men were either exclusively heterosexual or exclusively homosexual. There is no sliding scale, no continuum, no latent gayness and no universal bisexuality. There is no scary gay in the straight man's closet.[25]

The unisex ideal, which melds our male and female components, is beginning to look a little out of reach, yet some people still refuse to abandon the notion of bisexuality for they believe it is the route to universal toleration. Perversely, the argument that men with anti-gay attitudes are themselves gays in denial exacerbates the very thing it sets out to defeat. 'Common sense' suggests that most men and women are comfortable within their sexual orientation, and to suggest otherwise will irritate them. The non-gay male is being told that he is partly female, thus calling into question his masculinity, and if this annoys him he is accused of *protesting too much*. Thus he is twice impugned. He is annoyed – and small wonder. The attempt to dissolve stereotypes by imposing a unisex world can only reinforce prejudice. The explanation that we are all bisexual promotes the very reaction it means to abate.

But suppose there were another way to counter the average heterosexual's aversion to homosexuality? First we need to understand what is meant by 'homophobia', and it is our contention that it has nothing to do with fear. Gays, as a group, are not fearsome – indeed their popular reputation is the very opposite – and because the vast majority of men experience no secret homosexual longings it seems perverse to insist that they live in constant dread of such desires. Instead the prejudice against gays appears to spring from a vague feeling that homosexual behaviour is 'unnatural', and not so very long ago that was also the opinion of orthodox medicine. No wonder many ordinary folk persist in thinking of gayness as a deviant condition, a perversion, something immoral, even a sin.

Before gays lose patience with the apparent intransigence of public opinion they might like to remember that until very recently the same aversions were held about left-handed people. Left-handedness was sinister (from the Latin for 'left') while right-handers were dextrous (from the Latin for 'right'), and many older people will remember the painful efforts made in schools to force left-handed children to write with their right hand. No one would promulgate that nonsense today, for science has demonstrated that left- or right-handedness is not a choice, is not a deviant condition and does not reflect the malignancy or benignity of fate; it is a simple natural variation. As a result the prejudice against southpaws has disappeared.

So would anti-gay feelings disappear if people believed that gayness was a natural biological variation and not an unnatural perversion? Some research suggests that it would.[26] Yet despite evidence that abandonment of the bisexual theory would lead to greater public acceptance, much of the gay lobby still insists that 10% of the population is homosexual and, moreover, that the 10% is gay not because they were born that way, but because society and culture made them that way.

If gayness is promoted by cultural pressures then we could expect some cultures or microcultures to exert more pressure than others and that the incidence of homosexuality would thus be higher in those societies. Gays often claim that proof of this exists, and point to prisons and single-sex boarding schools as places where cultural pressures do produce much higher rates of homosexuality. This is true, but just because one extraordinary incidence of social pressure produces homosexual behaviour does not prove that all homosexuality is so caused. The 'prison' claim promotes a logical error; the common social science error of generalizing from the exceptional to the general. (Just because electrocution causes death, one can't therefore assume that all deaths come from electrocution!) Nor is there any evidence that prison homosexuality is a 'lifestyle' choice. Indeed, it seems that the most sexually active males in prisons are usually the most dominant men who, as soon as they are released from jail, go back to heterosexual partners.[27] Prison proves nothing.

If the gay lobby wishes us to believe that homosexuality is caused by societal pressure they need to point to cultures which are more 'gay-friendly' than others and thus produce more gays. Some research done in the 1960s did indeed suggest just that, but like much early sexual research, it suffered from skewed sampling and its results have been contradicted by later surveys. (Though that does not stop gay activists like Peter Tatchell from relying on the older figures to refute the idea that gayness is a biological phenomenon.[28]) The more recent research, so inconvenient to the gay lobby, demonstrates that the incidence of homosexuality stays the same across cultures and nations, and it stays at our baseline figure of 1% to 4%.[29] The conclusions of one leading researcher leave no room for doubt:

> The implication of a finding that the incidence of homosexuality is similar in all societies and that it remains stable over time is, of course, of considerable theoretical importance. In short, we are led away from social-structural interpretations toward the view that homosexuality is, for whatever reasons, a constant element in the spectrum of human sexuality.[30]

And:

> Societies do not create homosexuality any more than they create heterosexuality: they simply react to the ubiquitous emergence of homosexuality. Cross cultural examination of homosexuality leads us to the notion that homosexuality is a sexual orientation not a pathological and incidental manifestation of a particular social structural arrangement. It is rather a

natural, fundamental form of human sexuality ... the most obvious implication is that behaviour which up to now has been regarded as highly variable culturally, and thus socially determined, is less variable than previously conceived by most social scientists and at least in some important respects has a biological basis.[31]

The gay lobby may not like it, but the evidence suggests that homosexuality is a 'natural, fundamental form of human sexuality', is not 'socially determined', and its incidence does not change from one culture to the next. Being gay is natural; not being gay is natural.

Men do not fall on a continuum of sexuality, their sexual orientation is one way or the other. Nor is the world full of men and women who are as happy to bed one of their own sex as someone of the other. That, like the widespread incidence of homosexuality, is a myth of the 1990s and can now be safely laid to rest.

If gayness is a natural variation of the human condition, as ineradicable and inevitable as left-handedness, what causes it? One suggestion is that homosexuality derives from genes, the ancestral building blocks handed down from parent to child. Left-handedness is a genetic trait, though the process is more complicated than pure inheritance because other biological factors influence whether the genes that cause left-handedness are switched on in the growing foetus or are left unactivated. This means that many people carry the genes that appear to cause left-handedness, but are not actually left-handed themselves. If you are an identical twin and left-handed there is only a 12% chance that your identical sibling will also be left-handed, even though he or she will carry the left-handed genes.[32] Genes, by themselves, are not enough.

Is there a gene that causes homosexuality? In 1993 Dan Hamer and his colleagues announced the discovery of just such a gene,[33] but its existence is still controversial and Hamer's research has been under assault ever since the announcement. Some scientists complained that the sample from which he had drawn his genetic material was skewed because it comprised only self-proclaimed gays, while others believed he had over-simplified a horrendously complex process.[34] The gay lobby disliked Hamer's research because it suggested a frightening scenario: if gayness was indeed genetically induced then pregnant women might choose to abort a foetus if they discovered that it carried the homosexual gene.[35]

That concern is genuine. Parents regularly abort foetuses that carry the Down's Syndrome gene, and that process could easily be extended to provide 'designer' babies, tested in the womb and guaranteed to be free of any unwanted genetic trait – whether of hair colour, sexual orientation or left-handedness. The danger is real, but some way off because the process of how genes are expressed is still not wholly understood. Dan Hamer's 'gay' gene might not cause gayness at all, but merely predispose its possessor to the real causes of homosexuality. If that is true, then for the gay gene to be expressed requires further biological action, and that seems most likely because, confusingly, some homosexuals do not possess the so-called 'gay' gene at all. Something else, either an unidentified gene or a biological process, made them gay.

The most likely explanation is a biological process that occurs in the womb. Few scientists dispute the influence that is wielded on the developing foetus by hormones, and hormones are central to the process of sexual development. Hormones (among other things) are the 'switches' that activate genes, and in turn those genes instruct the growing foetus whether to be male or female. It is to that process, and to its effects on sexual orientation, that we must now turn.

It seems obvious that hormones will determine our gender, but, until very recently, the further assertion that the same hormones determined our brain structure into either a male or a female pattern was very controversial. The idea of a differently patterned brain was anathema to most hardline feminists, who wanted to assert their equality (by which they too often meant sameness) to men; if it could be proved that the brains of men and women were distinctly different in structure and function, then it was an alarmingly short step to believing they might be different in abilities as well. Their problem was that male and female brains did turn out to be distinctly different, and what was once a politically controversial theory quietly became the standard stuff of undergraduate textbooks.

Women might take some consolation from the fact that the basic human template is female. Every foetus begins as a female, but, at six weeks, boys begin to be made by a flood of hormones that drench the developing baby and so convert sugar and spice into slugs and snails. The male foetus is capable of making high levels of androgens – or male hormones such as testosterone. The male starts making the hormone at six weeks. It is not a one-off action: it goes on for months in the womb, each successive dose of hormones doing its bit to turn what was a female into a male. For our purposes, the crucial moment appears to come in the third month of pregnancy when a heavy dose of testosterone affects the developing boy's brain. Among other effects this dose of testosterone sets his sexual orientation. Up until now 'his' brain has been effectively female and like any female his sexual longings, if he had any, would be focused on males; the testosterone drench reverses his polarity and from now on he will be attracted to girls. But if the testosterone dose falls below a critical high level the brain remains female. All foetuses receive some testosterone, even those destined to be born girls, but samples taken from the amniotic fluid suggest that the 'brain-sexing' drench of testosterone is eight to nine times higher for boys than it is for girls.[36]

Now it does not take much imagination to hypothesize that a shortfall in testosterone at the crucial moment of pregnancy might leave an otherwise conventional male with a female sexual orientation. The result would be an adult man who is, quite naturally, attracted to other males. It is possible that a 'gay gene' influences the crucial testosterone levels, but whether that is the case or not, the evidence for this hormonal cause of homosexuality is overwhelming.

Overwhelming but not absolutely proven, for we cannot experiment on developing human foetuses to test the hypothesis. So the evidence, however compelling, is indirect. A study by Lee Ellis has shown that mothers who suffer from severe stress (stress reduces the levels of testosterone) during the third month of pregnancy produce a higher than average incidence of homosexual offspring.[37] We cannot prove this absolutely because, rightly, ethics forbids us to experiment on human foetuses, but animal studies support the biological explanation. Humans and rats share specific sex hormones and have similar areas at the base of their brains that control sexual behaviour (the hypothalamus). Roger Gorski and his team have demonstrated that a rat's sexual orientation can be changed at will by manipulation of foetal hormones.[38] A male rat deprived of testosterone in its early foetal stage becomes female in its sexual behaviour. No amount of male hormones given in later pregnancy can reverse this behaviour – the animal's brain has been permanently organized into the female pattern.

A female rat dosed in the same critical period with male hormones becomes masculine in its sexual behaviour and, again, no amount of later female hormonal influence will reverse the orientation. Gorski's work suggests that there is a critical stage during the development of the mammalian brain when male or female sexuality is established.[39] Once that critical moment is passed no amount of 'corrective' hormone will make any difference. The sexual orientation of rats, and most probably that of humans too, is determined in the womb.

The researchers went on to investigate whether there were any structural differences between the brains of male and female rats and discovered an area of the hypothalamus that was seven times larger in the male brain than the female brain. 'The difference is so large,' one researcher wrote, 'that you can see it with the naked eye.'[40] Other researchers agreed with the finding, and confirmed, moreover, that it was just this area of the brain that controlled sexual behaviour. 'Experimental damage to this area produces a marked and significant reduction in masculine sexual behaviour.'[41]

Roger Gorski and his team then experimented by manipulating the hormones delivered to a developing rat foetus to see if they made any difference to the hypothalamus, and discovered they could determine the hypothalamus's structure by restricting the hormone dosage.[42] This was a breakthrough discovery for, though it had been inferred that hormones changed brain structure and behaviour, it was the first time anyone had demonstrated that process in a laboratory. Gorski and his team had shown that sexual orientation was determined by hormones, and that the brain's physical structure could be manipulated by the same hormones, and all this in an area of the brain that was well established as central to controlling sexual behaviour.

These experiments have been replicated by many different laboratories and in other animal species,[43] and inevitably lead to the question of whether homosexuality occurs outside the laboratory in species other than man. For a long time this has been denied (thus providing ammunition to those who ascribe homosexuality to social or cultural causes), but more recent research has demonstrated frequent male–male sex in primates and in mountain sheep. Such sex is often 'rape', in which the dominant male uses sexual assault to demonstrate his higher status, but genuine, consensual homosexuality has been observed in domestic sheep. It was first observed in Iowa where farmers were disturbed by the number of 'dud studs': rams that were not interested in ewes, but in other rams.[44] Research is still going on into the dud studs, but it suggests that there are definite biological reasons 'that brain structures involved in sensing or perceiving potential mates may be different in homosexual and non-sexual rams'. The dud rams it seems have a different brain from the heterosexual rams.

But what about humans? Empirical evidence suggests that human sexual orientation is determined by exposure to testosterone during the third month of pregnancy, but is there any physical evidence? Again it is the hypothalamus that most interests scientists because the human hypothalamus, like the rat's, controls sexual behaviour, and, just as in rats, distinct differences have been found in the male and female human hypothalamus. There is an area in the hypothalamus called the sexually dimorphic nucleus of the preoptic area, and researchers have demonstrated that this area is always larger in male brains than in female brains; in rats it is between five and seven times larger, while in humans it appears to be two or three times larger.[45]

This same area was investigated in homosexual men. Simon LeVay, in a controversial discovery, announced that the sexually dimorphic nucleus of the preoptic area was twice as large in heterosexual men as in homosexual men, which meant, simply, that gay men presented a female brain structure.[46] LeVay's announcement made headlines all over the world and, not surprisingly, excited controversy. If he was correct, the gay lobby could no longer be confident that homosexuality was a 'social construct'. It looked more and more like a biological phenomenon, so it was with some relief that the gay lobby announced that LeVay's findings had to be wrong because the brains he had dissected had all come from gay men who had died of AIDS, and AIDS can cause changes in brain structure. That criticism lost its force after LeVay investigated the brains of homosexuals who had not died of AIDS, and once again discovered that they presented a typical female pattern.[47]

LeVay's findings are no longer controversial. Indeed, other researchers are discovering still more differences between the structures of the homosexual and heterosexual brains – the suprachiasmatic nucleus, also in the hypothalamus, seems to be larger in women and gays than in straight men,[48] while the anterior commissure, a kind of telephone exchange that joins the right and left temporal lobes of the brain and is significantly larger in women than in men, has now, it should come as no surprise, proved larger in gays too.[49]

The probability that sexual orientation is determined in the womb looks more and more likely, except to those blinded by sexual politics. Yet more proof of the power of foetal hormones to affect adult behaviour comes from studying children who, because of a genetic abnormality, were exposed to abnormal levels of sex hormones while in the womb. Certain girls have an abnormality in their adrenal gland that leads to an overproduction of androgens or male hormones. The condition is called congenital adrenal hyperplasia, or CAH, and CAH girls are born with internal female sex organs but partly masculinized external genitals. Surgery can usually correct the genital abnormality and drugs can control the build-up of male hormone, but many studies have shown that these girls still behave quite differently from girls who were not subjected to high foetal levels of androgens.[50] The androgen-affected girls are masculine in their general behaviour: they are more aggressive than other girls, more 'tomboyish', preferring male toys (guns and model trucks) to dolls, and are more interested in competitive sports. Even at a very young age children look to their own sex for playmates, but the androgen-affected girls instinctively seek to play with boys. In adulthood they are far less interested in men, marriage and sex than other women, 48% of them confess to having homosexual fantasies,[51] and 44% are actively lesbian.[52]

These studies provide further evidence of the power of foetal hormones to determine sexual behaviour and orientation, though some critics dismiss the CAH studies on the grounds that the affected girls, because they were born with male genitalia, were raised by their parents as though they were boys. This reinforces the postmodern belief that sexual orientation is constructed by societal pressure, though in fact there is no evidence that the parents of androgen-affected girls do compromise their children's sexual identities by treating them differently. The girls do not behave like boys because their parents treat them as boys, but because their brains were set into the male pattern in the foetus. More evidence of such hormonal influence is provided by a few cases where pregnant mothers were exposed to atypical hormones during medical treatment, and once again the results are clear. The more testosterone a foetus receives, the more male the behaviour of the subsequent child.[53]

If this is true then we might expect to see a reverse manifestion – the less testosterone a foetus receives, the more female the behaviour – and such a correlation does exist: 70% of male homosexuals displayed a preference for girl-type play as children.[54] The first such signs usually show when the child is a toddler. He will sometimes assert that he is a girl, perhaps favour cross-dressing, and he will frequently prefer the company of girls as playmates to that of boys. Parents frequently try to stop this kind of behaviour and sometimes take such children for psychiatric treatment, and it is from that caseload that most studies of homosexual childhood originate.[55] 'The differences in chilhood history between homo-sexual and heterosexual groups are striking', but they are also precisely what one might expect if the cause is biological and not societal.

Not only behaviour but also abilities are affected by hormones. Girls who are exposed to male hormones in the womb have better spatial ability than normal girls (spatial ability helps us to park a car in a narrow space). The significance of this finding is that differences in spatial ability are one of the largest measures of difference between the sexes. Boys and men, for example, are much better at judging size and distance than girls and women, and spatial ability translates into all sorts of practical differences. Sense of direction and hand-eye co-ordination are consistently superior in men, which is why a male darts team is consistently better than a female one.

There have been two studies of hand-eye co-ordination that measured how well the subjects could throw a missile and hit a target. The studies discovered that the homosexual's ability to throw accurately was much poorer than the ability of heterosexual men; in fact homosexual target throwing was like a woman's.[56] Another study, related to neither ability nor behaviour, has shown that homosexuals possess fingerprints of the female pattern.[57] Hall and Kimura conclude that these findings are consistent with a biological contribution to sexual orientation and indicate that such an influence may occur early in prenatal life – exactly what our other researches have discovered. An even more recent study found that lesbian women literally hear like men. There is a sex difference in the structure of the inner ear that is under the control of foetal testosterone. Lesbians have the male type of inner ear structure.[58]

The evidence for the foetal origin of human sexual orientation is indirect, simply because we cannot test the hypothesis by direct experimentation, but it is still overwhelming. Our sexual nature is laid down in the womb. It is possible that there might be some genetic predisposition to homosexuality or to heterosexuality, but it is not necessary to postulate a genetic cause when the hormonal evidence is so compelling. Society does not construct homo-sexuality, nature does, and it does so at a time when the homo-sexual has no choice in the matter. Being gay, then, is not a perversion of biology, it is not a conscious lifestyle choice and it is not a disease. It is a natural variation of human sexuality.

We are still a long way from understanding the full causes of homosexuality, though no serious scientist would any longer deny that those causes lie in biology. When it comes to sexual orientation, as with other inherited traits, it is the cumulative effect of evidence from different areas that proves the case. Single studies have their flaws, but the sheer number of studies all indicating the same thing makes it hard to understand why there is still any argument about the proposition that sexual orientation is an inborn biological trait.

At this point the critics will say: 'Yes that's right and it is all too complex to unravel. It is impossible to separate the cultural and biological influences.' They usually then add, 'And anyway cultural influences are so much stronger, so why bother with those little bits of biology?' But there is a stability in the gender divide. By that we mean that you do not change your sexual orientation as your social circumstances change (with the exception of the prison example). If cultural influences were stronger than biological ones, then we might expect to see individuals reacting to societal pressures, veering from homosexuality to heterosexuality and back again as their circumstances change, but we do not see it. The only reasonable conclusion is that biological influences are far stronger than cultural pressures, and that an individual's sexual orientation, be it gay or straight, is unchangeable. For the vast majority of men that pattern is heterosexual, for a small minority it is homosexual, and for most there is no in-between. Straight males do not fear the hidden gayness inside themselves because it simply is not there.

There is a divide between gay and straight; the two are largely distinct, though there is a bisexual minority among the gay category. The studies put the incidence of bisexuality at 3% (of gays), but it is probably far less.[59] We also need to clear up another popular misconception here. Some men are hormonally primed to be less competitive and aggressive than other males, but that does not make them gay. We are discussing sexual orientation, not general personality traits. Some gays are every bit as macho and aggressive as the most belligerent heterosexual males, while some straight males have a gentleness and passivity that is often labelled 'queer', a confusion that probably arises from Freudian-inspired 'pop psychology'.

The debate over homosexuality is mired in confusion. Much of it is generated by the gay lobby, with its insistence that gayness is latent in all men, more is generated by those who condemn homosexuality as an aberration, something unnatural, unhealthy and 'sinful'. That argument can only work if gayness is believed to be socially conditioned and thus 'correctable'. It used to be thought gayness could be 'cured'. In the 1950s the American Psychiatric Association declared homosexuality to be a deviant condition that could and should be treated. One, however, might as well try to 'cure' blue eyes.

Homosexuality is natural, just as is the aversion that heterosexuals feel for homosexual sex. It is equally natural for gays to resent the aversion, to feel condemned by it, but those with a troubling sexual identity too often generalize from their own state (it is a common failing to generalize from one's own experience to that of others) and find androgyny to be the biological template. That is a one-sided denial of male sexuality.

Are you bald if you still have one hair on your head? If you have ten? Or ten thousand? Or a hundred thousand? (There can be three hundred thousand hairs on a head.) Here a subtle fallacy nips at the retreating heels of the first. So there *is* an indeterminate middle? We all have a female template that is variously modified by male hormones, so how can any of us be either all male or all female? We must be both male and female. The fallacy makes the subtle error of arguing that because there is no distinct break between the gradations, then there is no distinction between the extremes, that all is grey. It concludes there is no real difference beween a one-haired man and a man with three hundred thousand hairs. Or between men and women. So they settle on an 'in between': neither one thing nor the other ... both/and. On the surface this may seem the essence of moderation, yet in truth it is to incorporate the peripheral into the centre. The 'in between' is, statistically, nowhere in the middle, but at the far end of the spectrum. And, having reasoned that the exception is the rule, they proceed (like social revolutionaries everywhere) to stamp out difference in the name of moderation, in the name of universal humankind. Thus they elide the critical differences between the male and female.

The conservative, or traditionalist, prefers plain black versus white. We must all be one or the other, and anyone beyond the categories is an unnatural aberration. No wonder that those beyond the categories resent their exclusion and, just as their opponents attempt to straighten the 'bent', they respond by trying to curve the straight. But the opposite to nonsense is not the opposing nonsense, it is good sense and sound science.

Assertions of androgyny, that the male has a 'female' side waiting for his embrace, is made nonsense by science. To tell a man to 'get in touch with his female side' is an insult, for it implies that his male side is inadequate. Do women alone show concern, love, compassion, sympathy or kindness? To suggest as much is as offensive as to suggest that only men possess courage, honour, audacity or determination. For a man to have compassion or for a woman to display courage does not require a peculiar internal facet of the opposite sex but common humanity, and within the pool of common humanity lies an extraordinary range and variety of people.

Some of those people are unrestrainedly masculine, others feminine, and a *very* few are in between, but none of them is a perversion of humankind. Until recently we thought homosexuality was such a perversion and we tried to 'cure' it with medical treatment, but the new orthodoxy declares that it is the unreconstructed heterosexual male who is in need of therapy, sensitivity training and de-clawing. We disagree, and this book is a defence of the male who, probably, is incapable of much change anyway. Many people wish he were more like her, but he isn't and he won't be, because he is what he is. 'If my grandmother wore rollerskates she'd be a trolleybus' (Old Yiddish saying).

SUMMARY
- The normal incidence of male homosexuality is 1–4%, not the 10% usually quoted.
- The heterosexual is no more part gay than the gay is part heterosexual.
- Homosexuality is natural.
- Heterosexuality, in the male, is also biologically determined – not socially conditioned.
- There is no intermediate female side in most males.
- The accusation of 'homophobia' is too often a form of inverted 'heterophobia'.

DESIRABLE AIMS

- Recognition from the gay male that the heterosexual needs his own sexual space would do far more to reduce intolerance than the delusion that he is hiding from his own gayness.
- Biological awareness is more likely to undermine than reinforce stereotypes.
- An early stage in preparing the ground for nondiscrimination is to deny differences. The mature stage is to respect differences: the bio-integrity of the heterosexual male and of the gay.

CHAPTER TWO

Foodsex I

Perhaps he's a rabbit

'What am I,' asks Bill, 'a f-f-fasting rabbit? All those raw leafies and tofuburgers. Even the meat – when it's on the menu – is fatless and bloodless, shapeless and tasteless. No skin. Not a bone to chew …'

'And I thought you were chewing on one,' says Anne. 'Where're you heading?'

'Out to buy some charcoal before the barbecue is banished. Food is going female.'

'Perhaps it's healthier?'

Two months later …

'I did a MedLine search on male and female, food and mood,' says Anne, 'and what the whitecoat world finds is that this health food diet isn't for him.'

'What are you on about?'

'What we were talking about. Whole food. Health food. I called up the research papers. Here are the first four boxes. Digest.'

A battle is being fought in the kitchen and the supermarket. The battle is about what we eat, and some of the heaviest guns are deployed by western governments which bombard us with health warnings, earnest advice and outright rules. Some of them ban unpasteurized dairy products, others refuse to let their citizens eat beef on the bone. If it were up to our governments, we would all live for ever. 'You are,' says the old adage, 'what you eat', and authority is determined that we should all munch our way into perpetual health.

Our mothers told us to eat up our greens, and that advice now haunts our adulthood. Not just our greens (preferably organic) must be eaten, but wholemeal breads, lentils, fruit and wholesome grains. Government mandates food labelling so we can be sure our diet is low-fat, low-calorie, low-sodium and high-fibre. It is not hard to detect a gender divide in these food wars. Broadly, he likes meat, she believes meat is bad and red meat is worse. Her diet is 'healthier', and no one seems to be pointing out how often that word dictates poverty of choice. But so what? Where once we chose our food for enjoyment and taste, now we are made to feel guilty if we do not regard our diet as a lifelong therapy. Eat up your greens, count your calories and beware of fat.

'We do a lot of vegetables, and a lot of fibre and a lot of fruit,' says Mrs Hillary Clinton. 'That includes the President.'[1]

'He *always* eat cheeseburgers,' says Mrs Lucille Robinson (cook at Doe's Eat Place, Little Rock, Arkansas) of Bill Clinton. 'He's just a burger lover.'[2]

President Clinton, like many other men, likes red meat, but Hillary Clinton, like many other women, shuns it. The drop in the consumption of red meat began in the late 1960s, and by the mid-80s it had dropped by half among well-educated, high-income American women. Even among low-income women it had dropped by a third.[3] The same trend occurred in Britain where, by the health-conscious 90s, 43% of the population were eating less meat and most of those were women.[4] A survey by the American government reveals that one woman in seven between the ages of 19 and 50 now avoids eating beef altogether.[5] Given the chance, she will also make sure that her man does not eat red meat, and, institutionally at least, women do control men's menus. The American Dietetic Association says that 97% of its 68,000 members are women, while women make up 98% of the British Dietetic Association.[6] No fewer than thirty-two out of every thirty-three practising dieticians are female, so it is hardly suprising that the diet revolution is led by women. Red meat is out, wholegrains are in.

'Where are these dieticians at?' asks Anne.
'A goat feeds and a man dines,' says Bill. 'And nutritionists cannot tell the difference.'

So what he likes (red meat) and what she provides (salad) are frequently different, and she usually wins the contest, for women, on the whole, have control of the family diet. It is also women who take a greater interest in the latest advice about nutrition in magazines and newspapers. Men are more sceptical, but a woman wants to keep her man healthy and see that he eats 'well'. That means he must eat like her, and she justifies the change of his diet on the grounds of his health. Hard to argue with that, unless of course she has misunderstood what is going on. Has she?

It's entirely possible she has, for there is little published material on the different food needs of the sexes. Texts on nutrition make little or no allowance for sexual dimorphism (dimorphism is the occurrence within a species of two distinct types of individual; 'sexual dimorphism' is the current jargon for male–female differences). In fact most of the male–female distinctions in food requirements have only recently become apparent, and very few of them are factored into current dietary recommendations. It is time, then, to distinguish what science has so skilfully detected. Time, perhaps, to rethink his menu, and the catalogue which follows is intended to provoke just such a reappraisal. It is a list of observed differences between the sexes, differences not only in how their bodies deal with ingested food, but why they might need different kinds of food in the first place.

First, though, we have to offer a health warning of our own. This chapter is not a discourse on dietetics or nutrition. It is an analysis of external social change set against what science has discovered about the inner nature of the sexes, especially the male, and the finding that the food he needs is not always the same as the food she needs. Sauce for the goose in not always suitable for the gander, because each has distinct metabolic mechanisms with different implications for diet, and the health police who increasingly hedge our foods with prohibitions do not yet understand the differences.

Men can lose weight by exercise alone

The normal woman cannot lose weight by exercise alone but must also go on a diet; this factor probably makes women much more sensitive than men about their food intake. Men can lose weight by increasing their physical activity even if what they eat remains the same. Research at the Lenox Hill Hospital, New York, found that: 'Unfortunately, while there is good evidence for such an effect in men, there is little if any evidence for a similar effect in women. Weight loss with exercise does not readily occur in women unless accompanied by caloric restriction.'[7]

At the University of Limburg at Maastricht in Holland, 16 men and 16 women were put through a five-month endurance training programme and their average daily metabolic rate – the amount of energy they each needed to keep their body functioning – was measured. All 32 of the subjects increased their physical activity by 60%, but the effects on the sexes were quite different. The men's metabolic rate increased markedly: at the end of the 20 weeks they needed an extra 800 calories of food a day just to maintain their body weight, but no such change was detected in the women. The increased rate of exercise was burning the calories off men, but not off women, whose metabolic rate scarcely changed.[8] Life is not fair. A man can jog away the pounds, but a woman cannot. She has to diet too.

It has long been known that men have less fat and more muscle than women. The average male body is one-seventh fat (15%), while fat makes up more than a quarter of the average woman's body (27%). Weight for weight, she has 80% more body fat than he does. If she tries to get her body fat below 12%, by diet or extreme pysical excercise, normal body functions are impaired. For the male, that lower limit for fat is 3%.[9]

Equally striking is the sexual difference in musculature. In men 40% of body weight consists of muscle. Women have only about half this amount (23%). In the adolescent female the fat to muscle ratio increases as she adds fat to the pelvic area and breasts (her breasts contributing only four per cent of that total). In puberty the male growth spurt is accompanied by a hormonally stimulated jump in muscular development which typically doubles his physical strength.

Normal exercise increases the male's metabolic rate. He then needs more energy from food to maintain a constant weight. The Lenox Hill Hospital study found that the female metabolic rate is little affected by exercise, so her exercise regime will not require more food. Nearly every man jack can lose weight by following the Jane Fonda Workout, but Jane can't. A possible reason for the personal effectiveness of her own regime is found in Ms Fonda's admission that her weight-reducing efforts had 'been accompanied by bouts of bulimia'.[10]

A survey by *Cosmopolitan* magazine found that a quarter of its readers were perpetually on a diet, and that one-third of those dieters vomited to make themselves lose weight.[11] That incidence of bulimia nervosa seems high; in the general population the figure is about one young woman in 33, while the occurrence of this disorder in males is a mere one-tenth of that in females.[12]

Women are fond of reminding us that food can spend 'a moment on the lips and a lifetime on the hips'. For them that is true, but for men it is not. They are different.

Men use more energy than women, even to breathe

Scientists at the National Institutes for Health in Phoenix, Arizona, have discovered that, adjusting for differences in size, body composition and age, the resting male's expenditure of energy is 5–10% greater than the resting female's.[13] Furthermore, since muscle is so much more metabolically active than fat, and men have more muscle, women more fat, the sex difference in body composition leads to even greater differences in resting expenditure of energy, favouring males. And not just while he is at rest; men generally expend more energy than women, even when they are engaged on identical tasks.[14] His motor simply turns over at a higher speed than hers does, and the difference begins early in life. Researchers at the Dunn Nutrition Unit at Cambridge University found that even at 12 weeks old a sleeping male infant uses 12% more energy than a sleeping female infant.[15]

Typically, men are more active than women. In a study of some 2,000 adults in South Carolina (431 blacks and 1,574 whites) it was found that between the ages of 30 and 60 men were 43% more active than women.[16] Higher levels of activity require more fuel, so his dietary needs are quantitatively greater than hers. If she eats too much the excess fuel will probably be stored as fat, while he has a greater chance of working it off.

Males need protein more than females

Canadian endurance athletes, both men and women, were put through a series of persistent and gruelling exercises.[17] It was discovered that the women needed to increase their protein intake by about one-seventh, but the men needed to nearly double it. Regular exercise increases the need for protein much more sharply in a man than in a woman.[18]

Exercise produces muscle, and the manufacture of muscle demands protein. The reason a man needs more than a woman is not just because he typically has more muscle, but because of his androgen hormones – the most common of these being testosterone. Androgens are made by both sexes, though in far greater quantity by the male (over ten times the amount after puberty), and they are responsible for the development of such male characteristics as facial and chest hair, baldness, the deep voice, increased libido, and greater aggression. A higher androgen level means a higher rate of protein synthesis (requiring, of course, a higher intake of protein). Men make protein faster than women, they use it faster than women, they need more than women.

Protein

Proteins are an essential part of every cell in the body, and they consist of 20 or so amino acids, eight of which are crucial to our nutrition. Proteins are continually broken down and resynthesized – the average adult reprocesses about half a pound (250 grams) each day – but in that process some protein is lost and needs to be replenished from our diet. We need about 2.5 ounces (70 grams) to do this. Proteins should form 10–15 per cent – one part in seven – of our daily diet.

The body of the average adult man contains between 25 and 30 pounds of protein, of which only 12 ounces (340 grams) is held in reserve. This slender margin means his body (and hers) is reliant on new protein from food. Protein lost through prolonged fasting, or because of an inadequate diet, can result in the wasting of body protein, and when that protein is drawn from the heart muscles the loss is irreplaceable and life-threatening. Children on an inadequate protein diet are often stunted and show poor mental development.

Animal protein is the best available source for humans. Without it, care must be taken to balance the food one eats to compensate for the consequent deficiencies.

Meat is usually 17–20 per cent protein; egg, 12 per cent; cereals, 10 per cent; milk, 3 per cent; potatoes and French beans, 2 per cent; carrots and lettuce, 1 per cent.

Dutch scientists recently examined older adults to see how quickly they used up protein. Even when corrections were made for differences in body composition, it was found that 'protein turnover rates were significantly higher for men when compared with women.'[19] It was also found that protein requirements do not drop with age, but may even increase.[20] Indeed, protein deficiency is the major nutritional problem of the elderly female.[21]

Another research paper reported that elderly people's intake of high quality protein needs to be twice the current recommendation.[22] However, the authors refer only to milk and eggs as 'high quality protein'. There is no meat in their recommended diet. But 'high quality protein' has long had a specific meaning in nutrition circles: it refers to those animal products that have an amino acid balance that is closest to human needs. (Amino acids are the building-blocks of proteins, so to make protein you need the right amino acids in your food.) Some vegetables have a similar protein quantity to meats, but they do not have the quality amino acid balance. Vegetarians, who eat intermediate or low quality protein, may need twice the protein intake of non-vegetarians to provide themselves with the adequate amino acids.[23]

'Didn't I hear of a vegetarian body-builder who recently won a contest in south-east England?' asks Anne.
'A one in 10,000 exception among muscle-men,' says Bill. 'Were it one in 20 we might take note.'

High quality proteins are, in order of merit: meat, fish, eggs and milk. Meat is by far the most efficient provider of protein, containing five times more than milk. Egg protein used to be the reference point for human needs; its amino acid balance is now found to be perfect for a chicken but not for a human, for whom lean meat or fresh fish is closer to the ideal.[24] We need protein, men need it more than women, and meat is the ideal source.

Brain neurotransmitters are affected by diet

Neurotransmitters are chemicals released from nerve endings. They transmit impulses – pass messages – from one nerve cell (neuron) to another. Mostly they work within the brain, but some are manufactured elsewhere in the body. In later chapters we shall see that there are differences in the levels of neurotransmitters used by men and women, but for now it is enough to note a few salient facts that are related to men's and women's dietary needs.

Serotonin is a brain chemical that is much involved with mood control. It promotes sleep and helps govern impulsive behaviour. Low levels, much more common in males, are related to aggressive behaviour. Serotonin, like the female hormone oestrogen, also acts as an appetite suppressant, which is why weight-reducing drugs are designed to raise serotonin levels in the brain. Women, on average, have slightly more serotonin than men, and many more men than women have the lower levels. (See Chapter six for more details about serotonin.)

Neurotransmitters affect far more than appetite. A high carbohydrate meal (starch or sugars, say) will raise the level of tryptophan.[25] Tryptophan is a chemical forerunner of serotonin, and an increase in its level acts as a sedative.[26] A high protein meal like red meat, on the other hand, lowers tryptophan and serotonin levels, thus increasing mental alertness. Men facing a challenging task can sharpen their edge by eating steak for breakfast and by drinking coffee. Caffeine increases our ability to concentrate.[27] What you eat changes how you think.[28]

Why men need iron

The body needs a host of micronutrients to function properly. Iron, for instance, is intimately related to the manufacture of blood: deny your body its fix of iron and haemoglobin levels drop, leading to lethargy. It was briefly thought that too much iron in the diet could lead to coronary heart disease,[29] but a study of more than 12,000 men and women found no relationship between iron stores in the body and death by heart disease in men. The results for women were more ambiguous.[30]

Research is showing that we have too few micronutrients – zinc and iron in particular – in our officially recommended diets, and a serious lack of either harms the body's immune system. Low intake of iron, especially for infants, can lead to irreversible brain damage. A weaning infant has no iron stores and must rely entirely on dietary iron. 'It is possible to meet these high requirements,' reads a leading textbook on nutrition, 'if the diet consistently has a high content of meat and ascorbic-acid [Vitamin C] rich foods.'[31] Vitamin C, just like red meat, is an anti-phytic agent. Phytic acid (phytates are found in brown flour: more of that later) impairs the absorption of some nutrients, including iron. Anti-phytic agents oppose the effect of phytic acid and so improve absorption of trace minerals. Too little iron in an adult can mean impaired memory and learning ability, though the effects are reversible.[32]

Tests on male vegetarians in New Zealand showed them to have little more than a third (35%) of the iron in their blood compared with the majority of the male population. Yet the vegetarians had a significantly higher iron intake. They were eating more iron, but absorbing less, and the researchers concluded: 'Recommended intakes of iron may need to be higher for vegetarians, particularly men.'[33]

'Popeye would have been able to absorb less than 2 per cent of the iron in his spinach,' Bill notes, 'whereas Dracula would have absorbed 20 per cent of the iron in his high protein snacks.'[34]

'Not quite,' said Anne. 'For some unknown reason, iron in blood that is not taken with meat is little more than 2 per cent absorbed.[35] Dracula should take a bite along with his blood.'

Lack of beef is directly and significantly correlated with the male lack of zinc and some vitamins

In 1995 three Arkansas nutrition scientists published an analysis of 43 menus that were to be used in a diet manual – a manual that conscientiously met the US Government's 1990 Dietary Guidelines for Americans.[36] To these health-conscious menus they added 11 more from various Arkansas hospitals and discovered that only one in nine of the 54 menus met the 1989 Recommended Dietary Allowance (RDAs) of zinc for men (set by the Food and Nutrition Board of the National Research Council). Four times more men than women were a fifth or more below their daily recommended zinc allowance. Low levels of zinc lead to a decline in the ability to taste and smell one's food.[37] Loss of taste can mean food is not enjoyed and so less is eaten and so the deficiency increases. Night sight deteriorates. New tissue growth slows. Mild zinc deficiencies have been shown to stunt the growth of Canadian[38] and American[39] infants and preschool children.

The Arkansas authors point out that the continued shift to fish, chicken and legumes 'may lead to zinc levels even lower than those previously found in the American diet'.[40] They conclude that the many dietary calls for the public to cut back on saturated fats may be having a negative impact on mineral utilization. 'Foods rich in zinc and iron may be further limited when people lower the fat content of their diet.'[41] In this they are supported by other research.[42] The Arkansas researchers discovered that the single main reason why there still seemed enough iron in most of the diets was because of the inclusion of breakfast cereals in the menus, and such cereals typically contain artificial supplements. Such a dependence on manufactured supplements seems at odds with the dietary grail of holistic, all-natural, 'organic' ingredients.

Half of the Arkansas menus failed to meet male needs for Vitamin B6. One in seven men – no women – were a third below the recommended intake. Vitamin B6 is involved in the brain's synthesis of neurotransmitters, and abnormalities can occur within two weeks of a B6-free diet.[43] The lack of vitamin B6 indicates a protein shortage, but instead of recommending more eggs or meat on the menu, the nutritionists urged an increase in the consumption of legumes: pulses, mung beans, lentils, chick peas, soya beans or tofu. The nutritionists recognized that there is a distaste for these foods, much more marked among men than in women,[44] but that was not thought to be a barrier. 'Legumes are not acceptable food items to many patients,' the nutritionists noted, 'this is clearly an area that could be addressed by nutrition education.'[45] Here is heard the clear voice of the female-dominated nutrition industry: men show symptoms of protein deficiency, meat will cure the deficiency, but legumes, though far less efficient providers of protein, are deemed to be 'healthier'. He needs red meat? Let him eat tofu.

There are deeply worrying aspects of the officially sanctioned American diet. Nutrition scientists aim to manipulate the average diet to make it ever more healthy, and some of them even accept that it must also be tasty.[46] So far so good. Yet when the diet fails to deliver the goods – when the needed nutrients are unavailable in the approved food – the nutritionists still refuse to increase the amount of meat in the diet, despite their own evidence that it was the reduction of meat which created the problem in the first place. Rather than rethink the diet in the light of current research, their advice is to increase the legumes and whole grains on the menu.[47]

What is not mentioned by the three Arkansas nutritionists is that the USA's recommended dietary allowance of zinc for men is a fifth higher than the Canadian recommendation and a third higher than the British. Canadian and British RDAs for zinc intake are based on a mixed diet of animal protein supplemented by unrefined cereals. The American RDA for 1989 was based on a diet containing foods with a moderate to low availability of zinc, which implies a near-vegetarian diet.[48]

Suggested daily vitamin and mineral allowances are set on the high side and are subject to constant debate. People's needs differ.

Most people need less than the recommended daily allowances, a few will need more, but there is common agreement that when a person consumes less than 70% of the RDA there is cause for concern.[49] Yet a survey of older Americans discovered that 40% of them, both men and women, were falling below this critical level for zinc ingestion. A high proportion of the men also failed to reach the critical level for consumption of Vitamin A.[50] There is a common belief that Vitamin A can be obtained from dark-green leafy vegetables, but even spinach, comparatively high though it is in Vitamin A, still falls far below the levels available from foods of animal origin.[51]

Men need 45% more zinc in their diet than women (unless pregnant or breast-feeding). He needs more zinc because its essential for making androgens – the male hormones that he has ten times more of than her. But where is he going to find that zinc? The problem is compounded because the body's store of zinc is negligible. We do store some, but most of it is in our bone and skeletal muscle and is difficult to release. Typically, only one-thousandth of our zinc is found circulating in the plasma (from where it can be taken up and put to use), so there is no 'store' of zinc in the conventional sense.[52] Fortunately it usually takes many months for a diet low in zinc to result in any deficiency,[53] but research presented to the Nordic Symposium on Trace Elements in Human Health and Disease in Norway, in 1994, warned that 'subtle deleterious changes seem to occur at much lower zinc intakes than was previously thought.'

The USA's officially recommended dietary intake for zinc is based on a semi-vegetarian diet. Yet if there is an adequate amount of meat in the diet, the level of zinc-rich foods you need to eat is far lower, because the zinc in meat is much more easily absorbed by the body than the zinc in unrefined cereals. There is a good reason. Unrefined cereals contain a substance called phytic acid.[54] Wholemeal bread, an obvious example, is phytate rich. Phytates, or phytic acids, block the uptake of both iron and zinc. The speaker at the Nordic conference found that 'from diets with a high content of phytate, less than 15% is typically absorbed while in refined animal protein-based diets up to 40% is absorbed.'[55]

> 'What if some readers think that they haven't enough of some mineral and go and buy iron pills or whatever to boost their intake?' asks Bill
> 'Too much zinc cuts iron in the blood,' Anne replies, 'causing an anaemia that won't go away with iron supplements. But at least on a balanced diet you won't overdose.'
> 'And vegetarians?'
> 'Better consult a sensible doctor.'

Male deficiencies, red meat and phytates

Back to the Arkansas study. If there were enough meat in the diet then men's zinc deficiency would soon be solved, yet by adding more whole grains to the diet, which is what the nutritionists recommended, the overall availability of zinc might actually decrease owing to the action of the phytates in the unrefined cereals.

> 'What's going on?' asks Bill. 'Bran, oats, fibre-rich cereals … horse food.'
> 'Health food,' says Anne.
> 'The phytates in them are zinc zappers. And they slurp up the iron the gut would otherwise take in.'
> 'Unhealthy health food, then.'

Men need a ready, steady supply of zinc in their diet because a lack of it impairs the metabolism of androgens which are the essential male hormones.[56] And where is zinc most readily found? In red meat. Not in white flesh. A lean piece of beef has six times as much zinc as chicken breast and ten times more than in fish.[57] Wholemeal wheat may have almost as much zinc as the beef, but the phytates in the wholemeal block the zinc uptake. Phytates also bind with iron and calcium, two other essential micronutrients, and so prevent their absorption. Phytates are undesirable, but the protein in red meat acts as an anti-phytate agent.

This was well known by the mid-1980s,[58] but somehow red meat has become demonized, even though research has shown that young males brought up on a diet low in meat and heavy on wholemeal bread and unrefined cereals, as is common in some poor countries, experience a high proportion of growth defects. An example is the epidemic of rickets that occurred among the children of Dublin in the 1940s. The Irish Republic, though neutral in the war against Hitler, had been forced to impose rationing and the main bread in Dublin was whole-grain. The combination of the phytates in the bran – which removed the calcium from the diet – and too little Vitamin D, resulted in an epidemic of rickets and after three years of rationing nearly half the children in the city were suffering.[59]

In Scotland the consumption of wholemeal bread has tripled since 1980. Women are mostly responsible for the increase and, unsurprisingly, a report on Scottish eating habits finds this trend 'healthy', while the males who continue to eat white bread are condemned as displaying a pattern of 'unhealthy eating'. This judgement ignores the realities. Wholemeal bread does contain more vitamins and minerals than refined white bread, but much of that goodness is locked into the bran, which is indigestible. Unrefined flour also retains its outer aleurone layer which contains the undesirable phytates. Nutrients in white bread flour, though fewer because the germ and aleurone layers have been removed, are spared the effects of the phytates and so more of those nutrients are absorbed by the body. Additionally, because white bread is thought less wholesome, the nutrients are artificially added. Wholemeal flour, because it is deemed 'natural', is left unfortified.[60] The Scottish men also ate a seventh more red meat than their womenfolk, and this too was deemed to be 'unhealthy', though the researchers made no effort to distinguish between lean or fat meats, just as they appeared ignorant of the deleterious effects of phytates in wholemeal bread.[61] Such is the current health-food wisdom: red meat unhealthy, white bread unhealthy – men are unhealthy.

> 'The label on my wholemeal bread tells me that it's full of goodness,' Anne says.
>
> 'What it doesn't say is how it's full of phytates blocking out that goodness,' says Bill, 'nor how the fibre in the bran speeds food through the gut and so acts as a mild laxative.'
>
> 'Truly,' said Anne, 'wholegrain bread is one of the original fast foods. The good news is that it shouldn't harm you if the rest of your diet is healthy.'

But what is thought to be healthy might very well not be. Current dietary recommendations do not take into account the poor bioavailability of minerals in the high-fibre diet so often associated with health food which, in its composition, is very like a Third World diet. They also overestimate the amounts of protein and energy that are available in such diets because too much fibre is assumed to be digestible.[62] In rural Mexico anaemia is found in a third of men and pregnant women and in over half of non-pregnant women. 'Low meat intake and poor dietary iron bioavailability were associated with anaemia in women.'[63]

> 'Health food ...' says Bill. 'I guess by definition all else is unhealthy: get-sick-and-die-quick food.
>
> 'Here's the definition in my *Collins Concise Dictionary*,' says Anne. '"Health food *n*. vegetarian food organically grown and with no additives, eaten for its benefits to health".'
>
> 'Eaten with a cupboard full of artificial vitamin supplements from the health food store? Yet many a vegetarian lives long.'
>
> 'Life outside the fast lane,' said Anne. 'Slow laps in the pool, aerobics and yoga: less risk and competition – more female

than male. It's not so much a lack of meat that makes for this long life, more a damped-down lifestyle. On the evidence to date, if the nice health-food people ate some nice red meat they'd live an even longer life. And be healthier too.'

Would nice-health food people be healthier if they overcame their repugnance for red meat? A diet containing varying amounts of lean ground beef was fed to young women by researchers in the Department of Home Economics at Illinois State University. For the first seven days all ate vegetarian. For the next three weeks they ate 3, 6, or 9 ounces of beef each day. Bodily iron increased the moment beef was introduced to the diet. Three ounces (85 grams) of beef a day was found to be the ideal amount, for there was no marked increase in the amount of zinc and iron absorbed when greater amounts of beef were eaten. This suggests that moderation is sensible. The researchers' conclusion was that 'zinc and iron utilization was enhanced after consumption of a diet including lean ground beef.'[64]

'A quarter-pound hamburger a day ...'
'... keeps the doctor away,' says Anne.

Except that adding a wholemeal bun to the burger decreases the available iron. So does overcooking the meat. Cook meat to a grey death (an attempt, perhaps, to disguise its blood-origin and now required by law in the USA for hamburger, because of deep fear of bacterial contamination) converts the iron into the equivalent of plant-iron – which is ten times more difficult for the body to ingest. (See above, 'Why men need iron'.) Medium done is better than well done.[65]

Men are short of zinc, women of iron, and both are most easily found in red meat, yet that is precisely what is most often removed from the diet. Her need for red meat is much like his, if for different reasons, but her distaste for red meat is much greater than his. Some people, of course, eschew red meat for moral reasons, and fruitarians take this belief to its logical end by not only rejecting meat but even refusing to consume roots or leaves that cannot be eaten without killing the plant. Karen Nobel, a shiatsu practitioner from London, likes to eat up to 20 mangoes a day. 'The thing about fruitarianism is that you are not murdering anything,' she says. 'It is delicious and it happens to be saving the Earth as well.'[66] Fruitarians tend to a dearth of iron, Vitamin B12 and essential fatty acids, and to flatulence and diabetes from the strain of producing insulin to break down the overdose of fruit sugars.

Karen Nobel turns orange during the mango season.

Men have a speedier gut transit time and greater stool weights than women

Fibre, we are assured, is good for us. Suppose there is a slight down side caused by phytates, so what? Everyone knows that fibre is good. Do they? It was once thought that cereal fibre protected against colonic cancer, but 'the large majority of studies in humans have found no protective effect of fibre from cereals.'[67] Vegetable or fruit fibre might help or, and this seems more likely, it is another, as yet unidentified, ingredient in the vegetables. At least the fruit and vegetables have a low phytate content and so, unlike wheat bran fibre, they will not block the uptake of essential minerals. Increased fibre is tolerable as long as one increases the intake of fruit, vegetables and, yes, meat.[68]

Fibre is also often recommended for the treatment of irritable bowel syndrome, reportedly the most common disorder of the intestine, which affects up to two in every five adults. The main cause is thought to be stress, and twice as many women as men are affected;[69] though food sensitivities, hormones and infections including candida may play a role. The syndrome accounts for half the patients seen by gastroenterologists, who frequently advise their patients to increase their intake of bran fibre. It is of no value. Experiments with three months' bran therapy resulted in a single conclusion. 'The beneficial effects of bran are due to a placebo response.'[70]

Men and women appear to respond differently to wheat bran and vegetable fibre, in regard to both excretion and digestibility. With an identical intake of dietary fibre men tend to excrete more of the fibre than women.[71] On similar diets women have much lower stool weights and a slower transit time than men,[72] and as the common reason for taking more fibre is to assist bowel movements, the current fashion for more fibre in the diet is seldom as appropriate for men as it is for women.

A large increase in male sperm tract abnormalities is linked to the increase in oestrogen-like substances, in both the environment and diet

Soya is the richest source of oestrogen (a feminizing hormone) in today's diet, and oestrogen and similar substances are known to cause reproductive tract disorders in men. 'Soya is the richest source of phytoestrogens and its consumption, especially as a substitute for meat protein, has increased enormously in the past two or more decades.'[73] Many men eat soya products without even knowing it (unless they read the small print on the package label) because it is used as a supplement in many pre-packaged goods. The can might be labelled 'stew', but some of the 'meat' will probably be soya. It is difficult, in fact, to escape this ubiquitous product. Soya beans, soya oil and soya derivatives are used in some 30,000 food products, including confectionery and margarine.[74] Crushed soya beans are used in 60 per cent of all processed foods[75] and are found in six out of ten products on the food shelves of our supermarkets.[76]

Yet Britain's leading sperm expert, Richard Sharpe, eschews soya products. 'I try to avoid buying anything with soya in it for my children,' he says.[77] The sperm decline in the modern male is undoubtedly linked to other factors. For example, at one time cattle were fed growth hormones that resulted in more oestrogen in the food supply. No one will know, says Sharpe, just how much oestrogen was circulating in the women of the 1950s who gave birth to today's generation of men with low sperm counts.

British bakers plan to manufacture loaves with soya flour, rich with plant oestrogens,[78] to be marketed to menopausal women. Four slices are said to provide a natural alternative to hormone replacement therapy. Food scientists are concerned that it might not be safe for men to eat this soya-rich bread. The pure soya flour is meant for menopausal women, but it is already almost impossible in Britain to find a supermarket loaf without soya flour added to it.

At least some people recognize that soya is a food better suited to women than to men. In Australia the 'Sheila's Bread' which is to be introduced into Britain, is claimed to put the waltz back into Matilda.[79] The essential ingredients of Sheila's Bread are soya flour and linseed oil, both rich in oestrogen, but maybe younger Sheilas should be wary: too much oestrogen in young women can inflict undescended testicles on their sons. Whichever way it is absorbed, oestrogen won't put the waltz back into Sheila's menfolk.

'But if soya feminizes the male –' says Bill.

'Perhaps that's why there's so little protest from some of the women's groups.'

'But these soya oestrogens are carcinogens, too.'

'Indeed,' says Anne. 'You know, the Food and Drugs Administration in America has already banned many carcinogens that are a lot less potent than these. If it weren't *natural* I'm sure soyas would have been banned as well.'

So far we have listed various factors that affect diet, and have tried to point out where they have a different impact on men than on women. Some readers may feel that, despite the undoubted importance of zinc and iron, our concerns are still peripheral. After all, we have not mentioned the real villains of the piece. We might claim that red meat is a superb source of protein and micro-nutrients, and so it is, but how can one talk about red meat without mentioning the dread subjects of cholesterol and fat? A man might struggle to get enough zinc in his diet, but too much cholesterol and too much fat will just plain kill him. Won't they?

It is time to deal with the real villains, and they deserve a chapter to themselves.

SUMMARY
- Men lose weight when they exercise – women don't.
- Men, taking the weight difference into account, burn 10% more energy than women. They need more calories weight for weight than women do.
- Men have more muscle and turn over body protein faster, so need more protein than women do.
- Men need 45% more zinc, and meat, especially red meat, is the best source of this crucial mineral.
- Men, without knowing it, are being fed a diet high in female hormones. The ubiquitous addition of soya to food may be literally feminizing them.

FUTURE TRENDS
- He is missing out on crucial minerals – we are cutting out just what he needs to operate at high energy. The meatless male is the lethargic male.
- Future long distant space travel has all-female crews, as the only astronauts who can bear the NASA space diet of soya nuts, tofu cheesecake, salad and pasta everywhere. 'A familiar, attractive and tasty diet,' says a NASA researcher.[80]

DESIRABLE AIMS
- It is time to take his needs into account – a healthy diet is none too healthy for him.
- It is time to take female hormones out of our food. Soya products are added because they are cheap. Wouldn't it be better to pay

the price for oestrogen-free food?

- *Hamburger medium rare, lite on the gamma rays*. Irradiated foods such as burger meat are a fair step to getting rid of nasty bacteria – as long as the consumer is told that the food has been zapped.

CHAPTER THREE

Foodsex II
Where's the beef?

'There are so many women in the place, the menu had got like a Kensington wine bar! They think three lettuce leaves and a spoonful of tuna is a good lunch. We don't.'

Joe Ashton MP was fighting back (successfully, too) against the feminization of the House of Commons dining room. Even there, it seems, the food police had struck. 'There was too much fettucine and penne,' said Mr Ashton, 'and not enough steak and kidney pie and stew.'[1] He was showing the same dietary preference as the male rats studied by researchers at Rockefeller University, New York, where newborn rodents were presented with a choice of pure protein, carbohydrates and fats. By week four the females showed a strong preference for the carbohydrates, while the males opted for the fats and proteins[2] – for meat. An instinctual choice? But let us be wary of rattomorphism, which is the practice of applying rat studies to humans.

Students at the University of Delaware were photographed by hidden cameras as they chose their evening meals in the college dining hall. The men chose bigger portions. No surprise. 'When protein-containing foods were limited men increased their selection of higher-fat items so that energy intake was unchanged.'[3] What the authors did not point out (though their own data shows it) is that the men consumed three times more burgers, roast beef, meat balls, and steak sandwiches than the women. You can lead a man to a salad bar, but you can't make him eat.

Men, given a choice, do what Joe Ashton does: they choose red meat. Yet those who take most of the diet decisions for men, women, choose to give them white meat instead. In the eighties, while beef consumption in the USA dropped from 91 to 73 pounds per person,[4] chicken consumption jumped from 30 to 43 pounds a person. Fish eating also went up, from 13 to 15 pounds a person. In the ten years to 1995 white meat consumption rose by nearly a third in the UK, while beef and lamb consumption fell by a quarter.[5]

Did the cost of red meat cause the decline? If it was purely a matter of economics then the greatest fall would surely be among lower-income consumers, but it was women with the highest incomes who reduced their beef intake the most.[6] So the reason for the sharp decline is not to be found in price constraints.

Perhaps it was fears of mad cow disease? No: the dates are wrong. The decline in sales of red meat predates the 1996 BSE (bovine spongiform encephalopathy) scare which, anyway, is confined to cattle raised in the UK. To date the annual rate of deaths likely to have been caused by BSE shows little or no difference from the rate of deaths caused by salmonella,[7] which is too often caused by cross-contamination from chicken skin. Somehow white meat does not inspire the same sense of danger as red meat.

Beef sales declined not because of price, and not because of BSE, but because the food experts kept telling us that it was unhealthy. 'For a healthy diet, choose fish and poultry instead of red meats,' is conventional nutritional and medical advice.[8] And the underlying reason for this advice is the popular belief that the saturated fats in red meat lead to a high cholesterol count, while those in white meat do not.[9] Beef kills you; what better reason can there be for avoiding it?

'GOOD' VERSUS 'BAD' CHOLESTEROL

The debate about cholesterol is confusing and contentious. Confusion lies at its heart because there are two kinds of cholesterol: 'good' and 'bad'. High density lipoproteins (HDLs) help to protect against heart disease, so they are known as good cholesterols. Low density lipoproteins (LDLs) may increase the risk of heart disease: these, then, are the bad cholesterols. But it is to be remembered that cholesterols, both 'good' and 'bad', are essential to the proper functioning of every cell in the body, and we derive them almost exclusively from animal foods. The catch seems to be that we can have too much of a necessary thing. We need cholesterol to live, but if we ingest too much of the 'bad' cholesterol then, according to the nutritional experts, we die.

It seems obvious that if we eat a diet rich in animal foods we will inevitably increase our cholesterol intake, including, of course, the villainous LDLs. But is that true? The October 1995 issue of the *Canadian Journal of Cardiology* is clear on the issue: 'Analysis of the results from over 30 years of cholesterol feeding studies in more than 2,750 patients indicates that for the majority of individuals modest changes in dietary cholesterol have little if any effect on plasma lipoprotein cholesterol levels.' So a modest increase in the consumption of animal fats will have little if any effect on most people's cholesterol level. Matters are made more confusing by the conclusion of a report in the *Mayo Clinic Journal* which reads: 'The total cholesterol level is a relatively weak marker for the risk of coronary heart disease.'[10] What these professional journals appear to be saying is that too much weight is placed on cholesterol levels and that the link between such levels and coronary heart disease has been exaggerated. Cholesterol was once reckoned the major coronary villain, now it is blamed in only 20% of heart attacks.[11] Fear is created that is either out of proportion to the risk or, when the risk exists, out of proportion to our ability to lessen the risk. The cholesterol card is too easily and too often overplayed.

Analysis of two decades of cholesterol-lowering studies has failed to show a related decrease in total deaths.[12] The most recent Scandinavian study on the effects of lowering cholesterol with drugs had too few deaths to show any significant reduction in total mortality.[13] Some other recent studies do show more favourable results from cholesterol-lowering drugs,[14] but it is also argued that yet more studies are needed if these results are to be accepted as conclusive.[15] The scientific jury is still out, so while we await the verdict it is instructive to learn of some findings by David Barker and his team at the Medical Research Council's Environmental Epidemiology Unit at Southampton. In a study of 6,500 men they found that a man's weight at one year old was a far better predictor of death from heart disease than his cholesterol level within a year or two of his death.[16]

The case against cholesterol, or specifically against LDLs, is unproven, but a prudent person might prefer to accept that LDLs are indeed dangerous and so avoid those foods which are high in them. Which, surely, means avoiding red meat? But is the bad cholesterol that results from eating beef really any worse than the bad cholesterol found in chicken? That is what 13 Texan researchers investigated in 1991[17] when they checked the good and bad cholesterol levels of 46 men given differing diets. Employees and students from the Texas Medical Center, Houston, were first fed a 'stabilization diet' of regular prime beef (13.6% fat) for four weeks. They were then divided by lot into two separate groups and for the next four weeks one group was fed with lean top round and loin steaks (both containing 4% fat) while the second group was fed chicken breast and red snapper (both containing 1.7% fat). The rest of the diet, vegetables, fruit, drinks, etc, were the same for both groups.

The researchers discovered that 'changes in total cholesterol and LDL [the bad cholesterol] were similar in the two diet groups ... percentage decreases in HDL [the good cholesterol] also were greater in the chicken and fish diet group than in the lean beef group.' In other words, the men who ate the beef had more good cholesterol at the end, and the same amount of bad cholesterol, as those who were forced to eat chicken and fish. Other studies also show that diets with lower levels of fat cause HDL, the good cholesterol, to decrease.[18] So the result of the Texas Medical Center study flies in the face of common prejudice: the beef eaters had the better cholesterol profile.

A recent experiment shows that low fat diets increase anger and hostility and makes people more depressed – and that a low fat diet had no total effect on cholesterol. A team led by Dr Anita Wells at the Centre for Human Nutrition at the University of Sheffield studied two groups of men and women. The volunteers spent a month eating a diet in which 41 per cent of the energy came from fat – a typical British diet level. Then for another month, half were given a diet with only 25 per cent fat – slightly lower than the health department's 'healthy eating' guidelines. The result: the 'good' form of cholesterol, which protects people against heart attack, declined, while the bad form showed no change – meaning that the low fat diet may actually increase risks in this case. Dr Wells concludes: 'Everyone says that eating low-fat diets will cut cholesterol, but the science doesn't demonstrate it.'[19]

Response to a low-fat diet may depend entirely upon a person's genes. Dr Ronald Krauss of the Lawrence Berkeley National Laboratory, California, told the American Association for the Advancement of Science in March 1998 that very low-fat diets reduce heart-attack risks in only a third of the people who adopt them. The rest –- two-thirds of men and five-sixths of women – fail to respond to the diets, or may even 'suffer increased risks because of the genes they carry'.

'It seems,' says Anne, 'that the less-and-less important the intake of cholesterol becomes, the more-and-more important it becomes to cut its intake.'
'That follows,' says Bill. 'To the degree its intake is found harmless, or meaningless, so it is safer to manipulate its intake.'

So the science does not condemn red meat in the diet – indeed, it appears to endorse it as a means of raising good cholesterol levels. If only it were that simple, for even more recent research introduces yet another level of uncertainty. Dr Ronald Krauss has found that the response to a low fat diet depends on the dieter's genes. Dr Krauss has further divided LDL, the 'bad' cholesterol, into two kinds and he finds that about one-third of men and about one in five or six post-menopausal women have what he calls Pattern B LDL,[20] and it is this pattern B that does the damage. So the minority of people who possess Pattern B LDL do benefit from a low fat diet, while the rest, the majority, do not. Indeed, if people without Pattern B LDL go on a low fat diet, they run the risk of converting their harmless Pattern A LDL into the deadly Pattern B.

This book cannot be the place to resolve the continuing debate over cholesterol and its effects, but we can note that there is nothing in any of these scientific studies to confirm the nutritional world's condemnation of meat. Eating red meat does not increase your levels of LDLs and does increase your HDLs, so if cholesterol is your beef, then the dangers have been hugely overestimated while the benefits of red meat have been played down. Not only is red meat a splendid source of protein and micro-nutrients, it confers other blessings. Dr Richard Petty of the WellMan Institute in London has been monitoring men who have switched from red meat to white, and his study discovered a significant decrease in haemoglobin, the blood component which carries oxygen from the lungs to the muscles. For men who insist on avoiding red meat the WellMan Clinic prescribes iron and Vitamin C in an attempt to restore their fitness.[21] Simpler to eat beef, perhaps?

But what about fat? Not cholesterol, but nasty, horrid, artery-blocking fat? If there is any one popular diet certainty then it is that we should all cut our consumption of fat, so surely we should be refusing red meat?

IS 'HEATHY' FOOD HIGHER IN ALL FATS?

Fat, we are told, is killer food, but we need fat's essential nutrients, which include fatty-acids and fat-soluble vitamins. Fat is also a rich source of energy, and it helps make many foods palatable. The average person can safely consume about three ounces of fat every day. Nearly everyone carries an adequate reserve (the obese have an over-adequate reserve), so we can live without fat in our diet for a while, but once the reserve is gone we must supply the body from our diet. We all need fat. Pity that it's a killer. Or is it?

The major cause of heart disease is impaired blood supply. The coronary arteries which supply blood to the heart are narrowed or blocked by plaques (cholesterol-rich deposits on the artery walls) that first compress, then cut, the blood flow. These plaques were investigated by researchers at the Wynn Institute for Metabolic Research in London. Their work studied the fats in the bodies of people who had died of heart attacks, comparing the fat in the blood and adipose tissue (which reflected the dead person's dietary intake) with the fat in the fatal plaque deposits. The British medical journal *The Lancet* carried their conclusions: it was not the saturated but the polyunsaturated fats which were implicated in the plaque formation. 'No associations were found with saturated fatty acids. These findings imply a direct influence of dietary polyunsaturated fatty acids on aortic plaque formation and suggest that current trends favouring increased intake of polyunsaturated fatty acids should be reconsidered.'[22]

A definition is needed here. Saturated fats come from animal foodstuffs: from meat, butter and other dairy products. Unsaturated fats come from vegetable sources like olives and, just as with cholesterol, popular wisdom divides the fats into good and bad. Saturated fats (from animals) are considered bad, unsaturated (olive oil and others) are good. The Wynn results seem to contradict that categorization; it was the unsaturated fats which contributed to the plaque, not the saturated.

A similar finding about strokes, published in the *Journal of the American Medical Association*, resulted from a study carried out by a team from Harvard Medical School which examined the link between diet and heart disease in a group of 832 middle-aged men from Framingham, Massachusetts. The researchers followed these men for twenty years and concluded (though they warned that their conclusions require confirmation from other studies) 'that restriction of fat intake among residents of Western societies, as recommended by the US National Cholesterol Program and others, does not decrease and could increase overall risk of ischaemic stroke'.[23] Ischaemic stroke, by far the commonest sort, is caused by a blockage of the blood supply to the brain by a fatty restriction in the arteries of the head or neck. The researchers also noted that a reduction in stroke risk is linked both to total fat intake and to the increased intake of saturated fats.

The Framingham study, like the Wynn results, suggest that our assumptions about fat, and about saturated versus unsaturated fats, need re-examining, but again, let us err on the side of caution and ask whether those who wish to avoid a high-fat diet would be sensible to keep red meat out of their diet? After all the standard nutritional texts commonly claim that a piece of raw red meat is one-quarter fat.[24] Meat is also said to provide a quarter of all the saturated fat people eat.[25] One authority even estimates red meat to be 40% fat.[26] These are scary statistics. They are also plain wrong.

Today's meat tends to be lean and so it makes sense to calculate the fats in beef from the figures given for the leaner cuts. Most of the best cuts of beef are one part in eight of fat (12.5%), less than half of which is saturated – yet still nutritionists exaggerate both the amount of fat in meat and its dangers. Look at the rankings of seven items drawn from a table in *The British Medical Association Complete Family Health Encyclopedia*:[27]

Food	Total Fat content
	(grams of fat per 100 grams, or 3.5 ounces, of food)
Sausage, pork, cooked	42
Beef, lean with fat, roast	40
Low-fat spread	39
Cream, whipping	38
Cheese, cheddar	32
Chocolate, milk	30
Egg yolk	30

We checked these figures against the individual rankings in the authoritative English nutritional text published by the Royal Society of Chemistry.[28] The ordering is seen to invert: a proper analysis of the fat content places the meats, not at the top, but at the bottom of the table.

Food	Total Fat content
	(grams of fat per 100 grams, or 3.5 ounces, of food)
Low-fat spread	40
Cream, whipping	39
Cheese, cheddar	34
Egg yolk, raw	30
Chocolate, milk	30
Forerib, lean and fat, roast	29
Sausage, pork, fried	24
Sirloin, lean and fat, roast	21
Sausage, low fat, fried	13
Topside, lean and fat, roast	12

How is it that a medical reference book, the main one for the British home, overstates the fat content of a sausage by some 75% to 200%? And exaggerates the fat in roast beef by between 40% and 200%? How does such overstatement go unchallenged? Red meat alone, it appears, is safely demonized.

'A simple mistake?' suggests Bill.
'Perhaps,' said Anne, 'the Royal Society of Chemistry got their figures wrong too?'
'Oh my god, should we check theirs as well?'

We did, and while we can accept that the figures provided by the internationally respected Royal Society of Chemistry are accurate, we do question the methods used to arrive at those figures. The method entails boiling down a complete piece of meat to discover its fat content: no allowance is made for any fat that might be trimmed off before cooking, nor for the fact that a good deal of meat fat is dissolved in the cooking process and then thrown out by the cook. Nor is any allowance made for the fat discarded by the carver or the eater. It is assumed that we eat all the meat, fat and all, that was sitting on the butcher's slab.

Yet in the real world we cook, trim and discard fat. One of the fatter cuts of beef, sirloin, is one-fifth fat when raw, but the actual fat eaten is much less than this. Let us err on the side of caution and imagine that a full half of the fat from the fattiest cut is eaten: even then the total fat in the meat is only 10%. And what that boils down to is that the saturated fat in the beef is less than the saturated fat contained in a digestive biscuit.

> 'Not four parts in ten fat,' says Bill, 'as in the medical encyclopedia.'
> 'Not even a quarter fat,' responds Anne, 'as in the other nutritional books.'
> 'More like two parts in ten.'
> 'And only then if you eat it raw with all the fat. Fat in the meat we really eat is often as low as one part in ten.'

The cholesterol and fat cards are most overplayed when it comes to red meat. Deborah Bull teaches nutrition to the students of the Royal Ballet School in London. She does not eat meat, preferring a diet of pasta, bread, starches, fruit and vegetables.[29] 'Lean steak,' she says, 'derives only 40 per cent of its calories from protein, the rest from fat.' That would mean that lean steak was 30 per cent fat, whereas in fact it is about 6% fat. Ms Bull overestimates the fat in red meat by some 500%. Meat fat content tends to be overstated in nutrition texts by 100% or more, and what do the authors recommend should be eaten instead? Foods that contain the same or even more saturated fats than lean rump steak (2.5% saturated fat):

steamed salmon (2.4% saturated fats)

Fruit 'n Fibre breakfast cereal (2.5% saturated fats)

instant dessert powder made up with skimmed milk (2.9% saturated fats)

oatcake (3.9% saturated fats)

avocado (4.1% saturated fats)

sunflower seeds (4.5% saturated fats).

Other so called 'diet' foods contain the same amount or more of saturated fats as a prime grilled rump steak which, fat and all, contains 5.2% saturated fats:

Greek yogurt (5.2% saturated fats)

Low fat potato crisps (6.2% saturated fats)

Dairylea Light cheese 'only half the fat content' (7.3% saturated fats)

Kraft Cheddarie Light (10% saturated fats)

Philadelphia Light 'half the fat' soft cheese (10% saturated fats)

Pact 'Between Heart and Hand' Reduced Fat Spread (15% saturated fats)

So if your aim is to reduce your intake of saturated fats, then replacing red meat by diet foods will not always do the trick. Anne watched customers buying their lunches from stalls in Covent Garden that sell baked potatoes. Men liked the meat-based chili-con-carne filling that gave them 11% protein and just 3% saturated fats. The women, and only women, chose potatoes filled with cream cheese, providing 1% protein and 30% saturated fats.[30] Something strange is going on with a woman's choice of healthy foods when, in her effort to avoid fat, she actually eats more of it. When people age 19 to 50 eat out, the women, though they eat smaller portions, eat a tenth more saturated fats.[31]

Are saturated fats in beef the real villains? Look at the following table we compiled from the Royal Society of Chemistry figures:[32]

Composition of food per 100 grams (3.5 ounces)

Food	Fats %	Saturated fats	Cholesterol (mg)
Grilled rump steak, lean	6.0	2.5	82
Beef stew	7.2	3.3	30
Roast sirloin, lean	9.1	3.7	82
Grilled hamburger (10% fat when raw)	9.1	4.2	82
Roast ribs of beef, lean	12.6	5.2	82
Grilled rump steak with all its fat	12.1	5.2	82
Vegetable samosas	9.9	5.2	16
Vegetarian cheese and tomato pizza	11.8	5.5	16
Macaroni cheese	10.8	5.6	28
Custard tart	14.5	5.6	95
Doughnut	21.7	6.3	24
Smoked mackerel	30.9	6.3	104
Croissants	20.3	6.5	75
Digestive biscuits	20.9	8.6	41
Roast sirloin of beef with all its fat	21.1	9.0	82
Reduced fat cheddar-type cheese	15.0	9.4	43
Wholemeal quiche	22.4	10.4	140
Cheese omelette	22.6	12.2	265
Polyunsaturated margarine	81.6	16.2	7
Plain chocolate	29.2	16.9	9
Shortbread	26.1	17.3	74
Vegetarian cheddar cheese	35.7	22.5	105

'Wholemeal quiche really does have more saturated fats than sirloin of beef.'

'And,' says Bill, 'because you don't eat all the beef fat your quiche may have twice the saturated fats.'

'So why is red meat off the menu?' asks Anne.

'Maybe it's a colour preference?'

'Strawberries? Raspberries? Cranberries? Sweet autumn apples?'

Officialdom, too, is prone to getting fat content wrong. A UK government committee announced in September 1997 that anyone eating over 3 ounces (80–90 grams) of red meat a day should consider cutting back for heath reasons.[33] The subsequent scientific ridicule of the recommendation was less widely reported. It seems likely that at least one of the scientists on the committee grossly overestimated the fat content in red meat. Much searching of the databases and scientific journals fails to reveal any other plausible reason for the government-approved scare.

Beef fat is not, of course, the only villain. When other meats are eaten, the now standard advice is to cut off the fat. 'Remove the skin before eating chicken,' says the Department of Health Nutritional Task Force.[34] 'Remember to remove skin from chicken before cooking,' says Marks & Spencer's magazine.[35] And if you forget? 'Remove skin from poultry before serving,' says the supermarket handout.[36] Most of that chicken fat drains away in the cooking and is then thrown away. There is an easy test: roast a chicken. What is that liquid in the base of the pan? It is fat, up to 95% of the chicken's fat that has run off the bird in the oven. The crisp skin that you eat is nearly all protein. But the nutritionists continue to measure the chicken or pork or beef fat in its raw state. Do they think cooks ladle up the fat and drink it?

The puzzle deepens. The so-called nasty saturated fats in beef are little different from those in chicken or fish. Something remarkable is happening; not only are saturated fats exaggerated in red meat, but what is substituted as 'healthy' is very often higher in saturated fats (see the table above). 'Low fat' products are thought good for you even though the fats in them are often higher than in meat. When women cease to eat fats in meats they maintain, and often increase, their consumption of fats, including saturated fats, in other foods. It is hard to maintain that the real concern with red meat is with its saturated fat.

Red meat is simply the best food for essential amino acids and thus for protein, yet it is rejected. And what is substituted? A typical piece of advice from a diet manual recommends, 'carbohydrates, such as potatoes, bread, rice and pasta, are not high in calories, and should form the basis of any healthy diet – including a weight loss one.'[37] Note that a potato is thought good to eat: no diet manual would ever recommend sugar, yet the starch in the average potato converts to six teaspoons of sugar within half an hour of eating and your body cannot tell the difference between that sugar and the demonized white granulated sugar that you have so carefully avoided. Six in seven people do not give up potatoes when they go on a diet,[38] despite their sugar content. Many will consume lettuce because it is regarded as a healthy food, but lettuce, nutritionally, is virtually non-food. Indigestible fibre, anti-food which passes blithely through the body, is considered especially healthy. Soya substitutes are thought to be far healthier than real meat. In 1995 the Food Commission, an independent consumer watchdog, found that 17 out of 21 popular brands of vegetarian burgers and sausages derived more that 50 per cent of their calories from fat. The fattiest vegetarian sausages derive 82 per cent of their calories from fat and cost more per pound than prime steak.[39]

Unhealthy health food. An obvious contradiction, but for many people today that is not a problem. Those who doubt everything give equal footing to the rational and to the fantastic.

'If science finds health food unhealthy,' asks Anne, 'won't those who eat it also find it unhealthy?'

'Quite the reverse,' says Bill. 'Here are minds that draw the line against drawing the line. To take sides is found wrong. So, by definition, those who side with science are found wrong.'

'Then how do we persuade our health food friends that they're wrong?'

'We don't. The better the case we make the more they will know they are right.'

'Fantasy wins.'

'To disbelieve the probable leaves only the improbable to believe in.'

Man can live by meat alone. In 1743 four Russians were marooned in the Arctic and for the next six years their entire supply of food was 150 reindeer and 10 polar bears with a seasoning of arctic foxes.[40] The four men were all in good health when they were rescued. We do not recommend emulating their example. This book is not attempting to switch men on to a wholly carnivorous diet, nor does it deny the beneficial effects of fruit and vegetables. We should all eat up our greens, but when we are told that we must also abandon red meat on 'health' grounds, we are justified in being very suspicious of the advice.

'Personally,' says Bill, 'I'm a two-thirds vegetarian.'
'You're a what?' asks Anne.
'Meat and two veg.'

The evidence demonstrates that some factor other than health considerations is implicated in the switch from red to white meat. Something about red meat deeply troubles the women of the West.

'Don't ignore the obvious,' says Anne. 'You see the fat in red meat. And women are more concerned with fat – with being fat.'
'Isn't is more obvious that red meat is red?'
'Deal with fat first.'

The mantra of the food fundamentalist is 'You are what you eat'. If the fat is visible then it follows that the fat-eater will end up visibly fat. Some nutritionists recognize the problem when they divide fats into 'visible' and 'invisible fats'. 'Visible fats are those that are readily apparent to the consumer: the spreads, the cooking oils and the fat on meats.'[41] Invisible fats are those which are locked up in the other ingredients; no one sees fat in a biscuit, so a biscuit cannot be as fattening as marbled beef. Fat, which gives the fullness of taste and the feeling of satiety, is found ugly.

To see the visible fat – most obvious in red meat or in the yellow layer under raw chicken skin – is to catch the enemy in your sights. Aversion to fat, or lipophobia, is linked to women's aesthetic desire for an hourglass figure, and to their belief that fat is ultra-unhealthy. Yet it appears that most women who cut meat fat from their diets actually gain weight. A study in Minnesota in the late 1980s found that most men kept their weight steady, but that women, who overwhelmingly had adopted a low-fat diet, were gaining weight.[42] Plainly something is wrong with the new diet when women who conscientiously reject fat gain weight and men do neither. A clue is gained from an Australian study which found that those who eat less fat, mostly women, were eating more fruit sugars and drinking more alcohol.[43] An American study similarly found that 'women are getting less fat from red meats and more fat from other foods such as dairy products, breads, legumes, vegetables and fruits.'[44] Women with the most education most reduced their fat intake from red meat – but have the largest increase in fats from other foods.

Women are thus trading sources of dietary fat. This is know as the Balloon Effect. Visualize fat intake as acting upon a partially inflated balloon. Cutting out eating red meat depresses one part of the balloon. 'The balloon responds by expanding in other directions, such as the increase in fats from dairy products.'[45] Men too will gain weight if they adopt the female diet.

> 'If she is what she eats,' says Anne, 'then she sure doesn't know what she's eating.'
> 'We are what we digest,' says Bill, 'in food as in thought.'

It is possible, even probable, that most women know nothing about fat content in food other than the misleading figures they read in magazines and diet manuals. Yet to argue that the science is little known leads to the obvious response: *Why is it not better known?* The question becomes more acute when it is realized that it is the most educated women who are in the anti-beef vanguard. (Does it take more education to sustain a fantasy?) These are women of whom so much more is expected, and who in turn influence other women, yet their new food mantra 'Eat to Live' is little more than the philosophy of an underfed goat.

'Men are so basic,' avers Anne. 'For them food that tastes good is good.'

'Women are, too,' says Bill, 'when they insist that "it's-good-for-me" food tastes good. Isn't her approach more in touch with the animal need to live? I mean, that's fairly basic.'

Results from three related studies on food selection show that females give consistently higher 'pleasure' ratings to the foods they believe are healthy. Women also give a higher pleasure preference for low-calorie foods than men. 'It should be apparent that males and females group foods quite differently when the criterion is pleasure,' conclude the five authors of a study from Kansas State University.[46] The female is much more concerned with the 'health value' of a meal, the male with the raw pleasure value.

Psychologists at Reading University find that enjoyment can boost the immune system and so protect the individual from disease. Professor David Warburton, founder of Associates for Research into the Science of Enjoyment, suggests that guilt about food can raise the level of stress hormones and so damage health.[47] If a woman finds enjoyment in her new health food then she may well live longer. But to give the same food to the male, the food he does not enjoy, might well shorten his life.

In the past, as now, women ate less meat than men. Did they prefer to eat less meat? Or was it because they were often served last, after the men had eaten?

Traditionally, in France, it was the women who chose chicken, salad and white wine, while the men went for steak and red wine. The traditional female meal, says Margaret Visser, a classicist turned food writer, has 'no red blood and little fat in evidence'.[48] Fish, too, was thought more feminine, partly because it was a picky dish for polite society. Men wanted solid bites of meat.[49]

Men prefer the hearty and tend to take a more sensual satisfaction in the food they eat. Pleasure is related to the palate, not the life-expectancy tables, and flavour, to him, is more of an appetite stimulant. The new woman almost seems to dislike the sensate qualities of food. Could this lead to the extinction of civilized desire? To the end of the ancient art form to which women have contributed so much: the pleasures of the table?

A word of caution is needed here. There remain many women who are untouched by the health-food fads, who enjoy a piece of beef as much as any man, who delight in a groaning table and in the pleasures of civilized eating, yet far too many women have been persuaded by the nutrition industry that whenever a man is left to his own culinary devices he sets about committing suicide. 'It's good for you,' they say to him as they present him with a limpid plate of nutritional vegetables, 'so eat it.' He is treated like a little boy. It might also be that he is being taken down a peg: if men do not always get what they want then perhaps it will be good for them. She takes pleasure in giving him her health food: in censoring what he wants. 'If it's good for you, it's not supposed to taste good,' says the author of the Paris guide to meatless cooking.[50]

Three out of four times one can tell men from women by their stated food wants.[51]

Men prefer steaks, roasts, burgers, ham 'n' eggs, and sausages with fries.[52] This is not just an American cultural phenomenon. Middle Eastern girls in Bahrain prefer to eat fruit, broad beans and chocolates, while the boys want their red meat.[53] In Britain twice as many men eat sausages as do women. Half the women report that they never eat a sausage.[54] Women show a higher preference for macaroni cheese, soup, salad, pasta, vegetables, fruit and white meats,[55] while men choose red meat. One in three Frenchmen, when eating out, orders steak.[56] Spanish men head to the *tapas* bar, a traditional male haunt, for their meat balls, stewed bulls' tails, and squares of blood (set solid with vinegar). Mighty medieval titbits 'to give men strength at night'.[57] In Ireland they like their blood-rich black sausage, the Frenchman's *boudin*, while in

Pennsylvania the men devour scrapple, rumoured to be the swept-up slaughterhouse scraps compressed into a delicious block. And nor do men just prefer such bloody foods, they are also more adventurous in all their eating tastes than women. The University of Cincinnati, Ohio, offered people 455 different foods and drinks and the most striking gender difference was the tendency of women to refuse unfamiliar items. A significant number of males scored higher in the intensity of how much they enjoyed foods, and there was no evidence that this was caused by sexual differences in ability to smell or taste.[58]

'"All of life is a dispute over taste and tasting",' quotes Bill.
'Nietzsche, right?'
'He was a vegetarian, you know.'
'Only briefly,' says Anne. 'He gave it up because it left him short of energy.'[59]

Does it matter that the professionals – the nutritionists and the dieticians – are so overwhelmingly female? Yes it does, for they are imposing on men a diet which is ill-based on science, ill-suited to the male's metabolism, and drawn more from feminine fantasy than from food science. Health food is largely a female concern, but one that is increasingly inflicted on men. To argue that nutrition is blind when it comes to the sexes – that dieticians treat men and women equally – is to point to a sexism that is intolerant of the masculine difference. The dieticians' health concerns are revealed as feminine, and never more so than in her untiring efforts to eradicate red meat from his diet.

The argument against red meat is sustained by concerns of 'health', which does at least sound vaguely scientific, but she can only make a convincing case against it by skewing the evidence. Why? The answer is obvious (perhaps blindingly so).

Blood is associated with killing, strife and the smell of death. Red meat is equated with nature that is red in tooth and claw: raw, gory, coarse, brutal, animal, uncivilized and male. It is men who are tainted with bloodletting (and eating red meat). The beef-eating male is seen as the taker of life.[60] Men shed blood unnecessarily (that many shed blood in the defence of peace, and that most shed none at all, is not taken into account). They are no longer perceived as a potential form of security but as a threat to all life. Blood in meat is linked to the beast in man.

'To oppose red meat is to damn the masculine presence in the world,' observes Anne.

'Shift it around,' says Bill. 'Those who want to turn the male into something else will not serve him red meat.'

In a single generation the traditional sources of meaning – right and wrong, good and bad – gave ground; most of all among those who are schooled in self-doubt. In an absence of meaning, life itself can take on meaning and the animal instinct to live becomes itself a right: the right to life. *Life is for living*. The circular logic is all-embracing. No longer are we talking just about human life, but about life in general. The line between humans and other animals is erased (even, in the case of fruitarians, between humans and vegetables). It is thus possible to seize the moral high ground (or, rather, climb into the moral highchair) by defending a cabbage's right to life or, more usually, a heifer's.

It is possible to date the growth in the female aversion to red meat by examining the studies of food aversions during pregnancy. In the two surveys prior to 1970 there is absolutely no aversion among pregnant women to red meat.[61] Quite the reverse. In the early 1960s a study of 900 first-time pregnant women in Aberdeen found a craving for black pudding – a sausage based on pig fat and fresh blood that is sliced and deep fried in fat.[62]

Ten other studies, done in different cultures since 1970, show that meat, and particularly red meat, became the most common food aversion during pregnancy. It is now shunned by a third or more pregnant women[63] (and that is in addition to those who already avoid it). This aversion occurs despite medical advice to eat more red meat because it helps the critical iron levels during pregnancy. So we must look to the late sixties and early seventies to find the causes for women's aversion to red meat.

There were two obvious changes in women's lives at that time, both of which were likely contributory factors to their change of diet. The first was the growth of the feminist consciousness – the feeling that women should have an equal chance to be in control. The second, a related development, was the greening of the female conscience: the one world, whole food, organic, wholemeal, holistic view of life. 'Tofu came in at a time in the 1960s when it was associated with peace, love and Woodstock,' says Bonnie Kumer, nutrition consultant and vegetarian.[64] With the greening there arose a guilt about the extravagance of Western diets compared to food shortages in poor countries, and that guilt led to a belief that because people in the world go short of food there must be a world food shortage (a concept much easier to grasp than why many people are too poor to buy food). The empathy with poverty translates into a wholegrain diet that is strikingly similar to poverty food.

This new consciousness led to repugnance. At Coombe Girls School, New Malden, Surrey, a quarter of the girls have given up eating meat. 'Most pupils, even the meat eaters, felt that they could not pass a butcher's shop without averting their eyes.'[65] It is not just visible fat which offends, but visible blood. Meat in the super-market is sanitized with a white pad. 'The pads are used to soak up the blood juice for hygiene reasons,' says a spokeswoman, 'and also to make the meat look tidier and more appealing.'[66] Even Baroness Thatcher, whose toughness as Prime Minister earned her the sobriquet 'the Iron Lady', shares this aversion to the sight of blood. Away! Away! She was so upset by several paintings that depicted bloody hunting scenes at Chequers, the PM's country residence, that she had them removed from her sight.[67]

Men and women drift ever further apart when it comes to the foods each wants to eat. Increasingly women eat what they want to eat (significantly, women who live without male partners consume even less red meat than women with partners[68]), but what women want to eat is not what men want to eat. Nor, and this is important, is it what either sex needs to eat. There is stubborn resistance to the new scientific knowledge. It becomes apparent that the reason for the shift in diet is less to do with nutritional needs than with psychological urgings.

Twice as many women are vegetarians as men.[69] Among teenagers vegetarianism rises to 20 per cent.[70] Two out of three of them are female.[71] Vegetarians increase as one goes up the social scale and, consequently, their influence is out of all proportion to their numbers. 'Vegetarianism is still dominated by women,' says the female chief executive of the Vegetarian Society: 'but as women still do most of the shopping they can have a disproportionate impact.'[72] This conversion to vegetarianism was, and is, driven by 'health reasons'.[73] In the 1970s it was more likely to be for religious or 'philosophical' reasons,[74] but today the words 'health' and 'moral' have become interchangeable. Still more women are quasi-vegetarians. Though, in truth, two in three professed vegetarians do not identify aquatic animals as animals and half of them appear to classify chicken as an honorary vegetable.[75] It is the red meat that deeply disturbs.

What commonly passes as health food is, literally, poor man's food. It is a medieval fast: a renunciation of the flesh, indeed, a renunciation of flesh itself. It is Dark Age fodder. It is a form of perverted Puritanism; remembering, always, that the best of English and American plain food was served by a Puritan gentry for whom God's bounty was not to be spurned.[76] The pleasure in today's health food is rooted in the denial of the sensuous: in the denial of male pleasure.

The modern female intellectual so much deprecates food that she cannot even bear to mention that some of her heroines were most famed for their cooking. Ann Douglas in *The Feminization of American Culture* tells the lives of three of her cultural stars – Sarah Hale, Catharine Beecher and Maria Child – without once alluding to the fact that they were, in their time, the all-time best-selling authors of American cookbooks.[77]

The women who write today's cookbooks spice their recipes with a high moral tone. In the mid-90s Philippa Davenport was twice named Cookery Writer of the Year by the Guild of Food Writers.[78] 'I am aware,' Davenport says, 'that three or four days may pass in a week without my eating more than a couple of ounces of meat. On the other hand I am aware of my growing need for grain protein.'[79] And this from a woman who, in the 1970s, was perhaps the best plain meat cook in England. The converted Davenport writes: 'New-wave vegetarianism is concerned not with cant but the pleasures of good eating without meat. Red meat, that is.' How nice to have cant off the menu. Frances Bissel, the cookery writer for *The Times*, tells us: 'Although I am not a vegetarian, I cook at least as often without meat or fish as I do with them. Sometimes I use no animal proteins at all.'[80] Hear the high moral tone in those last eight words. It is the commonplace of the new woman: 'We do not eat red meat these days.' The assertion, delivered with the bright-eyed assurance of the Born Again fundamentalist, brooks no contradiction, unless perhaps it can come from one of those superannuated Dead White European Males: 'Dost thou think, because thou art virtuous, there shall be no more cakes and ale?'

'Is life too short to give pleasure?' asks Bill.
'There's less and less generosity,' says Anne. 'That's what's worrying.'

The female increasingly serves the male her own brand of health food. What's more, if the male will not do 50% of every household chore, including the cooking, she is advised to 'go on strike'. This is the nineties 'relationships' advice of an upmarket woman's magazine, *Good Housekeeping*.[81] Not only must he eat her food, he must cook it too. Lysistrata lives, only this time she denies him his food.

There are real differences in food requirements. The male likes and needs more red meat – for energy, minerals and brain food –

and he is getting less. At a time when mainstream research finds that women, with their low intake of iron, would benefit from more red meat, she cuts it from her diet. She eliminates what males, young or old, want and need to eat. She even compromises her children's physical development and mental health by cutting out essential fats and proteins that are most economically found in red meat.

There is a balance to be struck, but it will not be found by imposing the desire of one sex on the other and so achieving the spurious equality of treating the sexes as the same, but by allowing for the splendid differences. Today the sexes grow distant, blinkered to each other's wants and needs. They are no longer on a collision course, as in the early days of feminism, but on courses that drive them apart; each in the belief that the other is made in the likeness of itself.

Traditionally the food on the table was the choice of the male. The meal was structured for him and, if he was affluent, it was meat-based. This is the Victorian diet of boiled mutton on Sunday, cold mutton chops on Monday, reheated mutton on Tuesday, mutton pie on Wednesday, mutton curry on Thursday, and so on. The male imposed his agenda, his preferences and his pleasures on the woman.

In the past she cooked for him, today she cooks for herself. Now her food – white, pallid and with pulses – is for him, and she declares that it is in his interest (self-interest is well justified as being in the interest of the other). Less willing to take risks, more attuned to scares, she puts the family's health at risk. As we will see she is less likely to take risks, so more susceptible to the arguments about negative consequences of eating red meat. Their differences in co-operation and empathy make females more likely to listen to 'expert' advice and to be more sympathetic with concerns about the lives of animals. Red meat has become a rare food for the well-off and health-conscious. There may be a delectable sense of revenge in this: doing to him what he too long did to her.

Her diet is hurting him, and hurting her too. Ironically, if she ate more of what he wants to eat, both would be healthier. But food is only one of the markers in the new state of relations between the sexes. It is time to move on to the other differences that can make for the distinct: the differences that make for the real difference.

SUMMARY
- Diet has little influence on cholesterol levels.
- Eating red meat increases the 'good' cholesterol without influencing the bad cholesterol.
- Saturated fats are necessary to health; they even protect against strokes.
- Low fat spreads have four times more fat than lean beef.
- Low fat products have more saturated fat than lean rump steak.
- His pleasure in food lies in the sensual, hers in its perceived health-giving properties.
- Red meat has been demonized – health has been the excuse, but politics is the reason.

NEGATIVE TRENDS
- *In the short term the growth in so called health foods will continue.* The butcher is already an endangered species. Are there only six butcher shops left in all of the United States? White bread, more healthy than wholemeal, disappears. Worse is on the cards. A tax on eating meat is seriously proposed by a green lobby in America.[82] Shopping for groceries on the Internet could lead to a monitoring of cholesterol intake. It is possible to build an intelligent fridge that refuses to open the meat section if someone has removed the weekly ration. The fridge could tell you to eat more fibre, and dispense it.
- Nutracerticals become the rage. Food and biotech companies combine to produce souped-up foods that go beyond claims to reduce cholesterol or low fats to promote health benefits, such as reduced blood sugar levels and improving the immune system. There will be even more snacks with 'extra bran', and 'health milks' will have genetically altered bacteria that colonize

the gut. None of these provide any extra benefits that could not be had by eating a reasonably balanced diet – but her 'healthy option' is on the menu.

DESIRABLE AIMS

- Sensible men and women, of whom there are still many, can fight back. The minerals and amino acids in the diet are best found in real meat as part of a balanced diet. There are still many women who give, not just take, pleasure. They will find, with a wealth of scientific evidence to support them, that the direction in which the health food world is heading bodes ill for both sexes.

- To continue on the present course is a recipe for nutritional and marital disaster. The table should be a place of compromise, a place for mutual pleasure; and, hope as she might, he is not going to eat her lentil soup and enjoy it.

- What she eats is a means of telling others what she is or would like to be: thinner, fitter, healthier, more beautiful and more knowing than others. She increasingly caters to her aspirations, not his. And she will be out of the kitchen, with more 'free time' and eating healthily. Strains in marriage are apparent. Gerhard Schröder, the German politician, divorces his wife Hillu when she goes veggie on him and refuses to serve him sausages.[83]

CHAPTER FOUR

Brainsex I
Bottom of the class

The last three decades have witnessed an extraordinary innovation in the history of humankind: a belief, at least in the West, that important sexual differences are moulded by culture. Not, of course, the obvious physical characteristics, but differences in behaviour, aptitudes and attitudes. This is much the same argument that we encountered at the beginning of Chapter One, that our sexual orientation is culturally determined, but culture is blamed for much more than our mere choice of bed-partners. Today's gender orthodoxy insists that men and women are 'equal', whatever that means, and that whatever he can do, so can she, so long as the playing field is culturally levelled. In the past there was a general acceptance that men were distinct from women, that the sexes behaved differently, each was less skilled at certain activities but more skilled at others and so worse or better suited for some occupations; but now we are told that those assumptions resulted from phallocentric thinking. The new orthodoxy insists we are equal, whatever the cut of our underwear.

'Remember Daph the Daft,' asks Anne, 'the schoolteacher near Oxford who protested when you said there are brain differences between boys and girls? She claimed that "the proper teaching method is to treat each pupil as an individual".'
'She probably got that from dear departed Dr Spock,' says Bill. 'He was wont to talk in soundbites about individuals, instead of about sex differences.'

'Then Daph said, "Each child's an individual, you know?"'

'One truism safely chases another.'

'Then she said, "Each different and in that the same."'

'Vacuous Daph. Without ever using the word "sex" she still
    managed to imply that there are greater differences within a
    sex than between the sexes.'

'But now,' says Anne, 'we are discovering the differences that
    make for a real difference. We are finding out what makes
    girls and boys distinct.'

'Then we might learn something useful,' says Bill, 'though I
    don't suppose Daph will.'

The new orthodoxy warns parents that they can ruin their
daughters' lives by 'sex-typing' them, which means that by buying
a doll for a girl you are dooming her to a life of motherhood or
nursing. Dolls are what boys should be given, while toy trucks and
fire-engines are the playthings that will expand the girl's horizon.
This attempt at deconstructing the sexual difference began in the
1960s and it failed, but the sixties parents blamed their failure on
the wider culture: on television, the cinema, newspapers and,
especially, schools, which were still mired in the old patriarchal
attitudes. That is no longer true; the wider culture has long fallen
to the new orthodoxy, which means that modern parents must
surely be able to mould their children exactly as they wish and
have the full support of the outside world as they do it.

School libraries have been rigorously censored for 'sexist'
material. Books which have been classics for years, like the works
of Enid Blyton in Britain or, in America, the adventures of 'Cherry
Ames, Student Nurse', have been consigned to the ideological
dustbin. Even the language reflects the new wisdom: firemen have
become firefighters and meetings to enforce the new vocabulary
are run by a chairperson or even a chair. History is her story, God
has undergone a sex change, and thus women have been freed
from the dead patriarchal hand that stopped them fulfilling their
potential. Or so we are told, yet despite this enormous effort to

persuade us that men and women are identical in their abilities and attitudes, the sex differences persist. Girls still buy Barbie dolls in their millions, read more than boys do and care more for their friends. Boys still love action-packed toys, war games and competitive sports. Cherry Ames is still a student nurse, despite all the efforts to make her a rocket scientist.

Common sense, not to mention the lessons of several thousand years of history, might give us pause about the underlying assumption that men and women are the same, but those with a social agenda ignore the evidence and insist that culture alone is responsible for our masculinity or femininity. Such pundits might not really matter – they could be classed with other eccentrics like those who still believe the earth is flat – except that these postmodernists have inordinate influence in education, government and, at least in the United States, in the media.

Yet research laboratories are producing evidence that contradicts this new orthodoxy. The evidence is compelling, and it shows that much of masculinity and femininity is not imposed by society, but is also influenced by our biology. The postmodernists either ignore this evidence or else contradict it with scientific evidence of their own. For example, they cite a celebrated case of a baby boy whose penis was irreparably damaged during circumcision.[1] The decision was taken to refashion the boy's genitals so that they appeared female and then to bring him up as a girl. 'John' became 'Joan', and we are assured that 'Joan' became a happy adult female without any physical or psychological problems. Here, the postmodernists assure us, is proof that society can change a person's biological sexual identity. *Time* magazine, commenting on the case in 1975, remarked that John/Joan 'provided strong support to the idea that conventional patterns of masculine and feminine behaviour can be altered',[2] and this case is still trotted out as evidence of the power of culture to overcome brute nature.

There is just one sad drawback to this otherwise impressive piece of scientific evidence: it is not true.

It took decades for the truth to emerge, but it was finally revealed in an academic paper.[3] John (his real name is still a secret) spent many hours with the researchers, as did his parents, and their tale proved to be very different from the happy outcome so celebrated by *Time* magazine. 'Joan' never did adjust to the female identity she had been so cavalierly given. As early as the age of five his/her parents knew that the sex change was a disaster. He ripped off the pretty dresses and asked if he could shave like his father. 'She' insisted on urinating standing up. Female toys were rejected in favour of guns. At puberty they tried treating 'Joan' with hormones to quell the male in her, and though they succeeded in giving her breasts they never persuaded her to like them, nor to wear a bra, nor, alas, to transfer her romantic interests from girls to boys. When Joan reached the age of fourteen her parents wearied of the struggle and at last told her the truth, whereupon this poster child for sexual neutrality made his own decision to revert to being what he had been born: a male. Surgery removed his hormone-induced breasts, more surgery fashioned him a penis, and today, far from being a happy Joan, he is a married John with three adopted children. So the truth of this story, which is still cited as proof of a culturally-induced sexuality, is the very opposite. Nature wins. John was behaving in the male-typical way even when he thought he was a girl and was indeed being treated as such.

At this point some people will protest that there is no such thing as 'sex-typical' behaviour; indeed, even to raise the possibility of such a thing is to invite the accusation of stereotyping. Yet anyone who has lived or worked with small children knows that boys and girls behave differently. By the time they are four years old children prefer to play with others of their own sex. Boys choose to play noisy, competitive games that test one against the other, while girls prefer verbal, co-operative games that exercise their personal skills. They are already behaving like men and women, as though their games are a rehearsal for adult life.

Scientific evidence backs up these common-sense observations.

Eleanor Maccoby has been studying sex differences for over thirty years and has conducted many experiments on how young children socialize.[4] Her results are consistent; girls are much more sociable, while boys are likely to be competitive and aggressive. Other experiments with young children show precisely the same thing. Boys like rough and tumble play, they use more space, they make more noise. Girls are quieter and more sociable. The psychologist Diane McGuinness tried an experiment in which pre-school children were presented with a range of new toys and games, and she discovered that the boys moved from one item to the next four times more frequently than the girls. Boys were bored more easily, interrupted each other more often, and were generally far less sociable than the girls.[5]

None of this will surprise pre-school teachers or the parents of young children, who daily observe the sex-typical behaviour that children display from their earliest years. Boys prefer toys that make a noise, they like activities in which they can manipulate objects and they enjoy boisterous play. Girls like much quieter activities and can concentrate for much longer. No wonder many teachers prefer to teach girls, for they are much more co-operative, and it is hardly a surprise that six to ten times more boys are diagnosed as having Attention Deficit Disorder (or hyperactivity). Boys do have a shorter attention span; girls aged between 7 and 10 typically spend twice as much time on a task as boys do.[6] This difference grows with age; a recent study concluded that the attention-span of a teenage boy is five minutes, while that of a girl given the same activity is twenty minutes.[7]

Girls are more compliant; they do as they are told more readily and more often than boys.[8] Boys play in larger groups, their play is rougher and takes up more space. Boys will happily colonize the streets or public places, while their sisters will prefer to play at home.[9] Girls tend to form close relationships with one or two other girls, and sharing confidences within that intimate group is a marked part of the feminine pattern. Boys' friendships are rarely so close, and tend to revolve around mutual interests and activities. And when boys are in a group they interrupt each other, issue commands, make threats and revel in annoying each other. They like jokes and insults, and are far quicker to use physical force. Girls, meanwhile, are more likely to express agreement with another speaker and pause to give someone else a chance to speak. Girls are not assertive among themselves. They do pursue their own ends, but more by persuasion and by trying to bring about agreement.[10] Boys, then, are more active, less attentive, noisier, and they display far more aggression. One result of this has been to label boyish behaviour as an abnormality and to prescribe drugs that will change that behaviour. Are our modern methods of upbringing making us perceive boyish behaviour as a disease? We shall argue later that this does seem to be the case, and that we are drugging boys to make them better-behaved – to make them, in fact, more like girls.

Even those who insist that our sexuality is culturally induced might, on being confronted with a classroom of children, agree that there is such a thing as sex-typical behaviour, but they would probably argue that it is produced by parents. Parents, the postmodernists claim, treat their sons and daughters in different ways and so encourage typical male and female behaviour. By this theory parents are, even if unconsciously, encouraging their boys to be rowdy, noisy, aggressive and inconvenient. The idea is a nonsense. If anything, most parents do the opposite; they are constantly struggling to civilize their sons. The research shows that parents spend far more time on their boys, expend much more worry over them and punish them more frequently, all in an attempt to curb that impetuous rowdiness.[11] As often as not they fail because that regrettably boisterous behaviour is wired into the male child while he is in the womb. We not only come into the world with a distinct physical gender, but with a sexually distinct behavioural agenda too. None of us is born sexually neutral.

A tale of chromosomes and hormones

At conception the 23 chromosomes in the mother's egg are joined by 23 more that come in the father's sperm to provide all of us with 23 pairs. The key chromosomes that determine our physical sex are, not surprisingly, known as the sex chromosomes and they form one pair. The male pair is XY and the female XX. The egg has a single X and the sperm couples it with either an X or a Y chromosome. If the egg is fertilized by a Y-carrying sperm then the foetus usually becomes male. If the winning sperm carries the X chromosome then a girl usually develops. So the sperm determines the sex of the child.

The Y chromosome is the key to masculinity, for it triggers the production of high levels of androgens, male hormones, in the foetus. These male hormones switch on a cascade of genes that are found on all the other 22 pairs of chromosomes that males and females share. The female foetus lacks the Y chromosome and so the androgens are not activated; thus her genes for masculinity are not switched on. She has those genes – within every woman there is the capacity for beards and baldness – but without the androgens that are the legacy of the Y chromosome, those genes should remain dormant. In a male foetus, however, the switches are thrown. The high levels of male hormones are the key to that process, and they are very powerful.

It was discovered many years ago that one could change the physical sex of an animal by manipulating the hormones during its very early development. A genetically male baby rat deprived of male hormones will develop as a female, behaviourally and anatomically. A genetically female baby rat exposed to male hormones will develop as a male.

continued overleaf

We do not manipulate hormones in humans (we can, but it would be seriously unethical); still, nature has provided her own evidence. There are genetic XY males who suffer a disorder that prevents their genes from responding to the activating hormones, and such men develop the physical appearance of a female (the disorder is called an androgen insensitivity syndrome). Then there are the genetic XX females who mistakenly produce high levels of male hormone during their foetal development. (This genetic disorder is known as congenital adrenal hyperplasia, or CAH.) These girls have an abnormality in their adrenal gland that leads to an over-production of androgens. They are born with male genitals, or with ambiguous ones, depending on the levels of male hormone they are exposed to.

'That's all a bit complicated, isn't it?' Bill suggests.

'Not really,' Anne says. 'It's just like the idea we discussed when we looked at the development of sexual orientation. The female is the basic human pattern, and it takes the addition of male hormones to create the male's physical appearance.'

'So the female is the basic model and he's the customized version?'

'Yes, and it isn't only his sexual orientation that is customized. Even a man's level of aggression is fixed in the womb. The more testosterone a foetus gets, the more aggressive he'll be as an adult.'

'A hot rod, eh?'

Not even the postmodernists would deny the crucial role of chromosomes and hormones in determining the biological sex of a foetus, but there is controversy over how far-reaching the effects are. Do the hormones simply mould the body? Or do they also affect the growing mind?

In Chapter One we saw how Professor Roger Gorski and his team could alter the sexual orientation of rats at the drop of a hormone. A baby male rat deprived of testosterone becomes female in sexual behaviour, while the female dosed with testosterone behaves like a sexually aggressive male. But it is not just the rats' sexual behaviour that is changed. The masculinized female becomes more assertive, more territorial and more skilled at finding her way through a complex maze. In real-rat life females are not nearly as good at males at negotiating complex mazes, but a masculinized female can do it just as well as a normal male. Humans, of course, are not rats, but we do share a similar nerve structure and use the same hormones, so is the human brain also sexed in the womb? Thus leading to the sex-typical behaviour we see in classrooms and playgrounds?

The most compelling evidence for the foetal determination of sex-typical behaviour in humans comes from biological accidents, from those CAH girls who were accidentally exposed to high levels of male hormones while they were in the womb. Congenital adrenal hyperplasia occurs in about one in a thousand births. In extensive research on the CAH girls the results consistently show that, in addition to altering the girl's physical body, the male hormones also alter her behaviour. CAH girls have a boyish play pattern. More than thirty studies throughout the world confirm this,[12] and the following story[13] illustrates just what these girls are like.

When Susan was born her genitals were slightly abnormal and this symptom alerted the doctors to a possible problem, leading to a quick diagnosis of congenital adrenal hyperplasia. Treatment with drugs was eventually successful in restoring her body's chemical balance to normal, and a simple operation corrected the genital abnormality, but Susan's mother vividly recalls just how different she was from her elder sisters:

They were never any trouble, but Susan, well, she was a nightmare. She was a noisy baby, she never slept and was quite uncontrollable as a toddler. I couldn't take my eyes off her for a second or she would be a hundred yards down the road all on her own. She could never sit still. She was always found playing with a group of boys, and the games she enjoyed most were rough and playful. She came home with her clothes filthy and torn.

Like other CAH girls, Susan preferred the rough and tumble style of boys' play. The toys handed down from her elder sisters were ignored: she did not want their dolls, except to use as weapons. Her mother remembers that at four years old Susan wanted a remote-control jeep for Christmas. She was fed up with all the dolls and things everyone kept giving her. She soon had a collection of trucks, cars and trains and she would spend hours making zooming noises and crashing them into each other. She was a wiz with Lego, building intricate three-dimensional towers.

Susan's pattern of behaviour continued to be much more like a typical boy's. Her favourite pastimes were climbing trees and playing ball with the boys. Her mother recalls:

'She really had very little interest in playing with other girls. So it wasn't always easy for her to find playmates. Sometimes she'd get into some awful scrapes trying to do the things the boys did.'

No one could deny that Susan's parents did their best to bring their daughter up as a girl, yet she persisted in behaving like a boy. Her father tried hard to persuade her to take up a nursing course, and she did try, but gave up after a few weeks because she simply could not cope with the caring side of the job. She eventually became a successful structural engineer, an area of employment that is 98% male.

The mirror image of CAH girls is a handful of boys who are born with a genetic abnormality that gives them an extra female chromosome, making them XXY instead of XY. Such boys are born looking male, but during their foetal development their exposure to male hormones has been abnormally low, as is their exposure to the second crucial drenching of masculinizing hormones which occurs at puberty. These XXY boys are feminine in their behaviour. They are far happier playing with girls, they hate the boisterous games of other boys, and are less aggressive and competitive than the average male. Other hormonal accidents occurred in the 1960s and 1970s, when thousands of women were given hormones during difficult pregnancies and, though their children showed no physical abnormalities at birth, they did display the same behavioural changes as CAH girls or XXY boys. These children have been extensively studied and those girls who were exposed to male hormones in the womb were found to be far more aggressive and assertive than their sisters, while the boys exposed to female hormones grew up more feminine in behaviour.[14]

What these 'accidents of nature' show is that we really are born with a behaviour pattern programmed into our brain. You can give a CAH girl all the Barbie dolls in the world, and all she will want to do is arrange them into battalions and mow them down with mock gunfire; try to toughen an XXY boy as much as you like, he will stubbornly insist on being gentle and considerate. Each is displaying sex-typical behaviour, albeit of the opposite gender, and they graphically prove that our sexual behaviour patterns are not inflicted on us by culture, as the postmodernists insist, but are imprinted in the womb. And if more proof were needed it comes from another group of children who are apparently born as girls, but who become boys at puberty (when the second drenching of masculinizing hormones occurs).

These children are not really girls at all, but boys who, although they are genetically male, were subject to an inborn metabolic problem which denied them an adequate level of the form of testosterone that is responsible for extruding the penis. They do possess penises, but they are very small and easily mistaken for a clitoris, so that at birth their genitals appear female. Such children are often raised as girls, and thus receive plenty of the social conditioning that might determine their feminine sexual identity, but at puberty the surge of androgens leads to an enlargement of the penis so that it becomes recognizable (though smaller than usual). The 'girls" voices break, they develop facial hair, and they become what in fact they always were: boys. This sounds a traumatic rite of passage, but Julia Imperato-McGinley has been studying these rare cases for many years and reports that the overwhelming majority have few subsequent problems. Most of them, indeed, switch to male behaviour with ease and go on to marry and have children of their own.[15] Why is the transition so smooth? Because their brains, shaped by androgens before birth, always were male and so the female social conditioning had minimal influence on them.

Some people might be ready to accept all this evidence, yet still baulk at the idea that levels of behaviour are determined in the womb. Surely, they might say, a brain can become male or female before birth, but how could a grown man's level of aggressiveness be set in the womb? Surely that depends on his upbringing? An opportunity arose to test this assertion because a maternity hospital had preserved blood samples drawn from mothers during their third month of pregnancy and Richard Udry, a sociologist, was able to examine the offspring born to those mothers.[16] By the time Udry discovered the blood samples the babies were all grown up, and Udry was able to measure the amount of testosterone present in the mothers' blood and correlate it against the adults' behaviour patterns. Those patterns were measured on a series of scales showing how much interest they took in things like clothes, do-it-yourself projects or jobs, and the results demonstrated that the level of foetal testosterone determined male-behaviour characteristics. The more androgens a girl baby received in the womb, the more aggressive the grown woman's behaviour. Male foetuses are exposed to 5–8 times the levels of females: men are even more aggressive.

The evidence is overwhelming, yet still there are parents who persist in trying to raise their children as 'sex-neutral'. Barbie dolls are inflicted on boys who would prefer to have toy guns, while little girls unwrap toy trucks on their birthdays. It does not work. Children have minds of their own, and those minds were powerfully shaped in the womb. Society can reinforce those minds, but it does not, cannot, reverse their orientation. The hormones are massively effective engineers of brain and behaviour, and their effect means that boys are not girls, and cannot be made into girls, nor girls into boys, nor either into something in-between. The brain-sculpting effect of the hormones also has a profound effect on the way that a boy's brain and a girl's brain work, and that, in turn, affects the way each sex learns. It is a difference that, as we shall now see, is largely ignored by the education establishment.

At the start of this century women were still considered too weak-minded to be academically educated. The vast majority of men got little education either, because there was small opportunity for them outside the middle or upper income groups, but there was even less chance for women. It was believed that young women would fall prey to neurasthenia or some other nervous disease if they strained their pretty heads with an intellectual challenge.

His education came first; hers a poor second.

His education was usually classical (Latin or Greek, and so on to Oxbridge or the Ivy League), while hers was practical (needlework and home economy).

That view seems ludicrous today, yet the current attitude to education is equally wrong. The unisex world contends that, given equal opportunities, there will be no differences between male and female in terms of educational interests or achievements. Equality is confused with sameness, and the confusion does neither sex any good. We do need to provide equal opportunity, but we must not expect equal outcome – especially between the sexes. Males and females are drawn by the biases of their brains to learn in different ways and to have different interests and enthusiasms, and any educational system that insists that boys and girls are the same, and must therefore be treated the same, is set to do damage.

Few would claim that education in the West is serving its

children well. 'The well documented decline of the quality of state education in America is an ominous sign,' the *Financial Times* reported,[17] going on to say: 'The social consequences and costs of a large growing underclass that is not fit to enter the modern capitalist economy may over time be the Achilles' heel in the drive for true political legitimacy and superior economic performance. *Most of those that leave school without reading or writing skills are male.*' (Our italics) The Industry Education Group claims that schools could be producing an 'unemployable generation'.[18] On 4 April 1997, *The Times* was reporting a chronic decline in boys' performance in British schools, and such stories became commonplace. Something is seriously wrong with the state of education, and most commentators see its most worrying symptoms in the manner in which education fails boys.

The classroom was one of the first institutions to be feminized and the effect has been to make the education system user-friendly to girls but hostile to boys. Naturally boyish behaviour is frowned on in this female-dominated world, a fact recognized by some males in the teaching profession. Martin Spafford, a teacher at an East London comprehensive, says that 'boys feel continually attacked for who they are. We have created a sense in school that masculinity is bad.'[19]

The feminization of the classroom means that boys are supposed to learn in the girl's way, and her way is verbal and non-competitive.[20] Boys are not as verbal as girls and far more competitive, so many boys find the female-dominated classroom an unfriendly context. Proof is in the results. In English schools girls are now more successful than boys in every subject except physics. 'Why?' asks Her Majesty's Chief Inspector of Schools. 'The honest answer is that nobody knows and it becomes increasingly important that we find out.'[21] He attempts an answer, blaming teachers, the lack of male role models and the anti-education culture of the working class male, but everything he adduces is social. He does not mention the vast and basic research on how boys learn differently from girls. More recently the Education

Minister, Stephen Byers, also acknowledged the problem: 'We must challenge the laddish anti-learning culture which has been allowed to develop over recent years and we should not simply accept with a shrug that boys will be boys.'[22] But boys *will* be boys. To think otherwise is to deny nature's ineluctable reality, and the challenge is not to change the boys to suit the system, but to change the system to make it as boy-friendly as it is already girl-friendly.

Statistics from around the world reveal a similar pattern – that when girls are given a chance to go to school they do better than the boys.[23] Learning in a typical schoolroom comes more naturally to girls, and they find the feminized teaching environment far more to their taste. Girls pay attention, boys fidget.[24] The modern classroom favours (in the US it requires) a non-competitive approach, which girls like, and relies heavily on verbal skills, which deploy the girls' natural strengths. Girls, too, are better organized; their schoolwork is usually neatly written and submitted on time, while boys are more likely to turn in careless work. Boys, as we have already seen, have a shorter attention span, which may be because of their lower boredom threshold, and without imaginative teaching they often begin to misbehave.[25] This is hardly surprising. Boys are naturally more active, aggressive and restless and so need more control.[26] Informal lessons do not work with most boys. They feel they are being let off the leash and use the freedom to make mischief.

In the early school years girls do far better than boys in every subject.[27] They learn to talk, read and write earlier[28] than the boys, and current teaching methods make it even harder for the boys to catch up. Why? Because the male's more natural skills are spatial, while the girl's are verbal. Boys are better at simple manual tracking tasks, at hand-eye co-ordination and at three-dimensional puzzles,[29] talents that are rarely appreciated in the classroom. Girls talk to their toys and the boys deconstruct them, but most teaching ignores a boy's spatial skills and depends on the verbal skills at which a girl excels.

These are, of course, average differences with vast overlaps between girls and boys – some boys will have high verbal attainments and some girls will show high spatial skills – but there is very little overlap at the extreme ends of the distribution curves. As always with statistics these observed differences do not predict individual performance, but they do foretell the likelihood that a girl or boy will behave in a certain manner. Thus we can be reasonably sure that most girls will perform better on tests of verbal fluency or on solving anagrams and, indeed, girls do outperform boys by a huge margin on such tests.[30] Throughout the world girls are better at this sort of test than boys.[31]

But girls do not have the same advantage when it comes to solving mathematical problems. These call for the male's spatial talents, and studies show[32] that the male brain uses his more visual right-brain skills to solve mathematical problems while the female's uses verbal skills to tackle what is essentially a visual test. We see this in everyday life, where most men have a (much vaunted) greater talent for parking a car (Americans call it 'parallel parking', the challenge being to reverse the car into a kerbside slot). He sees the space, sees in his mind just how the car will fit into it, and slots it home. She takes longer, because she first needs to put the problem into words. She estimates the car's length, gauges the available space, then juggles the two by asking which is larger, and by now he is already wondering how she ever passed the driving test in the first place. The difference also shows in the male's better sense of direction. Men carry a spatial image of a journey's geography in their brains, women do not, though she may well be better at finding the way next time because now she has reduced the answer to a verbal one ('turn right at the church, left at the post-office'). He nevertheless is more likely to have a better sense of direction,[33] though not an infallible one, as any woman knows who has sat beside a man who, most annoyingly, refuses to ask a stranger for directions. This basic difference between men and women is fundamental and is confirmed by an extraordinarily wide body of research; women are generally more verbal, men are more spatial. She is good with words, he is good with things.

This difference is even found in animals; male chimpanzees and rats are much better at finding their way through a maze,[34] but females (including humans) are better at remembering the landmarks.[35] These differences, both in animals and humans, have been demonstrated repeatedly, yet that has not stopped the argument about the influence of biology on sex differences in ability. Those who deny such variation are usually politically motivated, and the most vocal of them are the hardline feminists in British and American universities who, in their eagerness for political respectability (and, of course, funding), deny the existence of biological advantages for either sex. The very words they use betray their bias. All male/female differences are described as 'gender' differences, and in their terminology 'gender' is a matter of societal influences with no recognition of the influence of biology.

One of their camp, the psychologist Diane Halpern, decided to settle the argument for herself. She was certain that 'gender' differences were all caused by cultural bias, and that she could prove it.[36] 'It seemed clear to me that any differences between the sexes in thinking abilities were due to socialization practices, artifacts and mistakes in the research, and bias and prejudice.' But once she had studied all the evidence, she admitted she had been wrong: 'After reviewing a pile of journal articles that stood several feet high and numerous books and book chapters that dwarfed the stack of journal articles, I changed my mind ... there are real, and in some cases sizable, sex differences with respect to some cognitive abilities. Socialization practices are undoubtedly important, there is also good evidence that biological sex differences play a role in establishing and maintaining cognitive sex differences, a conclusion that I wasn't prepared to make when I began reviewing the relevant literature.' Gender is biology as well as society.

Professor Doreen Kimura has devoted her life's work to the study of sex differences and their biological underpinning. 'Scientific evidence for consistent sex differences in cognitive function between men and women has accumulated for well over fifty years. A solid body of research, carried out primarily in North America and Western Europe, has established that men, on average, excel on spatial tasks (particularly those tapping ability to imaginably rotate a figure), perception of the vertical and horizontal, mathematical reasoning and spatio-motor targeting ability. Women, on average, excel on tasks of verbal fluency (where words must be generated with constraints on the letters they contain), perceptual speed (in which rapid pattern-identity matches are made) verbal and item memory, and some fine motor skills.'[37] Kimura also notes: 'Women have larger colour vocabularies, better verbal memory and better performance on a test of finger dexterity.'

Those who deny biological advantages for either sex are flying in the face of the scientific evidence, and in one area that evidence is particularly striking. It derives from the work of Professor Camilla Benbow who has been researching highly mathematically gifted children for over thirty years and her results have been consistent over that long period.[38] At the top end of the ability scale there are thirteen mathematically gifted males to every one female. Males are much more likely to excel at higher mathematics, at physics and at economic studies, indeed at any area where mathematical reasoning is needed. Women have the skills to win the Nobel Peace Prize, but it is a rare woman who will win the Nobel Prize for Physics or for Economics, and that has nothing to do with society's bias, but all to do with the male's inbuilt advantage. He simply finds higher or abstract mathematics easier. Camilla Benbow says: 'Among the gifted there are sizable gender differences at age 13, favouring males in mathematical reasoning and in spatial and mechanical reasoning abilities – the very abilities required for the physical sciences. At the end of high school and college these differences remain.'[39]

Professor Benbow goes on to argue that these differences help explain the disparate male/female achievements in maths/ science, and also explain why men and women choose to concentrate on different specialist areas in higher education. Girls are frequently urged to focus on engineering, physics or mathematics, in order to prove that they are the equal of the high-flying male students, but not only are girls less well-equipped to tackle these subjects, their very inclinations guide them away from those areas into subjects more amenable to their skills. Even when the girls possess high mathematical ability, they will very often choose to study something that appeals to them more.[40]

The hardline feminists simply refuse to entertain the idea that boys just might be plain better at higher mathematics than girls. They insist that girls are scared out of being good at it, though they never really explain why anyone should want to frighten girls away (except to claim, of course, that there is a male conspiracy to keep women down). Their explanation makes no sense, except to conspiracy theorists, and the accumulated evidence from years of research demonstrates that the sex difference in higher mathematics, however regrettable, is firmly in the biological domain.

The truth is that the brains of the two sexes are organized in different ways, and it is that difference which gives rise to the differences in ability. When men are engaged in a verbal task they use only the left side of their brain, while women use both hemispheres to process language. Women simply have more of their brain set aside for dealing with verbal matters. Professor Ernie Govier, a psychologist at East London University, has been studying brain organization for ten years and has found that the most articulate of his subjects are using both sides of their brains, the female strategy, while the less verbally gifted use only one.[41] Professor Govier has found some males who are as verbally gifted as women, but it comes as no surprise to discover that those men had the female brain pattern. Govier argues that sex-typical academic choices (boys choosing engineering while girls study languages) are in part a result of sex differences in brain structure and organization. These differences in the brain lead to sex differences in abilities, interests, levels of aggression, motives and emotional characteristics, and these in turn will influence what boys and girls choose to do in school.

Drs Sally and Bennett Shaywitz at Yale University[42] have produced the most dramatic evidence of these differences. They took pictures of the living brain while it solved a language problem, using a Functional MRI Scanner which, through magnetic resonance imaging, produces images of both the structure and the neurological activity of the brain (the structure is a map of the brain, the activity is what traffic is moving on the map). The subjects, shrouded in the scanner's hood, were solving verbal puzzles like whether two nonsense words rhymed or not. The advantage of using nonsense words is that the subject cannot depend on previous knowledge, but has to think about the example presented. That thinking demands that the brain employ its verbal skills and the findings were striking. In all the male subjects the brain was active on the left side only. Women, however, were using both sides of the brain to solve the same problems. The results were highly consistent, so much so that you can tell, merely from the pictures, which brains are male and which are female. The Shaywitzes concluded:

> Our data provide clear evidence for a sex difference in the functional organization of the brain for language, and indicate that these variations exist at the level of phonological processing. We wish to emphasize that in a site uniquely serving phonological processing females devote greater right hemisphere resources to that task. We have demonstrated remarkable differences in the functional organization of a specific component of language, phonological processing, between normal males and females.[43]

These findings were compelling, but, because the Shaywitzes were using a very expensive, time-consuming technology, their sample was not large enough to detect the very few men and women who possess an atypical brain pattern. Several other studies, using a cheaper, indirect method, substantially confirm the results, but also detect that there is a tiny minority of people with reversed brain polarities – men with brains organized like women's and women with male brains. These are exceptions; most of us have brains that conform to our sex.

The difference between the male and female brain is now well attested by different researchers. Women have stronger connections between the two halves of their brains, men have stronger connections within each half of the brain.[44] It's possible to translate these differing arrangements by saying that a woman's brain is better networked. As we shall see later her brain sees more, hears more, communicates better and cross-references far more efficiently. Her brain possesses more verbal resources: the parts of her brain that are devoted to language are larger than the equivalent in the male.[45] And what does the male brain have that the woman's does not? He can focus its attention far more closely. She has a floodlight, he has a spotlight. There really is no escaping the conclusion that male and female brains are different. You can claim that men's and women's abilities are the same, but you must then explain how that similarity emerges from two such different organisms.

A girl devotes more of her brain to verbal reasoning, so does a boy do the same when it comes to a mathematical problem? Iowa State University runs a Programme for Gifted Youth, most of whose members are 10- to 12-year-old children who are already scoring top marks on the University's maths tests. Professor Michael O'Boyle, a research scientist in the Psychology Department at Iowa State, is conducting functional brain studies with these children to see how their thinking processes differ from those of their peers, and how they differ between girls and boys, and his findings are tantalizing. Most children, both boys and girls, employ both hemispheres of their brains to tackle a mathematical problem, but the highly-gifted boys shut down the left side of their brain and used the right hemisphere alone. That means that male mathematicians, the most talented, are using *less* of their brain to achieve more. Professor O'Boyle suggests 'that in the male gifted brain there is an ability to selectively inhibit-activate cortical regions necessary for specialized processing. They are putting all of their brain activity into solving the problem whereas girls are not.'[46] Note 'all of their brain activity', not all of their brain. O'Boyle discovered a similar contrast when children were asked to solve spatial puzzles (jigsaws are an easy example). The boys used one side of the brain only while the girls used both, yet the males consistently did better.[47] On the face of it this seems perverse. We have already seen that girls outperform boys on verbal tests, and in doing it they employ both sides of the brain, yet when they use the twin-hemisphere strategy on spatial or mathematical tests they come second. Why? Professor O'Boyle suspects that the girls are using verbal processes to help solve a spatial problem (like parallel parking the car), and verbal strategies are not going to be as efficient for purely spatial problems. The girl is complicating a spatial problem by translating it into verbal terms, while the boy is dealing with the problem in purely spatial terms. His mind is focused, hers is networked.

The Functional MRI scans, with their glowing red hot spots that show where the brain is working, reveal how differently the sexes use their thinking processes. But the differences do not stop there. It is not only the processes that differ, but the brains themselves. Between the brain's two hemispheres lies the corpus callosum, which serves as a kind of telephone exchange between the brain halves. The corpus callosum differs in shape between men and women: a man's is tubular, while a woman's is shaped like a bulb and is about one-fifth larger.[48] The size differs too, though this is harder to measure for it changes with age; but if ageing is taken into account, and the fact that on average a man's brain is larger than a woman's, it does appear that the corpus callosum is about one-fifth larger in women, while two specific areas of the corpus callosum, the splenium and the isthmus, are dramatically larger. It is these two areas that connect the verbal areas of the brain. One group of American researchers discovered that they could predict the level of a person's verbal fluency by the size of their splenium area alone: 'Our most consistent and dramatic finding is that the midsagittal surface area of the posterior corpus callosum, particularly the splenium, relates positively to verbal fluency.'[49]

So science, inconveniently for those who insist that the abilities of men and women are the same, keeps proving that the sexes use different equipment, and different equipment, whether we like it or not, is liable to produce different results. But how can we tell that these equipment differences in the shape and structure of the brain are not forged by experience? There is plenty of evidence that the brain is more malleable than we once thought, and that it can be altered by outside forces.[50] One experiment demonstrated that kittens raised in the dark never develop the necessary neural networks that allow them to see properly, even though they possess fully functional eyes.[51] Light was required to stimulate the brain to form the neural connections and, denied light at a crucial phase of their development, the kittens only ever developed a rudimentary vision. Does our cultural treatment of boys and girls similarly inhibit some neural networks? Do we deny girls mathematical light and boys verbal illumination and so permanently change their brains?

It appears not, for the evidence is overwhelming that the different brain organizations are set in the womb by the sex-determining hormones. The CAH girls who were exposed to male-typical levels of hormones in the womb have better spatial skills than the average girl, they are more proficient at higher maths and they tend to be more career-oriented, competitive and self-assured. They are, in short, more like males.[52] Susan, whom we met earlier, is typical. As a small child she was always taking things apart. She was fascinated by her father's car and was already an accomplished mechanic by the age of twelve. At school she was just average at English, but she was exceptional when it came to mathematics. Her teacher recalls:

Susan did not seem to have to learn how to solve problems, she seemed to just know. This was especially true for abstract reasoning, the really difficult problems I set her. I once asked how she did it. She just said she can see the answer in her mind's eye; she doesn't really have to work it out, it just comes to her as a visual pattern.

The research on these CAH girls produces consistent results; they have an ability pattern more like the boys. Dr Elizabeth Hampson is studying the spatial abilities of CAH girls and her hypothesis is that

> the high levels of androgens or male-like hormones that these girls were exposed to during the sensitive periods of early development facilitate the ability to process spatial information. We do not know what they have done to the brain, but we have some good ideas. We think the hormones alter the way the brain is organized, making spatial processing more efficient.[53]

Experiments on rats, in which growing female foetuses are exposed to male hormones, show similar results. The resultant females prove far better than normal females at negotiating mazes, a talent normally reserved for male rats.[54] The evidence of the CAH girls and the hormone-enhanced rats makes it very difficult to claim that the sex differences in spatial ability are due to social conditioning alone: biology plays a major role.

Even more evidence comes from a study of normal children.[55] A research team in a Toronto hospital measured the levels of male hormone in amniotic fluid, the liquid which surrounds the growing foetus, and they discovered that the fluid about a male foetus generally has five times the levels of the female's, though there was a great deal of variation in the female levels. When the resultant children reached the age of seven they were tested for spatial ability. The boys, as usual, did better than the girls, but what was more interesting was the discovery of a correlation between the girls' spatial abilities and the amount of testosterone to which they had been exposed in the womb. The higher the testosterone, the greater the spatial skills. Not only that, but when the researchers investigated the children's brain organization they found that the girls with high exposure to male hormones possessed a male-typical brain pattern, and along with that pattern they had received more male-like spatial abilities than the girls who had been exposed to the lowest levels of testosterone.

So what is testosterone doing to the brain? No one has yet revealed the exact process, but it is increasingly clear that testosterone is the architect of the sex difference in brain organization. The male brain begins as a female brain, but foetal testosterone changes its structure. It appears to take away the female brain's more 'networked' organization, leaving the brain more compartmentalized. Language skills are restricted to the left side of the brain, spatial skills to the right, and all this happens long before society or culture has had any chance to influence the brain's development.

Male and female brains are not the same, and are not equal, and the difference has consequences for the way boys and girls learn. Doreen Kimura summarized the consensus in the journal *Scientific American*:

> Men and women differ in the way they solve intellectual problems. It has been fashionable to insist that these differences are minimal, the consequences of variations in experience during development. The bulk of the evidence suggests, however, that the effects of sex hormones on brain organization occur so early in life that from the start the environment is acting on differently wired brains in girls and boys.[56]

The differences are enhanced when more hormones come on stream at puberty. Many studies have demonstrated that women perform better on spatial tests when their oestrogen level is low (during the menstrual phase of the cycle) than when it is high.[57] In contrast their performance on fine manual and articulatory-verbal skills is better at the high-oestrogen phase – that is, when their hormonal distinction from men is at its most marked.[58] It is noticeable that at puberty girls start to fall behind in advanced maths, a reason why so few go on to study technological subjects. Their brains, already biased against such spatial subjects, are being further tilted away from them by their hormones. Once at university, women are much more likely to be studying languages and related subjects (70% female–30% male), while 87% of the students in engineering and technology courses are male.[59] This might be regrettable to those who believe that anything a man can do, a woman can do better, but it should come as no surprise considering the brain differences between boys and girls.

Boys and girls are different. Their brains and their aptitudes are different, but there is still more to the story. We know only too well that ability is not enough to determine success; it takes something more to motivate an individual, and here again biology plays its vital part.

SUMMARY
- The brain has a sex just as the body does.
- The male brain is forged in the womb by exposure to high levels of androgens or male hormones.
- A girl exposed to male hormones in the womb acts more like a boy.
- There are thirteen mathematically gifted boys for every one girl.
- Boys excel in areas that require three-dimensionsal thought processing, girls in verbal skills.
- Girls and boys have different aptitudes because their brains are specialized for different skills.

FUTURE TRENDS
- The research is moving at a great pace, revealing more differences that make the difference – that make for the distinct male brain. Science is giving the ordinary parent the weapons to stand up to the nonsense that rules how children are taught.

CHAPTER FIVE

Brainsex II

The malady of boyhood

THE MALE'S SLEEPY BRAIN

Even the most dedicated egalitarian amongst teachers, one who is certain that there can be no biologically determined difference between the abilities of the sexes, will admit that boys are more difficult to teach. Figures from Britain illustrate the point. British schools are currently expelling pupils in record numbers and most of those unwanted pupils are boys. In the school year 1994–5 there were 1,445 children under the age of 12 expelled from schools (just four years earlier only 378 had been considered unteachable) and 90% of those children were boys.[1] Since 1990 the number of children expelled from all schools has quadrupled to 12,000 a year, and overwhelmingly they are boys.[2] There are six times as many boys as girls in special schools for pupils with behavioural problems.[3] Chris Woodhead, Chief Inspector of Schools, admits that boring lessons are part of the problem.[4] It is the boys who are bored, and they are being bored in ever greater numbers because too many classrooms have become feminized. Her teaching methods simply do not suit his brain.

To understand why, we need to look at three parts of the brain; the cerebral cortex, the reticular activating system and the limbic system.

The cerebral cortex is the grey tissue on the outermost part of the brain, the big wrinkled globules that villainous scientists keep in glass jars in science-fiction movies. Much of the cortex is devoted to analysing sensory information coming from the world outside us, but it is also the place where the functions of thought, consciousness and language are found. The portions of the cortex just behind our forehead, the frontal lobes, are most fully developed in the human species. Among other things, the frontal lobes are thought to be responsible for some uniquely human traits such as our self-conscious awareness, our ability to figure out what others might be feeling or thinking, to plan for future events, and to control our impulses. These frontal lobes are the 'sensible' brain, the rational governor of our wilder impulses.

Reticular means 'netlike', and the reticular activating system, or RAS, is a neural network that extends from the spinal cord up into the lower layers of the brain. We shall now indulge in a gross simplification and imagine that the brain is composed of homunculi who do different jobs; in this case the RAS is rather like the telephone operator who awaits your emergency call. If your house is on fire, you do not summon the fire service yourself but talk to an operator who makes the call for you. The RAS, hearing from the cerebral cortex that danger threatens, initiates the brain's response, and the production of the neurotransmitter dopamine is crucial to that process. Dopamine is the brain's wake-up beverage; it tells us to pay attention.

The RAS has other functions. One is to regulate our breathing, and this may well be a factor in why four times as many infant boys die from SIDS (sudden infant death syndrome, or cot-death) as infant girls.[5] Why? Remember that the RAS has to summon help, and there is evidence that the male RAS is less easily alerted than the female RAS,[6] so possibly the boy infant's RAS simply failed to pass on the alarming message that breathing had stopped.

The limbic parts of the brain consist of many different structures, but together they can be described as the emotional centre of the brain. The limbic system is responsible for initiating what are sometimes called the four Fs: fight or flight, feeding and sexual activity. Feelings like anger, rage, sadness, irritation and sexual attraction are all generated by the limbic system. It also contains the parts of the brain that are most likely to be different in males and females. And in most species, including humans, sex hormones affect how these emotional structures operate.

These three components of the brain work together. Suppose we see a bear. The first thing that happens is that our sensory cortex registers the news that a grizzly is a few yards away. It passes a quick message – growling, furry, claws, smelly, close, definitely not a teddybear – to the RAS and limbic areas. The RAS sounds the alarm. By now the limbic system, fizzing with fight and fear, may well be demanding a furious response, but the RAS has also sent dopamine to the calm, civilized frontal lobes. The frontal lobes may well override the panicked limbic system and hold its primitive reaction in check while the cortex works out a more thoughtful option. It could, of course, decide that flight is the best choice, in which case the limbic system rules, or perhaps it comes up with something smarter ('just shut the car door and the big bad bear will go away'). What the RAS has done with its dopamine is increase the governing power of the frontal cortex; it has strengthened the part of the brain that distinguishes us from other animals, the part that lets us think clearly and make a rational choice.

'The bear doesn't know that,' says Bill, 'and it's about to charge. So what do you do?'

'Depends on the bear, but I doubt I'd want to fight it,' says Anne.

'So you'd flee?'

'I sense advice coming.'

'The US Park Rangers advise you to freeze. The bear, my dear, will then mistake you for a tree, or possibly a shrub.'

'I'll try to remember that.'

The crucial step in the wake-up-there's-a-bear process is the cortical-RAS alert, and in a newborn baby such alerts come frequently. The child is, after all, in a very strange new environment, and any sudden sight or loud sound might be alarming. But the RAS-cortex gets wiser as it grows older by learning which messages to take seriously and which to ignore. It has to do this, otherwise we would be woken by every small disturbance in the night. Young children have broken sleep patterns because their alarm system hits the panic button too often, but in time the child's brain learns that a curtain stirred by the night wind is not the bogeyman coming for a snack. The alarm system doesn't just operate at night; it is constantly assessing the outside world, and science is now discovering that men and women react very differently to stimuli. The male's alarm system is less sensitive than the female's, so signals that alert her brain will be ignored by his, which is why, on the whole, women do not sleep as soundly as men.[7] Women are more easily disturbed by smaller noises (partly, as we shall discover later, because they have superior hearing, but it is also because their cortical-RAS reaction is more sensitive). So far we have called it an 'alarm system', which is misleading, for the cortical-RAS reaction is not activated only at times of danger, but serves as the mechanism that alerts us to our surroundings: to interest, to curiosity, to any stimulus that is out of the ordinary.

The key difference between the sexes is the male's higher arousal threshold. This has been studied with tests which measured the electrical activity of the brain under various stimuli such as flashing lights and loud bangs, and the tests show that women pay attention much sooner than men.[8] If the results of those experiments are applied to the classroom, it is obvious that girls will be more readily interested in lessons than boys. The girls' brains are telling them that the lesson is interesting, while the boys' brains are busy wondering when something will happen to break the tedium.

The RAS, remember, stimulates the brain's upper level which controls the more primitive limbic system. But if the cerebral cortex is not in control, then the brain is ruled by the limbic system, which is emotional, impulsive and a potential nuisance. If a boy is to behave properly in a classroom he must be in control of his behaviour, and that needs the engagement of his cerebral cortex, but too often he is simply not being stimulated into using the thinking part of his brain and so he slumps into being an antisocial irritant.

A child who is not under the control of the cerebral cortex is likely to be a nuisance and even diagnosed as hyperactive. Boys are four to nine times more likely to be so diagnosed than girls.[9] Hyperactivity is characterized by a tendency to restlessness and an acute inability to concentrate upon tasks for more than a few minutes; such behaviour is disruptive in the classroom and, in its extreme form, makes life impossible for parents, teachers and child. We will return to the extremes of this condition later, but for now note that the treatment given to such hyperactive children is a stimulant, not a sedative. That seems contradictory, but there is a good reason for it. Studies of hyperactive children have shown that they have an extremely high alarm threshold, so it takes a great deal of stimulation for the RAS-frontal cortical interaction to start working. An artificial stimulant can fool the cortex into thinking that it has been aroused by the RAS and so make the world about the child seem more exciting and thus worthy of attention.

We all need stimulation, but the male brain needs more than the female. He needs more extreme messages to kick-start the vital cortical-RAS processes, which is why he is more likely to take risks than she is. He becomes bored more quickly than she does and so he seeks ever stronger stimuli; he will climb higher or skate on thinner ice, all in an effort to keep his frontal cortex working at normal or optimal levels. It is hardly surprising, therefore, that more men die from accidents than women. That disparity shows from the earliest age and by adulthood the frequency difference can be in excess of 400%.[10] It obtains for virtually all categories of accident: falls, drownings, poisonings, firearm incidents or car crashes. The number one killer of 15–24-year-old males is accidents, and those accidents occur because the male brain craves the stimulus of adventure.[11]

That craving makes it much harder for boys to sit quietly and learn to read. They would rather be moving around and doing things, and that makes learning in the modern classroom difficult for them. It also suggests why boys are far more likely to become juvenile delinquents.

Boys simply do better if they are challenged. But modern educational methods downplay competitive tests, preferring continuous assessment, and this might be one reason why boys are doing worse educationally than in the past. Girls like non-competitive learning, but boys suffer from it, and it is no surprise that once boys reach a truly competitive environment, like Oxford or Cambridge where the all-or-nothing final examination still rules, they do better than girls.[12]

Any teacher will tell you that boys are harder to teach and harder to keep under control, but few realize that the fault does not lie in the nature of boys, but in the teaching methods that favour co-operation and diminish competition. Blame it, if you must, on the testosterone that shapes a male brain so that its possessor is more aggressive, dominant, competitive and hostile. We have seen how that process starts in the womb; it is completed at adolescence when a second rush of male hormones comes on stream. The boy's voice breaks, he grows facial hair, he becomes a teenager, and he now has over ten times as much testosterone as his sister.[13] There is no overlap between the sexes on this – her low level of testosterone remains constant at puberty, but this second drenching of hormones gives adolescent boys enormous problems because high testosterone levels are related to impatience, irritability and a low tolerance of frustration. One researcher records that high levels of testosterone in puberty 'made the boys more impatient and irritable, which increased their readiness to engage in aggressive behaviour of the unprovoked and destructive kind (start fights, say nasty things without being provoked).' High testosterone also increases 'the probability that the boys will initiate aggressive destructive behaviour … by making them more impatient and irritable'.[14] It is clear that high testosterone levels at puberty are intimately related to anger, rage, delinquency and destructive behaviour, and since adolescent boys can have up to twenty times the amount of testosterone as girls, then they are the most likely to display these undesirable attributes.

Not all adolescent boys are uncontrollable horrors. Many learn how to deal with their internal rages by playing competitive sports, but once again the modern educational establishment decries such activities. Most sports produce winners and losers and today's educational experts believe that the experience of losing lowers a child's self-esteem, so they try hard never to place a child in a losing situation. Such experts want all children to be winners, but that can only be achieved by banning all competition and entering that through-the-looking-glass world where all are winners and everyone gets prizes. Boys need the genuine rewards of winning, and the real agony of defeat, if they are to learn how to control their hormonal turbulence and deal with the vagaries of later life.

The boys that do succeed at school are those who have learned to channel their aggression. Some do it academically; as both sexes move into higher education the boys start to catch up and in some areas surpass the girls. In higher national examinations, typically, 15% of boys gain the high marks to 11.6% of the girls.[15] The difference becomes even more marked where examinations are based on a competitive system. Men take a higher proportion of first class degrees nationally,[16] and gain twice as many top degrees as women at Oxford and Cambridge.[17] It is partly for this reason, of course, that some feminists agitate for an abandonment of competitive examinations, though their general hostility towards all competition plays a larger part; but deny boys and young men the spur of competition and you risk leaving their abilities dormant. If we really are to level the playing-field then some mix of continuous assessment, favouring the girls, and competitive examination, encouraging the boys, would seem desirable.

The good news of the past century is that we have moved away from the old patronizing idea that girls cannot be educated without serious risk to their mental health, and women are now succeeding academically in ways that were unimaginable a hundred years ago. Some boys are succeeding, too, but only those who are fortunate enough to learn how to control the naturally destructive behaviour engendered in part by their biological make-up. The bad news concerns the boys who do not make it, the ones at the bottom of the heap, and the bottom of society's heap is overwhelmingly male and troublesome. There are biological reasons for that, too.

THE VULNERABLE MALE

It is the boys who fall to the bottom of the educational heap. They also rise to the very top, for boys are found at the two extremes, at the genius summit and at the idiot base, while girls (and, of course, most boys) cluster in between. But the failures of our educational system are overwhelmingly boys. Far too many of them leave school with only the scantiest of educations, doomed to lives of trouble, crime and failure. Popular wisdom places responsibility for their failure on poverty at home and a lack of discipline at school, an explanation that leads to the contradictory solution that if we can only be kinder to the poor and harsher to their sons then the problem will go away.

New research suggests that the structure and chemistry of boys' brains make them far more prone to learning disorders, which in turn suggests that their disruptive behaviour is not voluntary, but a symptom which can be treated. The commonest of these disorders is attention deficit hyperactivity disorder or ADHD. Sometimes it is simply ADD, while in Britain the condition is usually called hyperactivity. The confusion over the name is, perhaps, a reflection of the debate over whether such a disorder exists at all; some believe that labelling a boy's antisocial behaviour with a fancy name is merely to dignify idleness and bad manners as a fashionable disease, but among those who do accept the disorder's existence there is widespread agreement that far more boys are affected than girls. How many more boys depends upon how the condition is defined, about which, as we shall see, there is no agreement. For the moment it is enough to note that some researchers claim that nine times more boys than girls are afflicted,[18] others say it is only four times as many,[19] while a handful of feminists, eager to deny boys any distinguishing characteristics, claim that the syndrome affects both sexes equally. There is less controversy about the incidence of other developmental and learning disorders. Four to five times more boys are autistic,[20] three times more suffer from stuttering,[21] four times more are dyslexic,[22] twice as many are mentally retarded,[23] and four times as many boys as girls are afflicted with Tourette's syndrome (TS).[24] It is a catalogue of disorders which overwhelmingly afflicts boys and helps to explain why so many fail at school.

Perhaps the most distressing of all these disorders is Tourette's syndrome (TS), named for Georges Gilles de la Tourette, the French doctor who first described this hereditary affliction. Dr David Comings, an MD and a researcher in the Medical Genetics Department at the City of Hope National Medical Center in California, specializes in TS, and he believes that 1% of all boys suffer from the condition, but notes that it is frequently undiagnosed, especially in Britain and Europe where recognition of the symptoms lags behind the US.[25]

The symptoms of TS make up a formidable list. Most prominent are motor tics – blinking, grimacing, head-jerking, shoulder-shrugging and other spasmodic movements – and vocal tics like throat-clearing, spitting, barking, squeaking, humming, and other irritating noises. Symptoms which are not always present include a short attention span, dyslexia, poor handwriting and obsessive-compulsive traits (such as an insistence on touching things with both hands, or counting objects repetitiously, or constant hand-washing). TS sufferers will often display confrontational behaviour such as talking-back or temper tantrums, they are irritable and suffer from frequent mood-swings, anxiety attacks or emotional hypersensitivity. Some have sleep problems such as bed-wetting, frequent nightmares or apnoea (respiratory hiatus). Perhaps most distressing of all, in its severest cases (which afflict only boys) TS involves an uninhibited and compulsive use of sexually explicit language that is allied to precocious sexual development.[26]

It is hardly surprising that such symptoms are very frequently mistaken for innate wickedness and that TS sufferers are more likely to be punished than treated or, if treated, treated in an entirely inappropriate manner. This is especially true for the severe cases (about one-third of the total) whose sexually explicit behaviour and foul language often lead to a diagnosis of sexual abuse. The result of that misdiagnosis is that the child is removed from the family home and the underlying condition, TS, goes untreated. Other symptoms, such as temper tantrums and insolence, are more likely to lead to punishment, yet the behavioural peculiarities of TS are merely symptoms of a hereditary disease, the genetics of which are well understood. Many, usually all, of its distressing symptoms can be eliminated with medication.

Ryan Hughes suffered from TS, and his story illustrates the saga of misery, humiliation and anger that affects such boys and their families. His mother, Susan Hughes, in her book *What Makes Ryan Tick?*,[27] recalled that her son's symptoms showed up early in his life. By three years old, the hyperactive Ryan had been diagnosed as suffering from attention deficit hyperactivity disorder (ADHD), but the diagnosis and its associated treatment achieved nothing. 'By the age of seven,' Susan Hughes remembers, 'he was violent. He hit and kicked, threw objects, screamed, used profanity, and exploded with rage attacks. He was phobic and obsessive-compulsive. He was only ten years old when he expressed the desire to die because living, as he put it, "was just too hard".'

Ryan frequently attacked his mother. 'One day I sent him to his room for a sassy mouth. Not only did he refuse to go, he screamed, yelled and cursed me for several minutes. After letting him blow off steam, I tried to escort him upstairs to his room. He pushed me away and we ended up in a physical battle. He had me by the hair, pulling me down to the bed where we wrestled for quite some time. I ended up with a black eye, bruises on my arms and legs and losing a great deal of hair. At times he would seem almost possessed by an unknown force.'

Ryan had few friends because his behaviour was annoying and frequently unbearable. Not only did he hit his mother, his father and his teachers, he also spat at them and called them unrepeatable names. He lashed out verbally at strangers and flashed the finger sign to other parents, children, neighbours, teachers and even police officers. He possessed what his mother describes as a 'hair trigger temper'. He made holes in the walls of every room of their home and at school. During fits of rage he would often throw large pieces of furniture, and nothing that Susan or her husband tried made any difference. The rages seemed uncontrollable.

Susan and Jim were accused of being poor parents who simply let their child misbehave. On many occasions Susan would leave 'the doctor's office feeling like the world's worst mother'. The psychologist who was treating Ryan said that he was 'just spoilt', but spoiling a child was hardly likely to generate Ryan's symptoms. Susan recalls that he 'had the classic tics and obsessive-compulsive behaviour. He cleared his throat, pulled his crotch/pants, bit his nails, chewed his clothing, and licked his lips until they were raw. Our county Mental Health Department workers dismissed all of these activities as "nervous habits".' In the end, life became so unbearable for the family that Ryan had to go to a residential treatment centre for severely disturbed children. It was a terrible moment for Ryan's mother. 'I felt as though someone had ripped my heart from my chest with no anaesthesia. I cried a river of tears.'

It was not just the county's Mental Health Department[28] that was blind to the true nature of Ryan's condition, the Hughes's paediatrician had never heard of Tourette's syndrome, nor indeed had the next three paediatricians who examined Ryan. It was not until Susan discovered Dr David Comings that her own diagnosis was confirmed, but by that time Ryan was 13 and the family had been through hell. That hell ended with the diagnosis of Tourette's syndrome and Dr Comings's prescription of drugs. By his later teenage years Ryan had become bright, inquisitive and articulate. The ghastly symptoms of TS, the tics, tempers and sexual displays, had been replaced by a humorous, charming young man who loved school and achieved high grades. Ryan Hughes is now unrecognizable as the foul-mouthed, violent child he once was.

If severe cases like Ryan's can go undiagnosed for so long it is not surprising that milder forms of TS are frequently missed. Hundreds of thousands of schoolchildren, most of them boys, are being blamed and punished for behaviour which is purely genetic and entirely treatable.

TS might be frequently undiagnosed, but one of its symptoms, ADHD, is fast becoming one of childhood's most fashionable afflictions. It rates a large section in the American Psychiatric Association's *Manual of Mental Disorders*, where ADHD is described as 'a persistent pattern of inattention and/or hyperactivity – impulsivity that is more frequent and more severe than is typically observed in individuals at a comparative level of development.'[29] The manual provides a list of symptoms: messy or thoughtless work, failure to concentrate on either work or play, frequent shifts from one activity to another, inattention, forgetfulness, fidgeting, impatience and impulsiveness. 'Symptoms generally worsen in situations that require sustained attention or mental effort that lack intrinsic appeal or novelty (eg., listening to classroom teachers, doing class assignments, listening or reading lengthy materials, or working on monotonous repetitive tasks). Signs of the disorder may be minimal or absent when the person is under very strict control, in a novel setting, or engaged in especially interesting activities.'[30]

'Hold on,' says Bill. 'That list's a bit all-embracing, isn't it? Is there a child in the world who won't be diagnosed as hyperactive?'

'Which is precisely why some doctors refuse to recognize the condition,' says Anne. 'They think ADHD is merely normality labelled as a disease.'

'The poet Cowley claimed that "life is an incurable disease".'

'I'll take your word for it.'

The American Psychiatric Association's list of symptoms is indeed so all-inclusive that it is hardly surprising that some doctors refuse to recognize the condition at all, insisting that ADHD is simply psychiatric double-speak for plain bad behaviour. In Britain the number of diagnoses is much lower than in the United States and Australia. This is not because British children are better behaved than their American or Australian peers, but because British doctors are much less willing to accept the existence of the disorder, though Eric Taylor, Professor of Developmental Neuropsychiatry at the Medical Research Council's Child Psychiatry Unit and one of the few British specialists willing to recognize ADHD, has noted that diagnoses in Britain are increasing because of parental pressure.[31] Nevertheless many doctors remain suspicious, and no wonder, for if every child who was fidgety or unable to concentrate on schoolwork were to be labelled ADHD then the incidence of the syndrome would be almost universal. Even the American Psychiatric Association's manual recognizes that the symptoms it advances closely resemble the average behaviour of most boys: 'In early childhood, it may be difficult to distinguish symptoms of Attention-Deficit/Hyperactivity Disorder from age-appropriate behaviours (eg., running around or being noisy)'.[32] The normal is being labelled abnormal, and this suggests that in the USA toleration for naturally boyish behaviour is very low. Boys are labelled as sick simply for being boys and are then placed on behaviour-changing drugs. A recent article in the *Wall Street Journal* remarked that in modern times boyhood has become a malady.[33]

Boyhood is more than a malady in the USA, it is an epidemic, for a widespread survey of parents and teachers revealed that 33% of young boys are now considered excessively hyperactive or 'hyperdistractable'.[34] One-third of all boys are sick? The figure is ludicrous, but so is the incidence of drug treatment for ADHD in the United States.

ADHD is controlled by giving the child a stimulant which, as we have already seen, mimics the effect of the RAS on the cerebral cortex and so switches on the thinking part of his brain. The drug most frequently used is an amphetamine, Ritalin. In Britain, where diagnoses of ADHD or hyperactivity are rare, the incidence of Ritalin prescription is low (estimates vary from 2,000 to 6,000 children only), but in the United States one estimate suggests that 10% of all boys aged between 9 and 13 are being treated with the drug. Indeed, male patients under 16 account for 80% of the USA's consumption of Ritalin.[35] Canada is much influenced by its southern neighbour and prescriptions for Ritalin tripled between 1991 and 1997 to 486,000 per year, prompting one Canadian psychiatrist, Dr Thomas Millar, to describe it as 'promiscuous prescribing'.[36]

The whole subject of ADHD is fraught with conflicting claims, but the best estimates suggest that only some 3% to 5% of children have the disorder.[37] The disproportionate number of American boys being dosed with Ritalin suggests that many of them are being medicated solely for being boys. There is no doubt that Ritalin is very good for those children that do have severe behavioural problems, but is it appropriate for normal boyish behaviour? Diane McGuinness, a psychologist who has worked on sex differences in learning, comments that her own studies 'indicate that being "hyperactive", or having a short attention span, is perfectly normal for young boys, and what is being measured by hyperactivity questionnaires is much more likely to reflect the parent's inability to tolerate this behaviour than anything wrong with the child.'[38] There is a suspicion that, at least in North America, boys are being given drugs to make life easier for harassed parents and teachers, and there is an added suspicion that, to justify the treatment, the normally rambunctious behaviour of young males is being demonized with the label ADHD.

At present the diagnosis of ADHD rests on behavioural criteria (it looks like a boy, it sounds like a boy, it behaves like a boy, so drug it), but it is possible that a more accurate diagnosis could be reached using EEG wave patterns. A study found that certain boys diagnosed with severe ADHD have a very specific brain-wave pattern,[39] and this finding led to a suggestion that these children have lower than usual levels of dopamine in the frontal areas of their brains, the very parts that allow us to control our more primitive, limbic-generated emotions. The dopamine which forces our frontal lobes to pay attention stems from the RAS, and it is essential for concentration; lacking it, these children are unable to focus their attention for more than a few minutes, in some cases for more than a few seconds. Such children are, consequently, totally disorganized, even in such mundane tasks as dressing themselves or getting ready for school. They literally forget what they are supposed to be doing, so don't do it. The forward-planning, thinking area of the brain is not being brought into play to modulate and control behaviour.

It would certainly help if the psychiatric profession could agree on a definition of ADHD, and one, moreover, that does not depend on a subjective judgement of behaviour, nor on guidelines as vague as those in the American Psychiatric Association's *Manual of Mental Disorders*, but on measurable criteria like EEG brain patterns or dopamine levels. Such a definition would end the over-prescription of Ritalin in North America and also encourage British doctors to take the syndrome more seriously. And such an encouragement is needed, for research shows that ignoring the disorder might be more harmful than over-diagnosing the problem for, if ADHD goes untreated into adulthood, it has serious consequences. 'Long term studies on adolescents demonstrate that ADHD impairs school performance, limits participation in extracurricular activities, increases the risks of delinquency, and harms social relationships and family interactions. In adults it is frequently linked to psychiatric illness, incarceration, job failures, marital discord, and divorce.'[40] Thus, if the underlying disorder is missed, as it frequently is in Britain, then the failure to diagnose and treat the child can lead to a miserable life. Which is worse, to over-drug children or miss a serious condition that has lifelong consequences?

Tourette's Syndrome is the most dramatic and disturbing

learning disorder, while ADHD is the most fashionable and, apparently, widespread, and boys suffer from both far more than do girls. That is also true of dyslexia, a condition that affects between 5% and 10% of all children. Many dyslexic children have no other apparent problems, they can be well-adjusted, angelically behaved and very hard-working, yet they are consistently poor readers. The condition is an enormous handicap for any child, and it is significant that it affects boys far more widely than girls. A British study tested a sample of 9–10-year-olds from 51 primary schools and discovered that boys were three times more likely to suffer from reading difficulties.[41] In fact boys outnumber girls in all the disorders, which is why there are six boys for every girl in special remedial schools.[42] Children placed in such special schools risk being regarded as delinquent trouble-makers rather than as patients, yet there is increasing evidence that learning disabilities (like ADHD or dyslexia) and developmental disabilities (like autism and mental retardation) are *all* neurodevelopmental disorders.[43]

Why are boys more vulnerable to these brain disorders? One culprit appears to lie in the chromosomes. A boy, remember, has only one X chromosome, while a girl has two, and if the boy's single X chromosome carries a recessive gene that is associated with a disorder then the boy will suffer from that disorder. A recessive gene is one that has mutated, or changed, and is unable to express the protein to perform its function. The best known examples of X-linked disorders are colour blindness and haemophilia, and both are mainly found in males. The female, with her two X chromosomes, is much more likely to carry a normal gene that overrides or compensates for the abnormal one. Thus, by possessing two X chromosomes, a woman has a built-in protection against faulty genes, but the male has no such advantage. If he receives a faulty gene in his X chromosome then he has no replacement in the Y. Mental retardation is another disorder linked to recessive genes (many different genes in this case), and again it is much more common in boys because a girl possesses back-up genes in her second X chromosome and the boy does not.[44]

A further disadvantage for boys comes from the layout of the brain itself. Put very simply, the basic pattern of the brain is always female, but prenatal hormones reshape the male's brain. The very fact that the female is the basic pattern makes it less likely that something will go wrong during the development of a girl's brain, but the growing male brain has to make adaptations and cope with high levels of testosterone, and these powerful hormonal infusions must occur at exactly the right time and in the right concentration: a complex process that can go wrong. The possibility of such errors occurring has been demonstrated by a study of CAH girls (those girls who were accidentally exposed to high levels of male hormones while in the womb) and it showed a significant increase in learning disabilities.[45] Because the development of a CAH girl's brain is, like the average male's, much more complicated, more can go wrong.

As if that were not enough, the very organization of the male brain makes him vulnerable to language problems. A male relies on the left hemisphere for language processing and any slight damage to that area will affect his verbal abilities, while a female possesses a back-up system in her right hemisphere. This explains why, after a stroke in the brain's left hemisphere, women recover their speech far more quickly and more extensively than men do.[46]

Boys, then, by their biology and by the complexity of their brain development, are more prone to all the learning disorders, but as the over-prescription of Ritalin in the United States demonstrates, a boy does not need to have a neurodevelopmental problem to be diagnosed as a trouble-maker. His naturally boyish behaviour, boisterous and aggressive, is quite sufficient to have him labelled as a problem, and a boy labelled as a classroom problem is more likely to become the delinquent of the future. Yet all he has done is be a boy; but, crucially, a boy in an increasingly feminized educational system.

The process is not difficult to trace. At the beginning of the century education was male-oriented. There was an increasing and justifiable demand for equal educational opportunities for girls and, by and large, these had been granted by the 1960s. Yet that was also the era when any elitist or privileged establishment was seen as unjust and there was a rush to establish co-educational schools. Thus, for the first time, boys and girls were being educated side by side in large numbers. The boys, being boys, behaved like boys. They showed off in front of the girls, they tended to dominate classroom discussions when they were not disrupting them, and they were, generally, more assertive. This gave rise to complaints that education was 'male-oriented' and, to correct that imbalance, boys were expected to change their behaviour. The process continues. Boys are being pressured to become more tractable, to become, in fact, more like girls, and if their self-control cannot perform that biological miracle, then drugs will.

The huge majority of teachers want the best for all the children in their classrooms, but teacher education rarely, if ever, prepares them for the different ways in which boys and girls learn. The huge majority of teachers are also women and that creates an environment in which the female virtues of non-competitive co-operation and calm assiduity are appreciated and in which his noisier, more awkward presence is seen as an obstacle. No wonder he causes problems. He is unchallenged, he is frustrated and he is certainly bored.

WHAT IS TO BE DONE?

It is not hard to think of ways of improving education by designing it to suit the different brains and aptitudes of the sexes, but implementing those changes is a different matter. Any such actions would fly in the face of those who blindly insist on absolute equality between the sexes. Equality means 'sameness', so boys and girls must be taught exactly alike to make sure that neither sex has an advantage over the other. Perhaps the most ludicrous application of this doctrine is now to be seen in the United States where the law insists that sporting facilities must be precisely equal for male and female students at universities.[47] It does not matter that males are far more interested in sport than females, the law has spoken. In 1997 Boston University closed its football programme because it was a male-oriented sport,[48] and all across America other universities face similar dilemmas as they scramble to ensure that every dollar spent on any male sport is precisely matched by a dollar expended on some women's sport.

The world will doubtless survive the closure of a few American college football programmes, but the process of 'levelling the playing field' is doing damage at a much more fundamental level of education: reading. Children have been learning to read for centuries, and one might have thought the process was well understood, but in recent years the tried and tested methods of teaching reading have been abandoned. The old methods tended to be disciplined and relied heavily on testing, the new methods are non-competitive and flexible, but so far the results are not encouraging. A study by Dr Joyce Morris, a teacher and child psychologist, concluded that the new less structured approach is not proving as successful as the older method,[49] but that will cut little ice with those who believe that political orthodoxy in the classroom is more important than literacy. Far too many children leave school with inadequate reading skills, and again it is the boys who suffer most. Dr Bonnie Macmillan, another researcher, ascribes this failure to the way children have been taught to read over the past two decades. Boys responded to the tightly structured old methods and are at sea with the modern classroom's gentler processes where education is apparently expected to happen by osmosis.

Dr Macmillan was attacked for her conclusions, mainly because she had dared to suggest that boys learned in a different manner from girls. She wrote that boys have a 'greater risk of reading problems; they have a shorter attention span and are slower to acquire language skills'.[50] These assertions, as we have seen, are backed up by science in every particular, but nevertheless she was chided on the grounds that her theory *requires more evidence*.[51] The real objection to Dr Macmillan's case is not scientific, indeed it is scarcely rational, but rather a stubborn reluctance to abandon the idea that boys and girls possess identical mental attributes and abilities.

Most modern schools make a concerted effort to teach the sexes in the same way. 'Gender neutral' education is the aim, justified by the praiseworthy intention that boys and girls must be given equal opportunity, yet the gender neutral educationalists are doing exactly the opposite of what they hope to achieve. If the basic learning differences are ignored, then plainly you are not giving the sexes equal opportunity, but if any teacher dares implement such common sense, he or she faces opprobrium. A teacher was recently condemned by the Schools Inspectorate because he was using teaching methods that segregated the class into boys and girls; he was, in the judgement of the inspector, 'reinforcing gender divisions'.[52] Worse still, this teacher was running competitive team sports in the lunch break! Competition is now a dirty word in schools, because competition inevitably leads to winners and losers, and losers risk having their self-esteem diminished. Yet boys thrive on competition. It is noteworthy that, while the Schools Inspectorate disapproved of this teacher, his pupils and their parents were more than happy with his methods

The introduction of computers into the classroom provided another area of conflict for those who demanded that education be gender neutral. Boys, always happy with complicated toys, took to computers far more readily than girls, leading a lecturer at Keele University to complain that 'boys in school display the usual domineering behaviour and presumption of privileged access.'[53] The lecturer, Frances Grundy, proposed removing games from the computer on the grounds that 'games usually involve violence and destruction, and women are not encouraged to participate'. It is true that computer games such as *Doom* or *Quake*, which transport their players into macabre worlds of mutant humans and heavily armed aliens which have to be killed with chain saws and machine guns, are far more appealing to boys than to girls. Critics can argue about the societal value of such games, but their appeal to boys is undeniable and if boys are denied access to such mayhem then they are likely to lose interest in the computer altogether, just as most boys have already lost interest in the new breed of gender-neutral books. Why not keep the boys' games and add other features that will appeal to girls?

In fact there is no evidence that women or girls are being frightened away from computers by the male sex.[54] Girls do find most computer games boring, but have no reluctance to use computers when the programmes are tailored to their interests. The Internet gives the clue.[55] When it began only 15% of its users were women; now it is closer to 40%, and the biggest reason for that increase is the opportunity the computer gives for communication using the Internet's vast array of bulletin boards and chat-rooms. So it is not the boys who are the problem, but the subject matter, though to accept that rather obvious conclusion means abandoning the precious aim of gender neutral education and, as Ms Grundy's complaint reveals, the road to gender neutral education means removing everything which appeals solely to boys. The gender neutral classroom is an emasculated space. 'Boys feel continually attacked for who they are,' says Martin Spafford, the teacher in an East London comprehensive school we have already quoted. 'We have created a sense in school that masculinity is bad ... we have not succeeded in doing what we have done for girls; we have not found things for them to love about themselves.'[56]

The emasculation of the classroom is encouraged by the disappearance of males from the teaching profession. The Chief Executive of the Teacher Training Agency predicts that male teachers will have disappeared from primary schools by the year 2010,[57] and the process is well under way. Over the last decade the number of male teachers in England has fallen by more than 10% to just 30,000. In the same period the ranks of women teachers have grown by 10% and now number 140,000.[58] The gender gap is greatest among new teachers, which indicates that the gap can only grow wider. One educationalist at a teacher's conference in Britain suggested that the lack of male role models in the classroom could be to blame for declining standards of achievement among boys, while another complained that 'the teaching profession is becoming increasingly feminised'.[59] The conference concluded that men were deterred by the profession's low pay and by the possibility of being accused of child abuse. Little children want to touch, but the contemporary suspicion of any physical contact between an adult male and a young child leads to an uncomfortable environment. Perhaps the male is threatened by that fear, but we suspect that most men simply find the classroom an inimical workplace, and no wonder if you face condemnation as a sexist for encouraging competitive sports in the lunch hour.

SINGLE SEX SCHOOLS

So should we educate the sexes separately? It certainly seems from the success rates of single sex schools that children thrive when they are educated apart, as can be seen from recent British surveys of national exam results. Typically, out of the 100 schools which prove to be the most academically successful, 90 are single-sex.[60] Statistics from the Department of Education show that sixth-form (twelfth grade) boys in single sex schools do about 20% better than boys in mixed schools, while sixth-form girls from single-sex schools also perform better than their peers educated alongside boys.[61] If the exam results for the middle years of secondary education are compared then single-sex girls' schools dominate the league; in 1996, for example, not an atypical year, they took all top fourteen places.[62]

Such statistics seem overwhelming proof of the advantages of separate education, though there is an argument that single-sex schools are more successful because they attract more than their fair share of high-fliers. Nevertheless, in a world worried about falling educational standards it might be thought that successful schools would be encouraged; the opposite is sadly true. Single sex schools might be successful, but they are all under pressure to become co-educational on the grounds that everyone must have an equal chance at a superior education. The pressure is not coming from parents (who frequently like such schools), but from governments eager to display their egalitarian virtues. In the United States the vaunted Virginia Military Institute, a boys-only secondary school which once boasted Stonewall Jackson amongst its teachers, was forced by law to accept girls. The judge in this case called for a uniformity of treatment of the sexes at all times; to do otherwise, he said, is to violate the US constitution's Fourteenth Amendment which guarantees citizens 'equal protection' of the law.[63]

One doubts whether the framers of the constitution really believed that girls needed a legal right to be given crew-cuts and bullied by soldier-instructors, but what is sad about the decision, and about the pressures on other single sex schools to integrate, is that the very virtue that makes the school successful in the first place, the fact that its teaching methods are designed for a single sex, is destroyed by the addition of the other sex. Instead of offering all children a better education it ends up offering them a worse one. Gender-neutral education does not offer equal treatment. It offers lesser treatment, especially for boys. Nor does equal protection apply equally to males and females. Men only colleges in America are being forced to integrate while women's colleges are protected against the same process on the grounds that their product (educated women) is 'substantially related to an important governmental objective'.[64] Presumably educated men are not a governmental objective.

Our argument is not that all schools should be segregated, for certainly one of the important objectives of education is to teach the sexes to live together, but that boys and girls learn differently and recognition and acceptance of that fact will assist both. In an ideal co-educational school some lessons might best be given to single-sex classes, but only because the two sexes need different treatments. Boys respond to competition and strict discipline, while girls need neither. Put the two sexes together, then remove competition and discipline, and the boys flounder.

If classes were organized according to children's needs rather than on a strict adherence to treating boys and girls exactly the same, then we should discover that there would be a preponderance of boys in the classrooms offering special verbal and language training, just as the girls would require more help in those areas of the curriculum involving spatial concepts. The fear in all this is that education would return to the bad old days when boys were taught Latin and girls were instructed in cooking, but this is not a plea for such sexism, rather that teachers recognize their pupils' different needs. Most boys need more dramatic teaching to draw their attention, they need the equivalent of those outrageous video games that are full of doom, horror and, yes, competition. The sort of teacher they need may be loud, dramatic and extroverted. Pupils with longer attention spans (mostly girls) benefit from a more subdued teacher who uses quieter and more kindly methods.

A few schools and teachers are beginning to recognize this. Martin Spafford, from his East London comprehensive, remarks that 'boys need an immediate sense of achievement, and if they don't get it they switch off. Boys need the rewards of a structured framework that measures them and allows them to measure themselves against others, without it they don't care.'[65] His words are encouraging. He is not the only teacher who has looked at the result of thirty years of educational experiment and decided that changes are needed if we are to save boys from educational failure. In 1994 Mill Hill County School in Barnet, north London, divided its examination classes into single sex streams and over the next three years saw the proportion of pupils gaining five or more good national exam passes rise from 40% to 69%.[66] The experiment has been so successful that Barnet is now extending the idea to all its secondary schools. A handful of other education authorities are attempting similar experiments and, thus far, they are all proving successful.[67]

Education can never be gender neutral because the genders are simply too different. Girls will do better at subjects that are verbal and based on communicative skills. Boys will be drawn to the subjects that attract them, and it is vain to believe that we can shoehorn girls into the spatial subjects like engineering. Some girls, yes, but the majority, never. Each sex has different skills and different interests, and those aptitudes are not determined solely by societal pressures but are also influenced by biological factors. Boys are not failing because there is a feminist conspiracy to hobble their education, but because female values are being imposed on their schooling. Women are not so competitive as men, indeed many women deplore competition as the cause of much of the world's troubles, but by eliminating it from the classroom they risk losing the boys' interest. Boys are more competitive than girls, a trait which they carry into adult life and, as we are about to see, it affects the workplace just as much as the school.

SUMMARY
- Boys need greater motivation to activate the brain into working at full power.
- Boys are at least four times more likely to suffer from a learning disability.
- Boys are failing in school because of a failure to understand their biological needs.
- Boys have ten times more testosterone than girls – they are more aggressive, impatient and competitive than girls.

DESIRABLE AIMS
- We can continue to ignore the sex differences in learning – we can continue to preach sexual sameness in the classroom. If we do we risk increasing the numbers of boys who never make it above the bottom of the heap; risk condemning many with the

potential to do more to the never-never land of permanent unemployment.

- On the other hand we could apply the lessons learned from science to the classroom. Lessons designed for the male brain: lessons for the female brain. To be successful, teaching cannot afford to ignore the fundamental differences between the sexes.

- The gender gap in schools is widening. The underachievement of boys is a significant problem, and it will not be closed by the increased 'cissification' of our schools. The vast predominance of female teachers – and teacher training as to equality in all things – skews the emphasis to the feminine. In careers guidance (and in parenting classes) there is too great an emphasis on equal outcomes: as if the construction industry and the caring occupations would ever attract equal numbers of the same sex. For boys there should at least be more active and practical learning; more action and stress; a firmer structure and more competitive (virile) tests; certainly more knocking questions back and forth …

CHAPTER SIX

Brainsex III
The neurological edge

THE RISK-TAKER

Up to two thousand people throng the trading floor of the London International Futures and Options Exchange. To an outsider it looks like chaos – noisy, frantic and disorganized – but in the maelstrom fortunes are being won and lost in seconds. The financial rewards of such trading are enormously high; so are the losers' penalties, as Nick Leeson, who brought down Barings Bank by his dealing on the Singapore Exchange, could testify. A trading floor is a high-risk place, and it will put immense pressure on those who work there. More than 90% of those traders are men.

Why? The conspiracy theorist might answer that, because the rewards for a successful trader are so great, men have made sure women are excluded, but it is hard to detect any gender barriers among the banks and brokerage firms who employ traders. They desperately need people who can survive the pressure of the exchanges and do not care what shape those people are. A good woman trader is far more valuable than a mediocre male trader and the banks know that, so why do men still predominate?

The answer lies in the nature of the work. Just as in any job that demands recklessness, the chemistry of a man's brain makes him far more suited to the high-speed, high-pressure environment of financial trading. Indeed, many men are neurologically driven to risk. Risk, for them, is an addiction.

'Yet women gamble at bingo,' says Bill.

'A night out with the girls,' says Anne.

'They play the lottery?'

'Pin money. It's men who play high stakes poker, who gamble everything on the turn of a card.'

'Women play the fruit machines,' Bill says. 'Hour after hour, feeding the slots.'

'Boredom,' says Anne. 'Fifty pence at a time, not a whole fortune. Not the week's wages. You ain't going to win this one.'

'I fold.'

It is the high stakes that attract the male. 'They don't need drugs,' one organizational psychologist remarked of traders. 'The nature of the work itself and the levels of neuradrenalins it creates make outside stimulants unnecessary ... They become addicted to their own biochemistry.'[1] In other words, these male brains are producing substances which, if sold on the street corner, would be illegal.

The biochemistry of many males drives them to risk, even to the point of endangering their own lives. Such a man needs a mountain to scale, be it real or metaphorical, and his self-esteem is inextricably tied to that need. Few women, on the other hand, enjoy danger. Their neurological brakes are more active, and for that reason they do not secure the same pleasure from taking risks, on a trading floor or on a cliff-face.

The connection between risk and pleasure requires an explanation of neurotransmitters, the chemicals that allow messages to be transmitted from one nerve cell (neuron) to the next. The human brain is made up of billions of neurons which are linked to each other in circuits, not unlike electrical circuits. The neurotransmitters switch those circuits on or off. So far about 400 neurotransmitters have been identified, all of them apparently doing different jobs. Some activate emotional circuits, others switch on the neurons which control the body's movements, and all are under intense scientific scrutiny, for neurotransmitters, and how they operate, are at the cutting edge of brain research.

There is much debate about the researchers' findings, but it is apparent that women and men possess different amounts of some key neurotransmitters and, just as crucially, have different patterns and numbers of receptor sites. A receptor site is like an electrical contact – it lets the current flow – but in the brain such sites are keyed to particular neurotransmitters; thus serotonin will not switch on a dopamine receptor, nor dopamine a serotonin circuit, and those two neurotransmitters, serotonin and dopamine, are important to an understanding of how men and women react when faced with risk.

Serotonin, or 5-hydroxytryptamine, is one of the major neurotransmitters and it works in those parts of the brain that control motivated and emotional behaviour where it serves as the great inhibitor, or the universal nanny. It stops us doing things. Among other things it tells us when we are not hungry any more ('stop eating'), when we are tired ('go to bed') and, crucially, it curbs our impulsiveness ('whatever you're doing, stop it').

Specific neural circuits in the brain are governed by serotonin. These circuits connect the limbic system (the more primitive area of the brain, which controls elemental feelings such as anger, rage, sadness, irritation and sexual attraction) with the frontal cortex (the two lobes of the brain that sit in the forehead), which controls our ability to think ahead – to make a judgement before we take a risk. The two areas are in conflict. When faced with the grizzly bear the limbic system will be raring for a fight, or maybe it panics and wants to flee, but the frontal cortex imposes, we hope, a calm rationality and suggests that we follow the advice of the park ranger and freeze. At times, obviously, the limbic system is useful, but it would plainly be disastrous if its impulses were allowed to run riot. For most of us, most of the time, it is kept in check by the frontal brain areas, and that process is achieved by the serotonin pathways.

High levels of serotonin in the brain mean that a person's actions will probably be sensible and thoughtful (nanny is in control), while low levels will suggest the opposite.[2] Gamblers, risking fortunes on the spin of a wheel or the turn of a card, are less likely to be under nanny's control, suggesting that men, who are bigger risk-takers than women, have lower levels of serotonin. That seems to be true, but the difference between the levels of the average man and woman is a matter of some controversy.[3] Some researchers have found large differences, others small. This is because brain serotonin levels are difficult to measure. The most direct method is to remove and analyse a sample of spinal fluid, but the procedure is uncomfortable and, understandably, volunteers are reluctant to undergo the ordeal.

A much easier, albeit indirect, method of assessing the brain's serotonin levels has now emerged.[4] It uses an enzyme, mono-amine oxidase, or MAO, that disposes of used serotonin and is also found in the blood and so is easy to draw and test. MAO is not serotonin, of course, but low levels of the enzyme imply low levels of the neurotransmitter, and studies have shown that men have lower MAO levels than women. Low MAO levels, like low serotonin levels, are consistently found in those with impulsive personalities. 'Low levels may decrease the individual's ability or motivation to maintain self control. Low levels of serotonin are associated with irritability and tendencies toward impulsive responses to environmental conditions.'[5] In other words, low serotonin levels can lead to a hair-trigger temper and a readiness to indulge in stupid behaviour; both traits are much more associated with men than women.

Still more convincing evidence that women have more use for serotonin comes from a study that examined the number of serotonin receptor sites in the orbital cortex, which is part of the frontal lobes and associated with the regulation of anxiety, impulse control, meticulousness, hygiene, and perseverance. The orbital cortex is, if you like, the adult and responsible part of the brain, the bit that keeps us safe, clean and hard at work, and the researchers discovered that women had more serotonin binding sites than men.[6] 'One could speculate,' they reported, 'that the higher serotonin potential in the female brain may provide a physiological basis for the better impulse, aggression, and sexual behavioural control in women that, thank God, is expressed most of the time.'[7] Though even here there is still confusion. One study indicated that men metabolize serotonin at a faster rate than women;[8] however, that research was measuring the neurotransmitter's turnover, not the number of receptor sites in the brain. Significantly, men also show lower levels of neural activity in that same area of the frontal lobes, showing that their behavioural control area is activated less.[9]

The conclusion, despite the difficulties of measuring serotonin levels directly, is hard to avoid: that men have lower levels of the neurotransmitter than women, and that this disparity is reflected in their behaviour. Several studies of impulsive and violent criminals show that they have abnormally low levels of serotonin[10] and, it comes as no surprise, such felons are overwhelmingly male. This does not mean that low serotonin is a marker for criminality – many men learn to sublimate their risk-taking urges by indulging in sports or in other activities – but the low level is a marker for impulsive, dare-devil behaviour. People with low serotonin have impaired behaviour control because they do not engage their rational frontal cortex.

> 'Impaired behaviour control,' says Anne. 'That sounds a lot more like men than women. Have you ever heard of a female lager-lout?'
> 'Isn't that a bit unfair to men?'
> 'What has fairness to do with it? Who drives faster, you or me? Who takes bigger risks? Who wants to climb higher?'
> 'Maybe I was culturally conditioned?'
> 'In which case culture, or maybe lager, somehow managed to suppress the serotonin receptor sites in your orbital cortex.'

Common experience reinforces the findings of science: that a woman's brain is under more rational control than a man's. A woman is much less likely to do impulsively stupid things. And the difference is not culturally determined, it is not because society teaches boys to be risk-takers and cautions girls against dangerous activities, but simply because the brains of men and women are different.

That difference does not just exist in the serotonin circuits, but also in the way we employ another neurotransmitter, dopamine. In Chapter Five we saw how it activates the neural circuits which make us pay attention to our surroundings, and that the male needs greater stimulation to activate his dopamine neural circuits. If serotonin is the nanny-neurotransmitter, the inhibitor of impulses, dopamine can be thought of as its opposite: the motivator.

Dopamine's story begins deep in the hypothalamus where we all have 'pleasure centres'. If those centres are stimulated by an electric current they produce dopamine[11] which, in turn, intensifies the effect of our endorphins which are natural opiates. So a surge of dopamine boosts the endorphins which give a feeling of elation. People become addicted to cocaine because it mimics the dopamine-endorphin surge and so provides an ecstatic high.[12]

Dopamine, like serotonin, is difficult to measure directly, but again the MAO family of enzymes provides a method of assessing levels in the brain,[13] and what the studies show is that low levels of MAO not only indicate low levels of serotonin, but also high levels of dopamine. The MAO-dopamine relationship is slightly more complex than MAO-serotonin because the dopamine circuits are more difficult to activate, and so some low MAO levels will show low dopamine levels, but once the dopamine circuits are stimulated they tend to over-respond with an intense surge.[14] The dopamine surge turbocharges the endorphins and provides a cocaine-like burst of pleasure. It also gives the brain an ability to concentrate intensely.

We began by asking why there are more male traders on the high-risk floors of the world's exchanges, and the question is seen to be answered in the consistent research finding that men possess lower MAO levels than women.[15] Low MAO levels indicate low serotonin (the nanny neurotransmitter) and an over-responsive dopamine circuit (the opiate-inducing neurotransmitter). So low MAO levels suggest a person inclined, even addicted, to high-risk activity, and we should expect to find compulsive risk-takers (like gamblers) to have abnormally low levels of MAO; the studies do indeed reveal that such men (and they are nearly all men) do have low MAO.[16] Such risk-takers get intense pleasure (endorphin-induced) out of taking chances that most of us would avoid. The opposite is also true: more cautious people have high MAO levels, so they are more under the control of their serotonin circuits. Such high MAO people do not thrive in dangerous environments. To be a good trader (or fighter pilot or Formula One driver), it helps to have low, even abnormally low, levels of MAO.

'So low MAO, high risk?' asks Bill.

'Exactly.'

'And men, in general, have lower levels? Which is why so many traders are men?'

'Exactly, says Anne. 'It's the chemistry of our minds. She doesn't enjoy risk, and he does.'

'Because he's neurologically challenged?'

By women's standards men are indeed 'neurologically challenged'. The fact that men have lower MAO levels than women means that they will be much better adapted to the pressures of high-risk jobs, whether that job is trading derivatives or landing high-performance fighters on to aircraft carriers. The current orthodoxy denies this, and the US Navy is making strenuous efforts to enrol women among its carrier pilots, but it will be a very rare woman who possesses the low serotonin needed for her brain not to engage her caution-inducing frontal cortex as she hurtles in towards the deck. An F-14 Tomcat weighs 22 tons and lands on a carrier at 160 knots with its afterburners glowing because the pilot has about one-twentieth of a second to decide whether the landing is good or bad. If it's bad he or she can abort the landing and scream off up into the sky again, but get the decision wrong and he or she becomes a casualty statistic. It is not an occupation for the faint-hearted; not, that is, for individuals with high serotonin levels.

Our levels of MAO are mainly inherited,[17] but also partially depend on current experiences, diet, and our developmental history. More importantly, they rise with age, so that the young, on average, have less serotonin than the old.[18] This helps to explain why men calm down as they get older; some claim that the process happens because men learn to moderate their behaviour, but it is surely as much to do with the undeniable fact that the inhibiting effects of the cortex are being brought into play by their increased levels of serotonin.

These neurotransmitters affect our behaviour from birth.[19] Babies with low MAO are, once aroused, more active, they sleep less and are harder to pacify than babies with high MAO levels, and almost any mother will attest that baby boys sleep less and need more attention than baby girls. It is sometimes claimed that baby boys receive greater attention than girls because mothers are socially conditioned to care more for sons than for daughters, but in truth the mothers are merely reacting to the more onerous demands of a low MAO child.

The differences continue to show in childhood and it is significant that the most difficult children, those with behaviour and learning problems, show low serotonin levels.[20] And the MAO distinction persists into adulthood. Professor Marvin Zuckerman has studied the phenomenon and concludes that 'there is no question there is a relationship between sensation seeking and platelet MAO [the marker for serotonin]'.[21] 'Sensation seeking' is a term used by Professor Zuckerman to describe 'a trait defined by the *seeking* of varied, novel, complex, and *intense* sensations and experiences, and the willingness to take physical, social, *legal*, and *financial* risks for the sake of such experience'.[22] His research examined behavioural differences between men and women, and he summarized their propensities for sensation seeking by dividing the trait into four distinct areas:

Thrill and adventure seeking. This area is concerned with dangerous sports and physically risky activities involving speed or defying gravity (like parachuting or skiing). The ever-present risk of the thrill-seeker is physical injury, and low serotonin people (mostly men) enjoy the risks while high serotonin individuals (mainly women) do not.

Experience seeking. The urge to seek out new sensations and experiences involving the mind and senses (e.g. music, art, travel or social nonconformity). Professor Zuckerman detected no difference between the sexes in this area.

Disinhibition. Losing control in social situations such as parties, drinking bouts or sexual encounters. Disinhibition is strongly associated with drinking and drug-taking, and Zuckerman detected a big difference between the sexes in this area, with men far more likely to lose control than women.

Boredom susceptibility. An intolerance for repetitive experience (such as routine work or coping with tedious people); and Zuckerman discovered that men were more likely to be susceptible to boredom, though the difference was not so great as in thrill seeking or disinhibition.

The conclusion is that men are more likely to put themselves into danger, more likely to lose their inhibitions at a party and less likely to endure routine patiently. The only area where women score as highly as men is experience seeking, though it is noticeable that the experiences (music, the arts, etc) do not involve physical danger. Professor Zuckerman writes that 'the lack of difference on experience seeking suggests that while men are high on the more active forms of sensation seeking, women are just as open to novel experiences through the senses and life-style as men.'[23] So women are as likely as men to become hippies, to join cults or to indulge in a passionate commitment to the arts, but are less likely to go paragliding or bungee-jumping.

The process is still under investigation, but Professor Zuckerman suggests that male sensation seekers, once their interest is aroused, have a more dramatic dopamine response. He likens serotonin to the brakes and dopamine to the accelerator: the high-sensation seeker, mainly the the male of the species, has an overly responsive accelerator once it is engaged, but inefficient brakes. It is not only that his low serotonin predisposes him towards risky behaviour; his dopamine circuits reward him for taking the risks, and so he actually enjoys the danger. It is that love of the dangerous thrill that the low-sensation seekers, mainly women and of course some men, never feel. The effects of the dopamine are also modulated by testosterone; a higher T level increases the dopamine effect.[24] If a male animal is castrated then its capacity to feel exhilarated by dopamine is diminished, but if the gelded creature is injected with testosterone the ability returns. Men have at least ten times more testosterone than women,[25] so, plainly, their ability to be rewarded with a dopamine-endorphin high is once again enhanced.

The problem with dopamine is that its supercharging of the opiate-endorphin high has the same effect as any other drug. In time we become accustomed to it and so need higher and higher levels to achieve the same euphoria. This is the addictive mechanism that drives men to ever greater risks. 'The sensation seeker needs to search for new stimuli to reinstate the state of heightened arousal,'[26] or, put another way, the high-sensation seeker is hooked on his own arousal mechanisms.

The futures trader at work in the chaos of the market is being driven not only by profits but also by the need to feel the high of a successful risk. It is mostly male work because the male's brain is engineered towards risk-taking (lower serotonin, fewer serotonin receptors) and it rewards him (higher dopamine) for a successful coup. The process of competitive trading has been studied and the conclusion, unsurprisingly, was that 'males are more willing to accept financial risk than females'.[27] The study went on to say that 'sensation seeking is positively related to riskiness of auction and lottery strategies for men but not for women'. Another study demonstrated that traders with the lowest MAO levels took the highest risks, and that women were far more averse to risks than men.[28] The most successful traders are the sensation seekers, and it comes as no surprise to discover that such individuals were also enthusiastic about skydiving or racing cars. Their neurochemistry drives them towards thrills.

It would be wrong to suggest that all traders, or even the majority of them, are suicidal maniacs. A man or woman without any braking system would soon be dead or bankrupt, and most successful traders try to minimize the risks they take. Whether men or women (and the neurochemistry of our species decrees they will mostly be men), they will be capable of making better judgements under high pressure because stressful situations do not make them anxious, and anxiety impairs performance.

Which is not to say that men therefore make the best financial managers. A recent report concluded that women fund managers consistently outperform their male colleagues, except in those funds which specialize in fast-growth equities or other high-risk investments.[29] This suggests that a prudent investor should look for a woman fund-manager (it might be a difficult search; there are still six times more men than women managing funds on Wall Street), because she is much less likely to take risks with her client's funds. Men are more likely to possess a compulsion to seek new challenges, which involves greater willingness to tolerate failure. Their thrill, your money.

Our neurochemistry decrees that a woman facing a risk, whether it be physical or intellectual, is more likely to be cautious, which is why there are no top-level women racing drivers. It is not because women cannot drive cars fast, they can, but because in the moment of crisis their instinct is to avoid risk. The male sees an infinitesimal chance to overtake a rival and floors the accelerator. He either wins or crashes. Most women do not understand that impulse, any more than most males sympathize with the cautious approach preferred by the majority of women. Each misunderstands the other. The male is condemned as a reckless fool, the woman is decried as timid. Yet eschewing risk does not make a person timid or boring, merely sensible and, probably, longer lived. The young low-serotonin male is four times more likely to die in an accident before he reaches adulthood.[30] Equally, the low serotonin male is much quicker to anger,[31] because of the lower levels of control exerted by the frontal cortex over the limbic impulses. This means that a male will almost always be more impatient with other people and, as we have already seen, low serotonin levels can make a man brutally impulsive and dangerous, even more so when his neurological equipment is affected by alcohol or drugs.[32]

It is this dark side of the male that draws attention and gives rise to the impossible demand that he 'get in touch with his femininity'. Wife-batterers and child abusers are rightly detested, yet it is a nonsense to suggest, as the outer limits of the feminist movement does, that all men are abusers and rapists. The male very often is violent, and sometimes society needs that violence for its own protection. When a society is attacked or invaded it needs low-serotonin males who are willing to risk their lives to defend what they love. Yet the new unisex culture deplores masculinity, condemning it as 'patriarchal', violent and unthinking. That attitude conveniently ignores the fact that risk-takers are far more than just traders or warriors: they are very often the creative minds that are ready to challenge stereotypes and extend the bounds of the possible. It is not surprising that it is the male who invents the machines (even the iron and the washing machine), and it is the male's technological genius that took us to the moon. We need that risk-taking, and if it is shown mostly by males then that does not make men superior to women, merely different. And one of the greatest differences between men and women is in the hormones, in testosterone, the fuel of victory. Men, far more than women, play to win.

PLAYING TO WIN

In 1992 the scientific journal *Nature* published an article by two physiologists, Susan Ward and Brian Whipp, which claimed that women would soon outrun men.[33] The gender gap was closing fast, the authors said; they predicted that by 1998 women athletes would be the equal of men at marathons and, in the following few years, would catch up and even surpass male athletes at all other distances. It seems many people believe this; that given enough training and time the fastest woman in the world will match or even surpass the speed of the fastest man.

What has actually happened? The first major marathon of 1998 was run just as we were finishing this book. Moses Tanui of Kenya won the Boston Marathon in 2 hours 7 minutes 44 seconds. The winning woman, Fatuma Roba of Ethiopia, raced home in 2 hours 23 minutes 21 seconds, 15 minutes 37 seconds behind Tanui. In 1992, when the prediction was made, the winning man's time was 2.08.14 – 15 minutes 29 seconds ahead of the fastest woman. Nothing has changed; nor will it.

In track and field events, on the whole, males have a 10% advantage, and nature will keep it that way. It is true that both sexes have become faster and fitter over the years, an improvement that has much to do with better diets, better training and a gradual increase in height, but the male has certain physical advantages that make it impossible for women ever to catch up. Of course a woman athlete will beat a male couch-potato any day, but if she challenges a male athlete who is as fit as she is then she will lose, and her loss will have nothing to do with training, diet or the uneven provision of sporting facilities for men and women. It has to do with nature. Men run faster than women, almost a tenth faster, so if he runs a marathon in two hours and thirty minutes then he will beat her by fifteen minutes, every time.

Why? For a start, men are larger, but, size for size, his physiology is also more efficient in terms of utilizing energy than hers. He has the advantage of possessing proportionately more red blood cells, he has a greater lung capacity and a faster metabolic rate. What all that means is that he can burn energy faster than she can. Not only that, but women carry a higher proportion of body fat than men because women are more efficient at converting energy into storage. This makes the female of the species (probably of all species) more resistant to starvation, but, weight for weight, the male has more muscle. She might survive famine, but he will always run faster.[34]

He also has the advantages of his different brain which is equipped with 'triggers' that provoke his body to produce testosterone. The female also secretes testosterone, but only about one-tenth as much as a male,[35] and testosterone is to competition what oxygen is to fire. It is a male weapon, a driving force, and nature has given him a plentiful supply.

'Gained 20 pounds last night!' Bill boasts.
'You did *what?*' Anne asks.
'Not me, silly, the pumpkin.'

Men don't just grow vegetables, they have to grow the biggest. All across Britain, every summer, men (rarely women) compete at village shows to see who has nurtured the largest leek, biggest cabbage or plumpest pumpkin. A woman, more sensibly perhaps, will grow vegetables to feed her family, but a man also grows them to prove he can do it better than his neighbours. He needs to win, and if he does not have a winning skill of his own he will transfer the urge to his home team. Sports fans, giant vegetable growers, racing drivers; these are men at play and very few women have the desire to join them. Of course women do compete in sports, and of course many women enjoy watching them, but still, to the majority of women, men's pastimes and their passionate attachments to their sporting heroes seem ridiculous. That is because women cannot know the compelling drive of testosterone. For men almost all of life is a competition.

Are men too competitive? The male's competitive drive is often considered negative, especially by green feminists, but most men consider it a strength and this can cause problems. A man is quite ready to sacrifice his personal life, his family and his home while he pursues success. To a man the corporate ladder is an assault course that produces winners and losers. So it's his daughter's seventh birthday and she is having a party and he has promised to be there? A woman would move heaven and earth not to disappoint the child, but a man will balance his daughter against the desirability of attending the sales conference and the conference will probably win. He is not in competition with his daughter, but he is in competition within his business.

Men can and do co-operate. This cut-throat picture of an executive callously sacrificing his daughter's happiness for his own success (though he, remember, would say that his financial success is far more important to her in the long run) does not mean that men are lone wolves. They can and do co-operate. Just watch any university rowing eight to see a group of testosterone-rich males combining as a team. Men can work wonderfully well together, but they work best when they are competing with another team. And to be a member of a winning team enhances a man's subsequent chances of individual success.

Men's banter is one-upmanship (or one-downmanship). Men pick up on other people's mistakes far more readily than women. There is a combative bite to male-talk. In the House of Commons male MPs relentlessly barrack and banter with their political rivals, while most women find this difficult.[36] A man is always testing the competition, always ready to prove that he is a more successful male. Women are less likely to read a newpaper's political coverage because they dislike the conflict and aggression of parliament. A MORI poll showed that 47% of men found political news interesting compared to 29% of women.[37] The female editor of a high circulation Sunday newspaper noted that 'politics is reported in terms of conflict and controversy. I don't think this is appealing to women, who are not adversarial in the same way. We don't like a fight'.[38]

When do men not compete? When it does not matter. Gloria Steinem wrote in her essay 'If Men Could Menstruate': 'if men could menstruate they would brag about how often and how much'.[39] That depends. If a thing is not vital to self-esteem or to success, a man will let it pass. He will not waste his energy on what he sees as the mundane everyday things, even though those things might be crucial to his wellbeing. Few men have ever boasted of being a better launderer than another, or a more efficient house-cleaner.

'Men can be so useless,' Anne remarks.
'Don't be absurd, woman.'
'So what's that thing in the garden? A giant pumpkin! We won't even eat it!'
'But we will always know we grew it,' Bill says, 'and the knowledge will be deeply satisfying.'
'I'm right. Men are useless.'

Men's competitive drive comes from testosterone, and, because in real life not everyone can be a winner, it will come as no surprise that testosterone levels vary between individuals. They also vary enormously between men and women: the adult male's T levels (5,140–6,460 units)[40] are about 11 times higher than a woman's (285–440 units). Give a man the challenge of competition and his already high T level will rise, increasing still further his competitive edge.[41] In all of us, male and female, the T level fluctuates. It is highest in the morning, goes down to a low in the early afternoon, starts to rise slowly towards supper time to be back at its peak by morning. The base level also sinks as men age so that old men often have levels more like the average adult female.[42]

The men who have the highest base-rate testosterone levels are the most aggressive and the most prone to violence.[43] Such individuals seem to lack impulse control; they are all accelerator and no brake. Just below them are men with high-medium T levels, who usually possess a dominant, competitive personality, but have their anger and hostility under control. Such men are frequently found in professions that demand a competitive streak. Barristers (courtroom advocates) have higher T levels than those lawyers who stay in their offices. Ministers of the church have the lowest levels. The same phenomenon has been observed in women. Female lawyers have higher levels than women teachers or nurses, and female business executives have higher T levels than clerical workers or housewives.[44]

T levels can and do change under challenge, so how can we say that the high testosterone levels associated with success are not a consequence of the job? If you took a low T level minister of the church and made him plead a case in the courtroom, would his testosterone rise to barrister level? It certainly would rise under the challenge, but the rise would be temporary only because our T levels are largely inherited.[45] A high T level father is more likely to breed a high T level son, or a high T level daughter for that matter. There is also evidence to show that if a high T level boy has an undisciplined childhood then he will never learn how to cope with his surging aggressions.[46]

All this must seem very unfair to those who believe that the competition for success must be equal between the sexes. And perhaps it is unfair, for a large number of studies have examined how men and women react to competition, and the results show a distinct difference between the sexes. Many of the studies looked at sports, which provide a clear challenge with easily defined winners and losers.

If a man is about to enter a race or start a game his T levels can rise by 40%, while the woman's pre-competition level does not change at all.[47] His biology is preparing him for the contest, hers is not. So what advantages does his highly elevated T level confer?

For starters it makes him far more willing to take risks, it improves the speed of his reactions and it helps him concentrate. It enhances his mood, too, for a raised T level makes him feel good and persuades him that he can win.[48] So, even before a competition begins, whether that competition is a marathon or a chess match, the male starts with a competitive advantage. His chemistry has psyched him up and sharpened his edge.

Once in the competition the male's testosterone level will climb higher still, but perhaps the most interesting finding of the various studies is that success breeds more of the fuel that helps make a winner. If two male players begin, say, a tennis match with the same high T level, the winner will end the match with a much higher level than the loser. The winner goes into the next round of the tournament with his pre-match testosterone surge even higher than before, and so, concomitantly, is his self-confidence. Success engenders success.

Women's T levels also climb during a contest (though there is no change before the game), but they climb from a much lower level and do not reach nearly the same giddy heights as the men's. More interestingly, there is not the same correlation between winners and losers. Two women playing a tennis game will both end up with slightly elevated T levels, but the biggest influence on the rise is not the fact of winning or losing, but rather the feeling that they have played well. So even if she loses a game, a woman can still have a winner's feeling. Winning was simply not so important to her, but performing well was. She does not have that feedback loop of winning, feeling great, and wanting to win again.[49]

Men can also show higher T levels for having performed well, but only if they have won. And success does help success, for while male winners had even higher levels of pre-game testosterone before their next match, the losers went into the next round with the handicap of a lower T level.[50]

So is winning all in the mind? That leaves out natural talent, training and dedication, but undoubtedly a high T level will help make a champion. T levels suppress pain, which obviously helps in any physical activity, and a high T level also creates a feeling of euphoria and exhilaration. This is because testosterone is linked to dopamine, the neurotransmitter which stimulates the pleasure centres in the brain: you only have to watch a tournament-winning male tennis player, or a goal scorer in football, to see just how high the euphoria can rise.[51]

T levels are not just associated with pleasure. They also correlate with aggression and dominance. The more dominant a male is, the higher his T level will rise, and scientists suspect there is again a feed-back loop in the mechanism. A successful attempt to dominate others (whether at sport or in business or at politics) increases testosterone, and a higher T level increases the willingness to compete further. So the more you win the higher your testosterone goes and the more you want to win even more. Losers, meanwhile, suffer a lowering of the T level, which only increases their propensity for failure.

One study measured the testosterone levels of ice-hockey players through a season and, as expected, the T levels of the winning team went higher and higher, peaking at the triumphant end of the season.[52] But even watching sport creates the same hormonal ebbs and flows in the male. The male fan's testosterone rises when his team wins, and when the team becomes the champion the male shares his heroes' exhilaration of a testosterone-induced dopamine high. Perhaps this is one reason why so many more men than women are passionate sports fans. Their body chemistry offers them a much stronger reaction to winning (and to losing). Women simply do not get the same chemical high out of supporting a winning team, and so are not drawn to sports as men are.

Our own survey of the sports pages of two national newspapers from 8 to 16 August 1997 showed that 91% of the sport's reports were about men and only 9% about women's sports. In a postmodernist's perfect world, one, say, controlled by American courtrooms, that proportion would have to be 50/50, but the newspapers know their readers. They reflect reality. TV sport is watched by men, and it is only when there is a special game, say a Superbowl or a World Cup match,[53] or perhaps a championship final when the home team is playing, that women watch at all.[54]

> 'For women to play male sports is to define themselves as men,' says Bill. 'The semi-violent competitive sports are not for the average woman.'
> 'Maybe women don't participate in sports the way men do,' Anne says, 'but surely there are good reasons for them to play if they enjoy it – even if it's not the competition itself that they enjoy. What about tennis or volleyball?'
> 'Let them play! I'll even watch.'
> 'You will? Why?'

Men do watch women's sports, but not always for the competition. We can find no research, but it is a fair guess that men's enjoyment of women's tennis went down sharply when the broadcasters banned the 'low-behind-the-baseline' camera angle for the woman's serve.

Men need sport in ways that women do not. PET (positron emission tomography) scanners have shown that even when a man is relaxing his brain, unlike hers, continues to show high activity in those parts which control movement and aggression. His mind is restless, always ready for action, and sports provide that; which is why, to relax, he can watch hours of sport. He becomes one with the flow of the action: advance, retire, hold, pass – *attack, attack, attack*. This is him: his hormones and brain are at one – at peace.[55]

The tale of men and challenge is not solely about testosterone. Testosterone is the fuel that prepares him for competition, heightens his pain threshold and hurls him into the action, but as the contest continues, and if it goes badly, the body secretes a second hormone: cortisol. Cortisol provokes anxiety and counsels caution, it triggers the flight rather than the fight reaction. Plainly, too much cortisol will prove a disadvantage for a competitor;

indeed, it might be said that cortisol is the loser's chemical while testosterone is the winner's, but cortisol is also much more the woman's hormone. She is influenced by cortisol much more than the male, so much so that while high T levels are an indication of a man's potential for success, a better guide to a woman's chances is her C level. A low-level cortisol female is more likely to be successful then a woman with a high level.

The reason for the disparity of cortisol's effects on male and female lies in the geography of the hormone's production. In both men and women cortisol is manufactured in the adrenal cortex, but the woman also uses the adrenal cortex to manufacture her testosterone. A very small amount also comes from her ovaries, while 95% of the male's testosterone comes from the testes. In men, because the two chemicals are made in different places, there is no immediate link between them, but in women it seems as though their manufacture is linked. When her adrenal cortex secretes testosterone, it simultaneously manufactures testosterone's 'antidote', cortisol. This means that her competitive biology is intimately linked with her anxiety system and, not surprisingly, women report far higher levels of stress in competitive situations than do men. One researcher, summarizing the studies, suggests that 'only women, not men, who compete successfully against the opposite sex seem to get tense and nervous'.[56] A man's reaction to challenge is to compete, because that induces the reward of a testosterone-induced euphoria, while a woman's reaction is to become anxious.

If that were not enough there are still further differences in how men and women respond to a challenging situation – to stress. The human response to challenge is better known as the fear, flight or fight mechanism, and it is triggered by an adrenalin rush. The adrenal gland produces adrenalin and nor-adrenalin, and these substances are crucial if we are to respond to the challenge at maximum efficiency. The adrenalin rush is a summons to battle-stations; it sends energy to the muscles and shuts down biological functions that are not crucial to the moment, which is why men shot in battle frequently do not remember feeling any pain at the moment of wounding. The adrenalin rush adapts us to deal with imminent danger, and without it we would be far more likely to fail the challenge. Men's adrenal response is much larger than women's.[57] Not only that but, rather like T levels, the bigger the adrenal response the better. 'The more men's adrenalin increases during competitive stress, such as taking an examination, the better they tend to do. Women's changes in adrenalin are unrelated or negatively related to their performances.'[58] Both men's neurochemistry and their body chemistry mean they are going to do better under challenge, and they help make him into a much fiercer competitor. Women often find this difficult to understand, for their own chemistry militates against savage competition. Any contest requires the individual to have less regard for the welfare of the opponent and women find such an attitude more difficult to adopt. His brain structure, his neurochemistry and his hormones all help him become a ruthless competitor. (Though sometimes he likes to compete on the moral plane to see who can be the least ruthless. Either way, to men it is almost all a contest.)

The greatest prize is peace (on one's own terms), which makes war the ultimate challenge. Women often misunderstand men's fascination with battle, though by now we have covered enough of the male–female differences to see why the components of war – machines, dominance, contest, winning, humiliating opponents and dreadful risk – so appeal to men. That appeal does not imply approval; many men are pacifists and many of our bravest warriors preach against war's horrors, but men are still fascinated by battle. 'It is well that war is so dreadful,' said Robert E. Lee, one of history's greatest generals, 'or else we would grow too fond of it.' Fond of war? The thought is terrible to many, especially women, but men enjoy risk, they enjoy challenge, they even need those things, and war is the ultimate provider of them. There is, perhaps, nothing quite so pathetic as the well-meaning attempts of the western democracies to integrate women into their military forces. If an enemy wanted one way to weaken the armies, navies and air forces of the West, it could do no better than to encourage more women to enlist for combat positions, for a cortisol-rich army will be a cautious army. Women join up in the name of equal opportunity and 'human rights', men for the thrill. If the Visigoths are marauding down your road, threatening to rape your daughters and burn your house, whom do you want defending it? Testosterone-rich, low-serotonin young males? Or women? Answers on a postcard, please, to the politicians who espouse cortisol-rich armed forces.

Men are nature's warriors, but that is not to imply that all men are ruthless killers lost in a wanton love of battle. Perhaps man's strongest instinct is to protect those whom he loves. Most men are not potential rapists, they are much more likely to be protectors. Given the chance the male is a natural hero, but nowadays he is a most unfashionable hero. His qualities of single-mindedness and ruthlessness are decried in a world which insists that there is no difference between men and women, and that women, given the chance, can be just as effective as men at leading corporations or assaults on enemy positions. But the truth is they are not equal. The man is blessed, or cursed, with a brain chemistry that encourages ruthlessness and sets less store on emotional ties. Men dominate in the workplace because their whole being is concentrated on just that domination. Nor should we necessarily condemn it; tough and unpleasant though the male mind might be, it is the powerhouse of change when it comes to innovation or to taking the great risks that result in the conquest of new fields. Those who deny that he is distinct have a problem when they ask him to control the differences they deny.

'So there is no glass ceiling?' Bill observes.
'More of a testosterone barrier,' Anne says.
'Tough.'
'Not at all. Our brain chemistry offers us advantages denied to you.'

'Such as?' Bill asks.

'We excel at any job where people are important or where relationships need encouragement.'

'People skills! Sounds dull.'

'Go and mulch your pumpkin.'

SUMMARY

- Men are more impulsive, impatient and more easily bored than women.
- Men derive greater pleasure from taking risks.
- A man's enjoyment of risk is neurologically driven.
- Men are neurologically primed to respond positively to competitive situations – women are not.
- The effects of these biological influences on our working lives are so important that in the next chapter we must examine the impact they have, and in all probability will always have, on sex differences in the workplace.

CHAPTER SEVEN

Extremes Are Not Rules

Top and tail at work

Nine out of every ten great chefs are men.

So it stands to reason, doesn't it? Men are superior.

There is a fallacy in this kind of reasoning. It may not be easy to spot but it should be noted, for men frequently use it as grounds for declaring their superiority as a sex. It is the old misogynist argument that men must be the more talented because they succeed more often. Watch the reasoning: *Men achieve higher status more frequently than women. To rank higher is to be superior. Therefore men are superior*. Any man who uses that argument cannot reason clearly, for it is plain wrong.

Men grow the big onions. Does this mean women are poorer gardeners? Obviously not. It is the common error of social science: to generalize from the margins to the common middle ground. Some women use it too; a few men are rapists, therefore all men are rapists. You cannot explain the ordinary by the extraordinary, and the fact that a few exceptional men soar to dizzy heights of achievement does not mean that all men are superior.

It is true that nature does seem to have endowed men with advantages in some areas. He has better daylight and perceptive vision. He has a faster reaction time to moving objects. He has better spatial and directional ability. He has greater mechanical ability. He is far more obsessive and competitive. That list surely means that he must be the better driver. And so he is, if you want someone to drive Formula One cars round a race track, but does that make him a better driver than a woman? Not according to the insurance companies. One study in America concluded that male racing drivers, who represent the ultimate in skill, have more road crashes than any other drivers.[1]

Arguing that the male sex is superior because a few men are wildly successful risks a counter argument, one just as fallacious but equally convincing, that men must be inferior because more men fail than women. If you plot the spread of talents on a graph you will see that the female scores heavily in the mid-range of abilities while there will be far more men at the two extremes of the scale: at the highly talented end and at the utterly useless end.[2] His bell-curve of ability is broad and hers is slim, and the difference in the two profiles is striking; but, and this is important, most men share the middle ground where most of the women are. It depends on the subject, of course, and in some areas, like linguistic ability, women will occupy the highly talented end of the scale in greater numbers than men, but in most areas of human endeavour it remains true that men achieve more.

'What does that mean?' Anne asks.

'It seems perfectly plain language,' Bill says, 'well within your feminine verbal skills.'

'Isn't child-rearing human endeavour?'

'It's hard work, so yes, I suppose so. But in the high-status activities, which are precisely the ones the women's movement wishes to open up to women, men excel. You're the one who found the research, not me.'

'But there is a cultural element here, surely?' says Anne. 'The achievements of men are highly regarded *because they are achieved by men*. Women's achievements are valued less; indeed, if a man reaches the top level in a "woman's" field – nursing, teaching younger children, textile arts – his status will never equal that of the top dogs in "male" areas – surgery, university don, architect.'

'Precisely the point,' says Bill. 'Women will excel in the softer fields like the arts and caring – and, indeed, in being the watchdogs for male high achievers.'

In some fields, like higher mathematics, there may be little or no female presence at the extremities of the graph, which means that significant success and abject failure are the preserves of the male. So if you argue that his domination of the highly talented end of the scale argues for his superiority, then you must also accept that his near monopoly of the untalented extreme argues just as fiercely for his inferiority. After all, four times as many men as women suffer a mental or learning disability.

People rarely compete for the bottom place, which is why the arguments in the gender wars concentrate on the top places. Women's advocates talk of a 'glass ceiling', an invisible barrier which stops women from achieving success, but they never talk of the 'glass floor' which, by their reasoning, must also exist, or else as many women as men would be abject failures.

Men do both better and worse than women. Some of their success is due to inbuilt assets provided by nature; thus their superior ability to envisage three-dimensional shapes translates to a natural advantage in mathematical problems, and that, in turn, helps to explain why there are so few female engineers, Nobel Prize winners in physics, or chess champions (there are at present 6 women chess grandmasters and about 450 men[3]). The alternative explanation for that dearth is, of course, the cultural argument which expects us to believe that all over the world parents (probably fathers) discourage their daughters from studying mathematics ('put away your calculator, dear, and play with your dolls').

Another reason why the male excels more often is that his brain is capable of a much narrower focus once his interest is finally aroused. We saw that illustrated in the brain scans which showed how the male shuts down parts of his brain so that another area can concentrate on a problem, while a female keeps both hemispheres working during the problem's solution. This seems to contradict the other research that says he has difficulty in keeping his mind on one thing; that is true, but only up to the point when his fickle interest is aroused, and then he goes straight into higher gear. He is more distractable in that he constantly seeks novelty, but once he has discovered something that intrigues him he will pursue it with ruthless dedication. Challenge gives him a surge in testosterone, testosterone enhances his ability to concentrate, and once he is focused he has an ability to ignore distractions. It is usually the male who pursues hobbies to the extreme: twitchers (called birders in the US) are mainly male, and while many women like to watch birds, there are few who will drop everything, abandoning work and family, to travel a thousand miles to see a misty glimpse of a wandering albatross that has wandered into the wrong place. A woman writing a symphony is much more likely to be sidetracked by worries about her family and friends, while a man will ruthlessly let both go hang while he completes the task. The talent required for genius is probably possessed by many, including many women, but the organization of men's brains makes it much more likely that they will be equipped with the total obsession that will allow the genius to be expressed.

A musical genius is nearly always a man.
Yet women, in general, are the more musical.

It comes back to the two bell-curves. His is broad, with room at one of its ends for genius. Hers is slim, with less room for genius, but less space, too, for idiocy.

MEN ARE DAMAGED BY THE WORKPLACE REVOLUTION

The differences between men and women have translated into an enormous social change, and one, as we shall see, that has been to the male's disadvantage. That change has been the entry into the workforce of a huge number of previously underemployed women. The advent of the birth control pill meant fewer children and thus gave her greater control over her life. The Second World War provided another boost to women's employment as thousands replaced men in factories across Britain and the United States (though not in Germany, where the Nazis stubbornly encouraged the belief that an Aryan woman's place was in the church, kitchen and kindergarten). After the war came the great revolution in housework which, despite the best efforts of gender equalizers, remains a feminine preserve. In the past Monday was usually washday, and the family laundry would take all day and even spill over into Tuesday – a horrific chore with tubs, scrubbing boards, bar soap and mangles. Now the dirty clothes are popped into the machine. Cooking, cleaning, and keeping the home fires burning was a full-time job, and usually a woman's job, but machines suddenly made it all much simpler and released women to other occupations. Women, of course, had always been forced into low-paid jobs such as garment-making, but the twentieth century released hundreds of thousands of women into jobs that had previously been held by men. And employers have discovered that women make better employees than men; they are less argumentative, more co-operative, more flexible in their hours and, yes, will accept lower pay. Add to that the biological truth that a man's neurology makes him a less reliable employee. He is a risk-taker, he is easily bored, and he is more likely to cut corners. She is more reliable. Nor are his personal or social skills as great as hers, and as a result she climbs the employment ladder at his expense in greater and greater numbers.

Worldwide, men now make up 53% of the workforce; in 1990 they occupied 66% of the jobs;[4] by the turn of the century they will almost certainly be a minority of the workforce. While this trend has been good for her, it has been disastrous for him. He's been displaced from many of the lower level jobs. Indeed, everywhere except at the very top of the employment tree, men are losing ground. There is not nearly so much heavy manual work as there used to be because automation has reduced the necessity. Today's woman can do what her grandfather did because she has a fork-lift truck, and one obvious result has been the creation of a much larger male underclass. Boys are leaving school without any useful qualifications – often, indeed, without any useful education, and are then discovering that jobs are few and far between. There used to be work for these unskilled, unqualified males as general labourers, but the demand for such men has dropped dramatically. A farm that once employed a dozen men can now operate with two. Hod-carriers have been replaced by machines, roads are now swept by machines, and even machines are built by other machines. This means that a man who possesses no job skills has almost no chance of gainful employment, indeed, in some countries as many as a third of men who do possess job qualifications are unemployed.

One obvious result of this has been a severe drop in male wages at the lowest end of the pay scale. The bottom 10% of male wage-earners have been hit hardest: their real income (adjusted for inflation) remained static between 1978 and 1992, while those in the middle levels saw a 35% increase and the top 10% increased their wages by 50%.[5] The average hourly wage for American males without a high school education fell from $11.85 in 1973 to $8.64 in 1995.[6]

The plight of such low-skilled or no-skilled males can only get worse because employers neither want nor need them. Indeed, employers prefer women. Female workers do not make as much trouble as men and will accept worse conditions, and that is true throughout the world so that, as manufacturing jobs move to undeveloped countries, the new jobs go to women rather than to men. South-east Asia and Latin America are humming with new industrial plants, many of them in export zones. Typically such factories make or assemble toys, clothing or electronic goods, and 80% of their workers are female. By the year 2000 three-quarters of entries into the British workforce will be women.[7] It is hardly surprising. Men are much more demanding about their pay and their working hours, and far more likely to belong to an obstreperous trade union. Men dislike part-time jobs, while employers love hiring part-time workers because they are cheaper. Part-time work suits women for it gives them time to spend with their families. The Equal Opportunities report of 1997 described the new reality: 'Women working part time earn 58% of the hourly rate of male full-timers. One in five of the population, most of them women, work part time and most of the new jobs are part time.'[8] Five times as many women as men work part time: 45% of women in employment and 7% of men.[9]

This helps to explain a puzzle in Western economies: a high growth rate – especially in the US – despite low unemployment and low inflation. Today women predominate in nine out of ten of the lowest-paid full-time occupations: three-quarters of low earners in Britain are women.[10] With a large proportion of women in the workforce employers are able to hold wages down; when workers are less demanding employers need not pay a premium to hold on to them. Men drive a harder bargain when it comes to wage negotiations. According to a study by the University of Illinois, girls are worse negotiators than boys. When boys find they cannot get a new toy by asking they switch to bargaining techniques such as offering to pay for half. Girls, on the other hand, resort to sulking, begging and pleading. Dr Elizabeth Moore-Shay, the author of this study, calls this 'the emotional approach'.[11]

Female first-time job seekers are 'preoccupied with the quality of relationships, and will reject a career if they think they cannot combine it with a full personal life,' says Heather-Jane Robertson, director of professional services and development for the Canadian Teachers Federation.[12]

Women are less militant, less agressive, which in part explains the collapse of the trade unions in manufacturing and the service industries. They are more likely to seek and accept part-time or short-term contracts. In this the modern state co-operates: short-term state benefits are given to tide over workers – largely female – between jobs. The percentage of women claiming unemployment can vary twice as much as the percentage of men.[13] This, too, benefits the employer and makes for a more flexible economy. The growing pool of temporary workers also acts as a brake on wage demands. And the Third World skills needed for basic computer literacy – data or word processing – are provided by these women workers.

> 'But everyone points to the modern woman's success in business,' says Anne.
> 'So they do,' says Bill, 'and women are succeeding, and they stand tall in the middle ranks. But it's politic to sweep under the boardroom table the fact that their low wage demands carry the economy on their backs.'
> 'You mean there's a conspiracy?'
> 'Reality is not a conspiracy.'

Most men see their job as their career. They may even define themselves by their job and their success at it, but women are much more likely to think in terms of overall life-style; she is willing to take a lower-paid part-time job that gives her some spending money and time with her children.[14] Employers are quietly delighted by this trend, it releases them from the need to hire troublesome men, and it gives them a cheaper, more flexible workforce which some companies encourage by offering child-care facilities. This trend leaves the low-skill male with nothing: no pride, no status and no hope. The existence of that lumpen male proletariat already poses problems for society, and those problems are going to increase as the numbers of unemployable men at the bottom of the social ladder increase. Such men are bored and demoralized, and they form an underclass in a way that women never did. A century ago a woman may have lacked opportunity and been dominated by the male of the species, but she rarely defined her self-worth in terms of a job so she did not feel rejected. Men do. They have been made worthless by a failing education system and by changes in the workplace that are far beyond their control, yet they still possess the male's inbuilt aggression and have a biological need for risk, achievement and excitement. The thoughtless thug is partly a product of our inability to harness the male potential. Education could certainly lift some of the potentially unemployable out of the grim fate that awaits unskilled males, but that will demand the re-imposition of male-focused schooling with its emphasis on challenge.

It is not just the rump of unskilled men who have felt the effects of women entering the workforce. Women are increasingly filling jobs higher up the socio-economic scale and, once again, much of the reason for this appears to be that they make more agreeable employees. Women demand less, and evidence for this comes from comparing male and female pay packets. Female bank and building society managers earn 36% less than men in the same jobs. Women secondary school teachers receive 10% less pay than their male colleagues.[15] A Law Society survey of solicitors' salaries in England and Wales in 1996 found that men were being paid significantly more than women even after allowing for differences in age and experience. Male assistant solicitors were earning an average of £24,000 a year while women doing the same work were receiving just £21,000. At the top of the profession the gulf was even wider: he averages £51,000 a year and she receives just £36,000. Overall, in the private sector, a woman receives just 67% of a male's salary.[16] The gap is narrower in the public sector, yet even there women typically earn just 80% of men's pay.

These salary differences seem to argue for the existence of the glass ceiling, or at least for a massive unfairness, but who is exploiting whom? High-cost men are being replaced by cheaper women workers. One-third of those solicitors toiling away for unequal pay are women, but over 50% of new entrants to the legal profession are also women.[17] Why? Is it because women have suddenly become 'better' at law than men? The answer, probably, is much the same for a lawyer as it is for a woman who takes a low-ranking job. She demands less. She is not so obsessed as the male with pay and status. She does not insist on the carpeted office, the partner's desk and a Series 7 BMW – he does. That makes him more expensive to employ, so any company worried about its profitability might be tempted to employ a woman entrant because, in the long run, she'll do as much work for less money.

This gap in male and female incomes starts at the very beginning of their working lives. Typically a male university graduate will earn £2,000 a year more than a woman graduate, even if she has better academic qualifications.[18] But a close look at the jobs they take reveals why the difference might exist. He goes for the hard sciences while she tries for the soft. He goes for the practical and she for the 'personally satisfying'.[19] At least at the professional level, he thinks of a job as a lifetime career, and surveys show that he works longer and harder. Men in full-time jobs work nearly seven hours a week longer than women in full-time jobs.[20] Fathers in work – the vast majority in full-time jobs – average 46 hours a week. Full-time working mothers average 40. But include part-time working mothers and the woman's average working week falls to 27 hours.[21] Overall, fathers with jobs work 20 hours a week longer than women with jobs. Indeed the inequality between the hours men and women work has led one management researcher, Rhona Rapoport, to suggest that men should demand less work: 'The answer is for work to finish at the same time for everybody,' she says.[22] There is an endearing utopianism in the suggestion, or perhaps a sad disappointment in our world. In these days of downsizing, economic insecurity and global competition, we are supposed to tell our bosses we want more time off? Get real. More than eight out of ten UK managers regularly work more than 40 hours a week; four in ten work more than 50 hours a week, and the same number take home work at weekends.[23]

He is putting in more effort, so isn't it right that he should earn more? And is she doing exactly the same work for her smaller pay-packet? It may seem unfair that a woman assistant solicitor earns £3,000 a year less than a man, but is she as profitable? It appears that she is much more likely to be doing unprofitable legal aid work because it makes her feel useful to society and good about herself, while he is chasing the high-profit cases. We are told that women engineers earn less than their male counterparts, but that complaint turned out to depend more on the definition of 'engineer' than anything else. Engineeering, for obvious biological reasons, is an almost exclusively male preserve, but once the social scientists tacked on 'food engineering' to the engineer category, it suddenly appeared to have a considerable number of less well paid but highly qualified women. Food engineers, of all people, should be alert to the dangers of not comparing apples to apples.

Men might earn more, but they are also probably earning more for their companies, and the likelihood of this is indicated by the fact that men and women are still disproportionately represented in different occupations. Women are more likely to be found in the public sector – the so-called carers of society. Men are predominant in the technical, mechanical jobs that require much less contact with people. This is hardly surprising for, as we shall see in a later chapter, men are much less sociable creatures than women. This factor, men's relative unsociability, has hit them hard in the public sector where the focus, ideally, is on serving people, and there is much less room for the risk-taking, aggressive mentality that serves wealth creation. In Europe, since the early 1960s, 97% of employment growth has come in the public sector, and the vast majority of those new jobs went to women.[24] They are better suited to it, and they are cheaper.

Cheapness is not everything, or else men might expect to have no jobs at all. Suitability still counts for a lot, and biological aptitudes have kept some job areas almost exclusively male as the following list shows. It expresses as a percentage the proportion of men holding jobs in certain occupations:[25]

Bricklayers/masons	100%
Carpet fitters	100%
Mechanical engineers	99%
Quantity surveyor	98%
TV engineers	97%

Compare that with the percentage of men employed in occupations that do not play to a man's mechanical or mathematical
advantages:

Psychologists	31%
Welfare workers	28%
Librarians	18%
Receptionists	2%
Typists/word processors	1%
Dental nurses	0%

The good news for men in all this is that, while it is true that women
are taking more and more jobs, they are not taking those jobs for
which men are peculiarly suited, and nor, thankfully, are men
invading areas which favour women's talents. A high testosterone
male, full of challenge, will hardly make a sympathetic nurse or a
courteous receptionist. Yet some men do make good nurses – does
that disprove the rule? Hardly, for one study showed that brain
organization does indeed correlate with the job divide in the
workplace.[26] The study looked at the handful of women who were
successful in male jobs, as surveyors or engineers, and discovered
that their brains were organized in a male fashion. The same study
showed that successful male nurses (even heterosexual male
nurses) had a female-patterned brain. Some people argue that this
reveals only that the job makes the brain, but that ignores the vast
amount of evidence pointing to the role of hormones in the
growing foetus. Men and women who are successful in job areas
that are usually the preserve of the opposite sex come from the tiny
proportion of the population in whom the hormonal balance was
upset during the foetal stage. They are not pioneers for a brave new
world, but exceptions to a biological rule.

The one area where men do not face severe competition from
women is exactly where the male bell-curve would lead us to expect
it; at the high-ability end of the scale. Women are gaining everywhere except at the highest level, as these recent figures show:

89 per cent of politicians (world-wide) are men.[27]

89 per cent of managers (world-wide) are men.[28]

86 per cent of the top 1,000 UK companies have no female non-executive directors on the board.[29]

91 per cent of partners in City of London law firms are men, as are 84 per cent of the partners in England and Wales.[30]

92 per cent of British professors are male (women professors are more likely in medicine, education and librarianship).[31]

Celebrity architects are almost universally men (but a third of architectural graduates are women).[32]

95.6 per cent of UK company board members are male.[33]

96 per cent of those running advertising agencies are men and 91 per cent of the agencies' directors are male (though over one-half of the graduates entering advertising agencies are female).[34]

97 per cent of all the executives named in a survey of the financial pages of the *Financial Times* were men.[35]

97–99 per cent of executive and board positions in the 70,000 largest German companies are male.[36]

97.6 per cent of top management jobs at Fortune 500 companies are held by males.[37]

98 per cent of executive directors of FTSE 100 companies are held by males.[38]

98.1 per cent of the top earners at Fortune 500 companies are male.[39]

91 per cent of the top three grades of UK civil servants are men.[40]

94 per cent of High Court judges in Britain are men.[41]

94 per cent of cabinet ministers (world-wide) are men.[42]

(FIGURES FROM FINANCIAL TIMES '96, 97, 98)

There is a consistency in these figures which suggests a power-rule: that for every high achieving woman there are nine men. Some, of course, will object to that statement and scream 'glass ceiling', but until some hard evidence is adduced for that ceiling's existence, we prefer to believe that the disparity reflects men's biological advantages.

The idea of the glass ceiling owes much to the pervasive illusion of sexual sameness; but, short of enforced 'equality' in public institutions, the breakthrough will not become a reality, despite the streams of press releases from various business institutes which try to present a rosy picture of women breaking into top business ranks. This is done by either cherry-picking the figures, or else by expanding the number who are labelled 'executives'. Take the Dun & Bradstreet press release: 'Nearly one third of company directors are women'; once broken down, the figures suggest that there must be one executive for every five workers.[43] Other recent headlines have trumpeted women's gains: Strong rise in the number of women executives. More women in the boardroom. Cracks grow in the glass ceiling.[44] But what the accompanying articles rarely reveal is that the gains for women are almost exclusively at the lower management levels.

In the US women make up 46 per cent of the managerial workforce and only 2.4% of the highest management jobs in the top 500 companies. Earnings of the US women managers were 68% of their male counterparts'. World-wide the average female participation in managerial jobs is 20%.[45] The number of women gaining jobs on the boards of the largest companies is levelling off. Sheila Wellington, president of the research organization Catalyst, says: 'Many already have one token woman, and see no need to add another.'[46] Indeed, the figures for women directors are not significantly changing. It was observed at a management school women's workshop that 'the lack of women at director level can be explained by women's ambivalence about power, conflict and politics at work.'[47] At the same time the competitive corporate woman is and will be in demand as never before. She will have more chances than ever before, yet the reins of power in the more compeditive sectors will remain in the hands of those most inclined to competition.

The highest-earning businesswoman in Britain, Margaret Barbour, prefers to use the word 'family' rather than 'team' to refer to her workforce. 'Team play' is a term much used in business, but it is a bad metaphor in terms of describing a woman's style of management which, as Barbour observes, is more family-based than team-based. Is there a difference? A big one. A team is organized for competition, to outscore or outrow another team, while a family co-operates. Boys like team games, girls rarely do. Boys play in teams from their earliest years; they learn to compete, they learn to win and lose, and they take those attitudes into the workplace where their aim is to outperform their competitors. A recent report on business methods again suggests sport as a metaphor for business with its emphasis on purpose, deter-mination, singularity, and sheer bloodymindedness in the pursuit of achievement.[48] Men are team players, competitors, and their inbuilt drive and aggression are invaluable in the pursuit of corporate victory and wealth creation. In other areas, like personnel management, the woman's family style works better, but place most women in the piratical world of cut-throat business savagery and she shows she is not neurologically primed for it.

A report commissioned by the British Conservative Party emphasized that women were not as 'aggressive and pushy' as men. Virginia Bottomley, a former cabinet minister and author of the report, says that while men are fascinated by political intrigue, women are more interested in areas such as health and education.[49]

Men are more likely to possess the biological equipment to compete, yet it ought to be remembered that very few men actually break the so-called glass ceiling. A man has less than one chance in 10,000 of becoming a senior manager, while his chances of sitting on a major board are only one in 55,555. Hers are one in a million.

There was a time, undoubtedly, when a ceiling did exist which prevented women from rising to the top, but it was not made of glass. It was very visible: an array of old boy networks, clubs, prejudice and social attitudes (remember that it was once thought women would become neurasthaenic if they were challenged by a serious education). That has changed and, at least in the West, there are no real barriers to a woman's success, no more than there are for a man. So why are more women not at the high-flying end of the employment scale? Most probably because they are not born with the male's driving need to compete. They lack his biological ruthlessness and single-mindedness. A recent survey by the Henley Research Centre discovered just that; most women did not even want the top positions.

The percentage of women in the topmost jobs is probably never going to go above the one in ten mark (unless the field is rigged by quotas) because her biology and neurology make it nearly impossible for her to compete with testosterone-driven men. A man enjoys a neurological high when he is faced by competition and the more he competes the more his pleasure centres are stimulated, so he fights even harder to receive still more pleasure. A woman is not equipped by biology to receive this neurological reward. Indeed, if anything, her reaction to competition will be anxiety. These days, when the courts are alert to any prejudice against women, companies are more likely to encourage them to break through the glass ceiling, yet the women are not taking up the challenge because it does not suit their biology. Men love challenge; from their earliest days they have been playing games that demand winners and losers, while women, from their earliest days, seek co-operation and agreement; valuable things, to be sure, but not best suited to the aggressive accumulation of wealth, power or advantage. Of course some women, a few, do make it to the top and their success is used as an argument for the existence of an artificial barrier that has impeded the rest. That is similar to the fallacious argument with which this chapter began – some women succeed, therefore all women could succeed if only they had the chance. Even governments take this nonsense seriously which is why, in countries like China and Sweden, there are rules that ensure the legislatures are 50% women.

Quotas do neither sex a favour. Indeed, legislating for equality merely reinforces the old argument that men are superior – so superior that women need a helping hand to equal them. Yet it happens all the time, and not just in politics but right across the public sector where rules are changed so that women can be firefighters or police officers. A survey in Britain concluded that one-third of all women police officers had been unfairly promoted: they simply were not good enough, but political pressures demanded their promotion. The same survey concluded that some men were also unfairly promoted, but the proportion was much lower, just one in seventeen.

The pressure for 'equality' in the workforce continues, and inevitably it becomes a matter of quotas. Rosabeth Moss Kanter, a professor at Harvard, says a 'token group' is anything less than 15 per cent of the workforce.[50] But women are not necessarily under-represented on the boards of large corporations even when their representation is under 10%. Indeed, it would be fairer to say that, at the top, a representation of women to men at a ratio of one in eight is not discrimination on the basis of sex. To seek a 50/50 representation is to show prejudice or, at the very least, ignorance of what it takes to get to the top. Corporate heads may ask themselves if it is possible for their firm to be half-heartedly competitive and still hold its own, on the grounds that a competitive corporation that is headed by the less competitive is heading for a fall. The same is true for nations. They compete. At one time nations competed for empires, now they fight for 'inward investment', for jobs, and competition is a rough business. Men like it, women do not. Women do better when they are asked to regulate society, but they are not biologically driven to stretch the rules or even break them. Of course some women can compete with the best of men (our power rule suggests one in nine), and when a Margaret Thatcher reaches the top of the tree you can be certain it was not a quota system that put her there. She got there the hard way, beating the males at their own game.

Power seekers go to where the power is. Even in Scandinavia, where women's rights are enshrined in laws and quotas, the big corporations are headed by men. This is not an accident. Biology decrees that a few men have the ruthlessness and ability that will leave most men and women standing.

Always finding that it is 'bad news' that women play a smaller role in the running of big corporations is to fail to ask difficult questions about the progress of women – it is to construct a battle line where there is none; or rather, the lines drawn are ideological and utopian. Women have made remarkable headway towards genuine equality with men in the last generation. It does not follow that equal results follow from equal opportunity.

The current feminist phase for networking with fellow females in for promotion and mentoring fellow female executives is a recipe for managerial disaster. It is a way of telling those who would hire you on your merits that you are in fact part of a quota. Similarly with the 'aspirational' aims of such companies as Royal Dutch Shell, when they claim to seek 20% senior female executives. Quotas are not an answer (though they may in an individual case be politically astute). To expect the same results in a competitive world, when talents differ as to competitiveness, will soon be recognized as prejudice.

The very top is a rarefied place. What are the chances of a man being a genius, of possessing an utterly brilliant mind like that, say, of a major philosopher? Great philosophers occur extremely rarely, maybe two per century, which means that 2,500 years of human history has yielded perhaps 50 such exceptional men. All men. That incidence suggest that his chances appear to be about one in a billion, and while it is possible that she might also be such a rare creature, we would prefer not to calculate the odds. Mary Warnock argues that philosophy must be gender indifferent, and that the male's lead in the field has nothing to do with philosophy proper but all to do with male drive. This implies that the woman's thinking ability must be as great as the male's and, to support her claim, Warnock offers Elizabeth Anscome as an example of a woman philosopher worthy of ranking with the all-time greats; but the suggestion seems a little disingenuous when you consider that all Anscome did was to interpret a great male philosopher, Wittgenstein. Perhaps the answer lies in the nature of philosophy:

as one practitioner writes, 'The disputatious nature of the subject certainly seems peculiarly male.'[51]

The great philosophers are all men? (Even worse, they are mostly Dead White European Males.) Does this mean that men are superior? That is where this chapter began, and we have seen the fallacy of either sex claiming superiority on the basis of a handful of exceptional individuals. Those are rare people. The rest of us occupy the common middle ground where men's general competence is no greater than women's. And in that common middle ground where most of us live, women are making huge advances. The low and middle male is in retreat, yet the noise of battle is not to save his jobs, but rather to apportion a handful of the few top jobs to women. But you really think men will yield power? Will the canary eat the cat?

Nine out of ten of the great chefs are men.

Therefore men are superior?

But more than eight out of ten cooks are women.

And men, in general, cannot cook.

SUMMARY
- Nine out of ten top jobs are held by men.
- Men dominate the top and bottom of the success scale.
- Women's move into the workplace has made it hard for the average and less than average male to find employment.
- Men are less attractive to employers because they are more demanding and are less likely to take a low wage.

FUTURE TRENDS
- Women's pressure groups, failing to achieve equal results at work for the individual woman, will shift the emphasis to equality for groups of women workers. This is already happening in Britain where the chairwoman of the Equal Opportunities Commision, Kamlesh Bahl, asks for a 'fundamental shift in emphasis' from individual to collective remedies. She also wants all boys' school sports open to girls. The EOC

further proposes that excepting women from sections of military duties under the term 'combat effectiveness' should end.[52]

- Legislation for public equality of pay and power.
- Downsizing, a commitment to long hours and intense global competition (itself resulting in the undercutting of men's wages by women) mean that even though most of the new entries into the workforce are women, even the middle management will continue in most fields to be dominated by men.
- Feminism, which encouraged women into the workforce, still refuses to accept any responsibility for the increasing breakup of marriages, for the general lowering of wages in the middle and lower income groups, or for the devaluing of motherhood and domestic work. The common feminist solution is that the male should spend less time at the workplace and take on more domestic chores – as if he were the same as her (even as we find that he is not).

DESIRABLE AIMS

- The male underclass is now far larger than it need be because we failed him in school. The probability is that this will continue. One can but hope that in the 2000s the knowledge about the influences of biology on ability and learning will change how we teach boys – so fewer men will fail.

CHAPTER EIGHT

Painting Him Green
He resists her dream

Just up the road from our house lives a couple who have divided their large garden into two. She is organic. He is not. He grows the vegetables and flowers on his side of the line, while she cultivates snails, slugs and weeds on the other. He uses every modern advantage, while she hunts snails by moonlight and deters greenfly by washing her weeds with soap and water. His garden could win prizes, but not from those, like his wife, who abhor mixing chemistry with horticulture. She prides herself on being 'green', and so harvests a moral reward.

The green world is the prime alternative to an increasingly complex and technologically driven world; and the green vision is undoubtedly attractive for it is co-operative, non-aggressive, nurturing, and free from contest and conquest. It is powered by 'alternative' energy which is non-nuclear, non-polluting and free of danger. What science underpins the green world is often described as 'alternative science', and is praised for being non-analytic and free from any bias towards the rational. The green world is holistic and healing. Who would not be green?

Many men, for a start, which is hardly surprising, for if there is a snake in the green garden it is man. Not woman, man. Competition, risk and conquest are, as we have seen in earlier chapters, male traits, and it has become axiomatic in the green movement that such behaviour is destroying the earth. Greens favour an environment that is free from antagonism, exploitation and the hard-driven logic that excludes the picture of a holistic earth. Eco-feminists are the philosophical gurus (gurettes?) of greenery, and their intention is to nurture a constructive, non-polluting, eco-sustainable and shared environment that will replace the current male-dominated and exploited world. The green premise is that our environment is all-important because it shapes us; and we, in turn, can shape it, so the goal is to eradicate the dominant and oppressive male and so liberate the planet to the healing and beneficent influences of femininity.

But the external environment is only half our environment, and the green case ignores the natural environment within the male of the species. Differences are reduced to externals which, like unwanted suckers, can be lopped off. The green's ideal world stands opposed to men as they are and wants to shape them into what they will not be. The eco-feminists, far from getting in touch with nature as a whole, have lost touch with the nature of men.

There are men who are green

The alternative world is deeply attractive to some men. Take competition out of the environment and the world suddenly becomes a place without fear or defeat, a world in which none needs strive and none can fail. There is a magical feeling of release. Ailments disappear, the air is for ever clean and the waters pure. It is a world in which waste, ruin, and war are things of the past. Who is not green for a time?

Feminists are the guiding green light

To be green involves planning the defeat of the aggressive male ego and replacing it with a more inclusive, holistic and feminine approach to the world. This is noted by many. It is well observed by a Californian academic, Richard Tarnas, in *The Passion of the Western Mind* (1995). It is the core of the green politics of the late Petra Kelly in *Thinking Green: Essays on Environmentalism, Feminism, and Non Violence* (1995). The feminist signature is green. 'Ecofeminism sees our ecological crisis as the outcome of the patriarchy that follows the "logic of domination",' writes one author. 'Dismantling patriarchy will free human relations and nature alike.'[1]

Ecological feminists plan to right our capsizing world (assuming, always, that it is capsizing in the first place).

> 'It's a dream, isn't it?' says Anne. 'A nice dream, so where's the harm in it?'
> 'Only in the practice,' says Bill.

Radical feminists have always allied themselves with radical ecologists, giving rise to some tension within the environmental movement: a divide betwen the 'deep ecologists' (who include men) and the ecological (eco-) feminists (who exclude men). Today the eco-fems battle with the deep ecologists for the hearts and hard core of the greens. But who are the eco-fems? And how important are they? They are less important in their numbers than in their influence, and the attitudes of radical feminists towards men have infused the green movement. The eco-fems have supplied the greens with an enemy, and the enemy is male.

In her book *Ecological Feminist Philosophies*, Karen J. Warren sees 'feminism as a movement to end all forms of oppression'.[2] All 'systems of oppression', for instance heterosexism, ageism, classism or racism, are found to be connected by the logic of domination. Included among Professor Warren's many 'systems of oppression' is naturism, which is not the practice of nudism, but rather the 'domination or oppression of nonhuman nature', and she finds that 'the logic of traditional feminism include[s] the abolition of "naturism".'

Professor Warren cannot be accused of naturism. She goes rock climbing above the shores of Lake Superior where, she tells us, she chats with the cliffs. 'I began to talk to the rock in an almost inaudible, child-like way, as if the rock were my friend. I felt an overwhelming sense of gratitude for what it offered me – a chance to know myself and the rock differently, to appreciate the unforeseen miracles like the tiny flowers growing in the even tinier cracks in the rock's surface, and to come to know a sense of being in relationship with the natural environment. It felt as if the rock and I were silent conversational partners in a longstanding friendship.'[3]

'I care for your welfare ...' says the Prof.
'I think you're slipping,' warns the rock.
'But I care for you!'
'Who cares?' asks the rock. 'It's time to let this conversation drop.'

The professor's friendship with a lump of rock typifies the emotional aims of a movement that, it is claimed, 'can be traced to feminist-vegetarian communities' in the academic dreamland on the Cambridge–Boston frontier.[4] It is a formidable green trinity: the sisterhood of women, the lone-parenthood of nature and the Harvard holistics, but wherever it began, eco-feminism provides the blueprint of a green dream; an amalgam of mysticism with nature, organic, pantheistic, anti-militarist, socialistic, communitarian and vegetarian, and, mixed with the aim of eradicating patriarchy, it makes for a heady blend. Men are not really part of this giant vegetarian commune, though 'for men in a patriarchal society moral vegetarianism can mark the decision to stand in solidarity with women. It also indicates a determination to resist ideological pressures to become a "real man".'[5]

The belief that women are somehow 'closer to nature' than men is crucial to the authority of eco-feminists, but the only qualification adduced for this proximity is that women, like nature, are apparently 'oppressed' by men. It is sometimes averred that a woman's natural functions of menstruation, parturition and lactation give her an affinity with nature, but it is hard to see why such things privilege her while a man's natural functions do not.

Nor is it more or less natural that women tend more to vegetarianism, when eating meat is natural to both sexes (vegetarianism is more obviously a cultural construct) unless it is accepted that man is not a natural predator.

Yet eco-feminism knows that man is a predator, and that is the trait which condemns him. Men do look for a certain dominion over nature. That is part of a man's nature, and at the root of the green distaste for the *real* male is his competitive, striving, aggressive, dominating, demanding and predatory nature. The eco-feminist preference for a male who is purely a social construct is understandable, even if it goes against all that we know about the male nature. But a rejection of his *natural* nature in favour of his potentially *social* nature (he can start by becoming a 'moral vegetarian' perhaps) is more a matter of hope triumphing over reality. This is not to argue that the male should not on occasion temper his aggression; only to point out that the natural male cannot be got rid of by sweeping him under a social realist carpet woven by feminist-vegetarian communities. By denying the real nature of the male, the eco-feminists deny the real environment. In its place they can only offer a dream-world that is sociable and co-operative, integrated and holistic (by which they mean that the whole is greater than the sum of its parts). These are traditional feminine traits, and the only way in which they can become the dominant traits of mankind is if the male makes his nature like her nature.

If the eco-feminists are one potent source of the green ideology, then the deep ecologists are another. The essential difference between them, writes deep ecologist Robert Sessions, 'seems to be that while deep ecology focuses exclusively on human domination of nature, ecofeminism insists that a proper analysis must also emphasize the intimate, logical and historical connections between the various forms of domination – the same logic and attitudes of superiority and practices of domination humans (men?) display in their relations toward the nonhuman dimensions of the world are found in men's relations to women …'[6] In other words: the analysis of eco-feminism is male centred, whereas deep ecology is human centred. 'Deep ecologists look to pre-modern and/or holistic tradition for suggestions about how to experience the world – to American Indians, Buddhism, Spinoza and others [like the Nazi philosopher, Heidegger, says an endnote], or to the science of ecology.'[7]

Andrew Kimbrell, in *The Masculine Mystique*, also advances a form of deep ecology.[8] He argues against 'dangerous "misandry", a belief that masculinity itself is responsible for most of the world's woes.' Which is fine by itself, but to free man of his responsibility for the world's ills Kimbrell gives us a Wimp's Charter. His male is non-competitive: a back-to-earth, organic, caring, holistic, healing, hand-holding sort of guy. The image is one of mythical male-bonding: of ageing boy scouts hugging trees, drumming in sweat-lodges, holding hands in men's groups, or guiding younger men through the stages of manhood.[9] Kimbrell thus claims to have uncovered the lost elements of masculinity.

Deep ecology males, like the lost-in-time males of *The Masculine Mystique*, look backward to a sub-Marxian male who lived in perfect harmony with his environment; a species of male never yet found by any anthropologist. But if the patriarchal male is not responsible for the world's ills, as the eco-feminists insist, who is? The deep ecologists blame the 'recent' competitive ethos. This is a paean for the New Man based on an idealized image of a non-competitive humanity, a vision of the future unrestrained by knowledge of science or of mankind's history.

The eco-feminists blame man. The deep ecologists blame competition, and men are patently more competitive than women, so, if the world is going to hell in a handbasket, plainly the male is to blame. But the complaints merely demonstrate that the green world is not the real world. The green's alternative reality is the alternative to reality. It is a dream. The eco-feminists, far from getting men in touch with nature, have lost touch with the nature of men. The green world has lost touch with nature. How? Because the greens, whether their roots are ecologically deep or mulched in eco-feminism, leave a man's inner nature out of their argument.

The green aspiration is a rejection of the world as it is in favour of the world as they believe it ought to be (which is why their environmentalism is a subject more for propaganda than for the education of the mind).

But isn't the male part of nature itself? So shouldn't his nature be part of the environmental equation? Instead man is decried as a thoughtless exploiter and polluter, and the supertanker, surely one of the greatest achievements of technology and responsible for a great deal of human happiness and comfort, has become the symbol of all that is worst in the world.

Man makes supertankers, and he cuts down trees to make roads, and he builds factories, yet he also wants to protect and improve the world. He is also, far more than woman, motivated by power, and he finds that to control natural resources is to generate productive growth. The hungry can be fed, the unemployed put to work and the rigours of a northern winter ameliorated by technology; in return he is decried as 'unnatural', a 'polluter', the enemy. He knows that some, not all, of nature can be tamed, so that the rest can be free. That is his nature – to control, to tame, to use. He does not always get it right, but it is his nature to shape the world to his ends, and his nature is as valid a part of the environment as an eco-feminist whispering to a rockface.

By nature he is not the safe player she is (Chapter 6).
He is not as co-operative as she is (also Chapter 6).
His logical focus is not as diffused as hers (Chapter 4 and others).
His female side does not exist (Chapter 1).
So the scientific bet is that his green is not her green.

THE DIVIDED GARDEN

Our neighbours, with their divided garden, typify the differences between the male and female ideals of the world. The husband wants his patch to be productive, and does not mind using chemicals and technology to help him, while the wife finds merit in being organic. Another near neighbour of ours has just returned from her second course on organic gardening at the Henry Doubleday Research Centre in the west of England. She reports that nearly all the students (on one of the courses all the students) were women. The British marketing intelligence firm Mintel, in their special report *The Green Consumer* (1994), found that 60% of women consumers were willing to pay more for 'environmentally friendly and humanely produced food'. Men are not nearly so particular.

This would seem to justify the green argument, that men exploit to produce while the eco-friendly nurture the soil without hurting it. Would it not be better, the idealists say, if we could all be organic?

Many parts of the world are all organic, because they cannot afford the luxury of agro-chemicals. In sub-Saharan Africa the staple diet of maize (corn) is overwhelmingly grown without the assistance of artificial fertilizers or chemical pesticides, and a recent survey revealed that one-third of the crop is infected with a fungus which produces a poisonous substance or aflatoxin which might well be a bigger killer than AIDS. A World Bank report calculates that the average person in sub-Saharan Africa works for only half his or her potentially productive life because of the disease.[10]

The aflatoxin was found in the blood of 98% of the people sampled in West Africa. They acquired the toxin from their maize, but their health could have been protected by a chemical spray that would have prevented the fungus from infesting the crop in the first place. In this case organic methods of husbandry kill.

'I just read in a women's magazine that an "organic vegetable doesn't contain anything that can do you harm,"'[11] says Bill. 'She doesn't know anything about the highly dangerous toxins that fungi produce when growing on vegetables,' says Anne.

The idea that organic-is-natural-is-good is based on a 19th-century belief that chemistry divides into organic and inorganic.

Organic dealt with substances that exist 'naturally' as constituents of living matter, while inorganic chemistry dealt with inert mineral elements and their compounds. The organic stuff was supposed to be formed under the action of vital forces and thus was considered natural and good.

But as early as 1828, a young German chemist, Friedrich Wöhler, developed the animal product urea synthetically and so created the organic from the inorganic. By the 1850s this process was common with many other substances, leading to the end of any scientific distinction between substances made from vital forces and inorganic lumps. But what the scientists discarded, the Victorian theologians treasured and so the distinction persisted until today when it is the green ecologists who insist that there is a difference between the 'natural'. or organic, and the 'unnatural'.

'She, her, the green gardener up the road,' says Anne, 'still believes in vital forces.'

'And she'll also be the one to seek answers in alternative medicine,' says Bill. 'Cutting out chemical pesticides and fungicides is the equivalent of cutting out conventional medical help.'

'A carrot full of maggots is as natural as a head full of lice. We go to a pharmacist for chemicals to treat the one … why not the other?'

Back-to-nature feminism is closer to the Garden of Eden than the real world of nature. Holistic, sustainable, green … The organic logic is part of her Green Dream. It is 'a saner healthier, sustainable future'.[12] The clichés cling as unexamined subclauses attached to the green prose like pests to a cabbage head: Nature is natural; Poisons pollute; Nature's way. It is not our way to draw a lesson from a truism, nor to argue against one. Her organic case seems safe from refutation (try punching air). It might also seem immune to scientific analysis. For example: urea excreted in the urine (along with toxins) is acceptable as an organic fertilizer, while industrial urea, first manufactured by Wöhler, is not. But a plant cannot tell the difference, nor can a chemist. Whether it is urinated or scooped from a packet, it is exactly the same chemical, the same organic compound. Yet the organic lobby condemns manufactured urea as inorganic because it comes from a factory. An understanding of the organic way of life may depend less on chemical analysis than on linguistics.

Not that organic gardeners shun all scientific experiment; indeed, they proudly proclaim the results of trials in companion planting, when you grow one plant close to another so that it protects its companion from pests. Thus, if you cultivate garlic next to potatoes, it will ward off aphids, and so it does, but it also unfortunately encourages another destructive insect, thrips. Researchers at the University of California find that 'white fly populations on beans planted close to American marigolds, summer savoury, basil and nasturtiums – all favourite companion plants for deterring pests – were higher.'[13] And this double planting can halve the yield by inducing competition for water, light and food. Most companion plants tend to be as effective at combating pests as wearing garlic to ward off Dracula.

Organic vegetables are frequently under more stress because they are given less protection from pests and diseases. They fight back by producing higher levels of pesticides or poisons. But surely, the organic consumer argues, those 'naturally produced' plant toxins are 'safer' than the chemical poisons we spray on our crops. Many consumers are blissfully unaware that vegetables produce poisons at all, though Bruce Ames and Lois Swirsky Gold of the Biochemistry and Molecular Biology Departments of the University of California report that 'about 99.99% of all pesticides in the human diet are from natural pesticides from plants. When plants are stressed or damaged – e.g. during a pest attack – they increase the levels of natural pesticides many fold (as their own way of resisting the attack), occasionally to levels that are acutely toxic to humans.'[14] Professor Ames has also pointed out that, without pesticides, far more land would need to be brought under cultivation, a move that would inevitably decrease biodiversity and make food far more expensive.[15]

'So what does an organic farmer do when faced with a major pest epidemic?' asks Anne.
'Goes bankrupt' answers Bill.

'Organic' pesticides manufactured by plants are not subject to the same tests and government regulations that are applied to 'artificial' pesticides produced in chemical factories, even though 'natural' substances like nicotine or pyrethrum are highly toxic. 'In the absence of any quantitative data,' says Professor George Lunt of the Biochemistry Department of the University of Bath, 'one could reasonably conclude that, under certain conditions, organically produced crops represent a greater health hazard than their conventionally grown counterparts.'[16] Organic farming is just a load of:

FARMYARD MANURE

Fresh manure (much loved by green gardeners) depletes nitrogen in the soil because soil organisms use the nitrogen to break down the manure itself, so causing a temporary nitrogen deficiency. The nitrogen and the potash in farmyard manure are washed out if exposed to rain, causing 'natural' manure to be so low in phosphorus that it must be added as a supplement. It is reckoned that half the nitrogen is washed out of farmyard manure, and so never has a chance to be utilized by plants at all. And where does it go? Soil scientists find that nitrogen leached from manure is two to four times higher than nitrogen leached from industrially produced fertilizers, and the wasted nitrogen is often washed off into streams and rivers where it causes ecological mayhem.[17]

The alternative is to fix nitrogen in the soil with crop rotation, and many organic gardeners swear by it. In truth the idea is a load of green manure. Green manuring means sowing a crop of, say, nitrogen-fixing clover in the autumn and digging it into the soil in the spring. A lot of work. And, as with fresh manure, the soil organisms use the new nitrogen to degrade the newly added decaying clover plants resulting, again, in a temporary nitrogen deficiency. Green manure is more commonly used to build up the organic reserves over a period of time. How long a period? To increase the organic matter in your soil from 2% to 3% will take 36 years (and you need at least 5% organic matter in the soil).

Very little of this is understood by the vocal green lobby, which attacks farmers for using 'inorganic' methods. One danger of such attacks is that farmers, reluctant to be villains, use too little and too few agro-chemicals. One product, Opus, a most effective disease control for wheat and barley is being used at half its recommended rate.[18] The result is a loss in production, but not nearly so great as the loss caused by pure organic farming which typically results in vastly lower yields. The Department of Land Economics at Cambridge University estimates the average loss of output from organic farms at 50%.[19] A member of the department, Michael Murphy, says that the cost to the nation if all farmers went organic would be between 20 and 40 billion pounds a year in the form of lost income and increased import bills. The manager of one of Britain's largest farms, 45,000 acres, tested organic methods for the Co-operative Wholesale Society. Mike Calvert found 'in organic farming the overheads per unit of production were double those of conventional methods'.[20]

So, in return for more work and higher costs the organic lobby are able to halve the yield while doubling the amount of land needed to achieve a poorer product. It is a hobby – a hobby-horse – for those who can afford the land, the time and the money: for those who need not or cannot tally output against input. It is life made tougher, not easier, a luxury available to those who live on the capital of earlier generations, and we are meant to be persuaded that it is natural and wise.

'Natural?' says Anne.

'The real artifice of organic farmers is to remove themselves from the century,' says Bill.

The green dream demands a back-to-nature level of science which, if generally adopted, would make the Dark Ages a period of enlightenment. It is a cry from the heart for an earlier, simpler world, a pig rooting for wild food in the primeval forest through which a prince sallies forth to save the world. It is a medium of fantasy, like living in a palace or vegging out in front of a television. The mind turns off to relax, becomes a blank screen free of the day's clutter and anxieties, and set to believe anything except what is real. Naturally we want a green and pleasant land. And there, before us, is the original garden, uncorrupted by knowledge or unnatural practices … the Garden of Eden without the snake.

The real world is undeniably confusing, and a common way of coping with its complexities is to fix upon an explanation. Not any old explanation, but one that cannot be falsified (or shown to be true). From then on there is no need to keep up with the world. Add a pious aspect – concern for life, the mystery of existence or nature's quiet wisdom – and your position is secure. What remains is to accuse those who disagree with you of arrogance. If they insist on facts, just ask, 'how can you be so sure?' and if they don't quickly back down then it is they who are being dogmatic.

Ignorance and piety; a truly lethal mix, and organic gardening offers both.

THE WORLD IN DANGER

The green gardener struggling with her small patch of land no doubt believes she is helping to save the planet. She, or he, also knows that she labours on behalf of a good cause. We all want to breathe clean air and save the rainforest, and those large causes are the driving engines of the environmental movement. Most of the green focus is on the glamorous, the big environmental topics like global climate ruin or species extinction. The world is in danger! We are constantly warned that the world is running out of oil and we must therefore spend money on renewable energy sources like windmills or tidal barriers, but in truth the price of oil keeps dropping and the amount of the stuff available in oil-tar shales gives oil executives sleepless nights.

Another standard green scare is that there will soon not be enough food to feed the world, but we hear little or nothing about the near tripling of the world grain harvest since 1950, or that in the past generation we have had the lowest food prices on record, or that food science will enable farmers to at least double their yield in the next generation.[21] Instead an apocalyptic future is laid before us. We are destroying the earth! Or rather allowing greedy men to destroy it! Amoco Cadiz, Three Mile Island, *Exxon Valdez*, Chernobyl! We have bought a one way ticket to disaster. Those who would save us from ourselves first present us with a nightmare scenario so that we can become dependent on them for the solution. It was always thus. The snake-oil salesmen, the Elmer Gantrys and the doom-is-upon-us environmentalists play the same old trick: they define the disease then claim that only they can cure us.

We are not denying that the world faces grievous problems; fish stocks are declining and many parts of the Third World lack fresh water or adequate sewage disposal, just as they lack effective pesticides and fertilizers. Many of these problems will prove solvable thanks to technology and science, but the environmentalists mistrust such solutions. Science has been wrong before, they say, and why should it be trusted again?

If science is not about certainty, it is surely about best bets. Science is also about judicious probabilities; and so it advances our knowledge of what is likely, or not likely, to be the case. Things work (and we work) on this basis. Science makes the best case as to what is or will be; greens make the worst case. Their caution is healthy. It is part of the odds that science can get things wrong.

Biotechnology is not a universal panacea, indeed there are no quick fixes, but to reject science and technology can engender a dangerous cynicism and disenchantment. If the answers to the world's problems are holistic and even mystical, then it follows that hard logic and reason must be discounted. This has been the achievement of the eco-feminists; to equate reason with the predatory male and to depict a male-dominated civilization as mere savagery or animality. In the non-competitive green world the wrongs of the world result from 'men solving the world's problems'. Most men see little wrong with this. He finds that to surrender science to nature could soon result in two billion people going hungry (and his never seeing a steak again). His idea of nature is part wild, part tamed. The wild part is there to explore. It is a place in which he can test himself and take risks (even if only in the mind). It is whitewater rafting, bungee jumping, blue-water sailing and caving. It is competition with the elemental, it is shooting and fishing. A man's green is hunter green.

The eco-feminists see red in his green, decrying those parts of the world that have been tamed, and warning us that the process is inexorably destructive. In its place they offer first an analysis, then a cure.

A world problem is identified

The rainforests are shrinking. The desert is growing. The climate is threatened. Species extinction is found real, rapid and ominous. All life is at risk. The world is too aggressive for its own good. Children become alarmed.

The main cause of the problem is identified

Men are in control. Men are the war makers and the earth rapers. Men are to blame for the destruction of the environment and the threat to life. The distinctive green touch is to blame today's problems on the dominant male environment.

The solutions are generated

An extreme answer is to do without men (a woman needs a man like a fish needs a bicycle). A less drastic one is to gain control of the home and workplace in order to tame men. Yet to seek control is to play his game; he is the more aggressive and competitive; so the odds are against winning a direct contest (an indirect admission that equal opportunity may not give equal results). In any case the point is not to compete in the male's competitive world but to change that world.

The most promising solution unfolds

To develop – as an alternative to his aggressive world – an alternative non-aggressive world. The eco-feminist answer is to reshape his environment for the common good. This vision has great appeal, and the basic message is clear because she is a good communicator. The logic is obvious and persuasive. It positively impresses. The green wave is not going to dry up, as a chat with most children will show.

Why does the vision appeal so much? Greens oppose waste, pollution, the anti-social, war, the unsustainable and the destruction of our environment. They support peace, sustainability, recycling, clean air, unpolluted water, social responsibility, the environmentally friendly, life itself.

But so do most of us. We prefer the favourable to the pejorative. That the phrases are banal does not make them any less valid. We are all friends of the earth. A truism is beyond refutation. Green logic is self-sustaining (as befits the user). Yet the green focus is often negative; and perhaps too much so. The green warning is of a dark future – final things – a spiralling into catastrophe. We all know that accidents happen. We know that knowledge is used both for good and bad, and that science can be abused. We know we will never know everything. Things can go utterly wrong. So the focus is not on the Best Bet – as is much of science – but on the Worst Case (like the strategists who plan a nation's defence). It is good to play safe.

Playing safe seems the safer bet, but is it the scientific one?

Who cares? Science, we are assured, is a 'man-made construct'. Science is nuclear bombs and agro-chemicals. Science is mercury-polluted seas and ravaged ozone layers. What is needed, and what the greens provide, is an alternative science.

ALTERNATIVE SCIENCE

Many greens no longer use the phrase 'alternative science'; they prefer 'complementary science' which happily suggests that their science does not contradict traditional science (it being a law of logic that contradictory propositions cannot be true). This acceptance of traditional science proves that greens are open-minded, and it is nicely argued that it is their opponents, those hostile to unconventional views, who are dogmatic in their rejection of fresh perspectives. There is nothing fresh in the argument, for those who do not draw a line against what is sense or nonsense or, for that matter, between science and non-science, first set up a travesty of their opponent's views by accusing them of being dogmatic, of being fundamentalist in their opposition to what cannot be understood. But drawing the line against nonsense – taking the best bet – is what science does best. What alternative science does best is to fill a gap between what we understand and what we do not understand: that is, multiple inanities take the place of ignorance. It is a role green science admirably fulfills.

It takes hard work to understand science, says the physician-philosopher Raymond Tallis, hence the ignorance of the idle.[22]

Complementary science does not take hard work to understand, just faith, and examples of it can be found in almost every issue of women's magazines that eagerly advertise and feature alternative clinics, hydrotherapy, aromatherapy, vital oils, new techniques for relaxation and shortcuts to health and beauty that fit in with every changing fashion on the outer, or rather the far-out, fringes of science. In this fabulous world of change the probable is given short shrift. The editors are charged with giving the impression that change is easily possible; an impression that the advertisers dream of and readers demand. This is prefigured in Nietzsche's 'Nothing is true, everything is possible'. Equal weight is thus given to countless improbables and, consequently, the probable recedes. The dumbing down of science procedes – giving way to the unreal alternatives.

Those who prefer the alternative versions of reality have some reason on their side when they find that the likes of alternative medicine are not capable of scientific testing. By definition, if they were capable of passing rigorous clinical trials they would not be alternative medicines. And, of course, alternative courses in therapy do sometimes work; just as, sometimes, astrological predictions come true. This is not validation.

More often it is said that if the alternative works then it must be a legitimate treatment. 'Therein lies the source of much of the erroneously placed faith in alternative medicine,' Dr Max Prola wrote to *The Times*.[23] 'The amelioration of symptoms following some kind of treatment does not constitute proof of the treatment's efficacy, not until the possible role of other influences has been ruled out. Ninety per cent of people suffering from headache would report a cure the following morning if they were to sing a chorus of 'Onward Christian Soldiers' before bedtime.'

Royal jelly, garlic, the water cure, nutritional supplements, reflexology, aromatherapy oils … these are not on the male menu. An article in the *New England Journal of Medicine* has estimated that in 1990 Americans made 425 million visits to unconventional healers, compared with only 388 million to all primary-care physicians. 'Most of those who consult alternative practitioners are the "worried well", female, middle-aged and middle class.'[24] At least there are no known toxic effects in most of the unconventional 'cures', thus avoiding any risk that they are actually bad for you, though that does not mean they are good for you. Many people consume vitamins in order to prolong their lives, and then they do live a long time and conclude that vitamins are a source of longevity. They might, of course, have lived even longer had they sung a chorus of 'Onward Christian Soldiers' every bedtime, but the results of the clinical trials are not yet available. What is available are the results of a survey in the south-east of England that found that 38% of all general practitioners had patients who had suffered adverse side effects from manipulation, acupuncture, homeopathy or herbal remedies.

Why do people take them? Most of these 'natural' therapies share common premises. There is an emphasis on body 'harmony', on health ('wellness') as balance, on the body 'life-force' and on the blockage of 'vital' energy by 'toxins' or 'pollutants'. To say that they are all quack remedies is to come up against the How Do You Know? brigade. How can you be so certain you are right? How can you be so dogmatic?

What is scary is the failure to quantify risk. Instead a world without risk is demanded. But to manage risk is also full of risk. As chaos theorists have taught us, even small changes can produce massive effects (for example, the Beijing butterfly responsible for some tornado in the US). Even to stay one's entire life in bed is to risk starvation or, more likely, death by apathy. A bit of chaos is part of the order of the day. It is on these grounds that John Adams in his book *Risk*[25] attacks the view held by many 'greeny', holier-than-thou intellectuals that while the world may be an increasingly precarious place to live in, it is possible for humankind, with the help of alternative science and ever stronger governments, to create perfect pockets of safety. With so little of their lives under control or understandable, and dreading the unknowable, they would bring more and more of our lives under nanny's management.

'Thou shalt not tolerate risk,' says Anne.

'Not even the risk of a risk?' asks Bill.

'But the alternative therapy people always ask, "What are you afraid of?"'

'Me?' asks Bill, 'I'm afraid of fools.'

'Or perhaps we fear the mystery of it all?'

'The mystery is what remains when we admit our igorance, not when we fill up great gaps in our knowledge with fanciful, or mysterious, explanations. Then all connects – you have connectivity – even among what doesn't connect.'

'What the fool is afraid of,' says Anne, 'is the sensible ground upon which sense is made.'

Two out of three members of Friends of the Earth are female.[26] But the feminizing influence on the greens is largely independent of the membership of the various green organizations who, on the whole, are content to follow the vigorous lead of green 'thinkers' who, both male and female, find solace in the general feminine approach to the world; an approach that is non-confrontational, non-discriminatory (especially when it comes to evidence), unaligned, and opposed to male certainties and the competitive ethos. The green ethos is the mystical side of the postmoderns, where they deny the traditional existence of the dividing line between the conventional and the unconventional. Their push is not upon the frontiers of knowledge, but upon the frontiers of ignorance.

We know that tigers are near extinction. But it is not the great white hunter who threatens the species. Instead the tiger is hunted to death to provide remedies for alternative therapies. 'A rapid increase in the demand for traditional Chinese medicine in the Far East has intensified the trade in tiger parts,' reports the Environmental Investigative Agency in London.[27] Nor is it greedy men who are responsible for wiping out rare animals. 'More than half the world's endangered animals are Australian and we have lost more species in the past 200 years than the rest of the world combined,' says the conservationist John Wamsley.[28] So what is responsible for this species decimation, if not man? The domestic cat, Wamsley finds, has wiped out 23 native Australian species.

And a calm, logical view of species depreciation is required. It is not just the greens who support the living museums of tropical forests. That they are vitally important to our well-being is almost universally acknowledged, and the fight to save them will continue to be just as important with or without the greens. But we must also bear in mind that 90% of all plants that have ever existed are now extinct, and, what we rarely hear about, that thousands of new species, like orchids, are being created every year. And there are many species, not least among the viruses (and perhaps the spider family), that we could willingly live without. Extinction is part of evolution. It is natural.

Perspective must be kept. Some evidence suggests that even if 90% of the tropical rainforests were to be destroyed, all the species of animals, birds and fish would survive.[29] 'This is a quite surprising finding,' Andrew Johns of Aberdeen University told a Royal Society meeting. 'The reasons may be that even in heavily logged areas, some tree cover survives on slopes, near streams and in other places where access is difficult.' This is not a justification for ravaging the rainforests, and the estimate provides little ground for optimism, but it is a corrective to the doom-laden predictions fed to our children. They should also be taught that, contrary to the prophets of ecological doom, forests do grow back, as they have in the north-east of the United States where, 100 years ago, most of the tree cover was cleared for farming; today, as farming has spread westwards, the regenerated forests cover about 80% of the region (where they are causing a surge in the spread of the potentially dangerous Lyme disease). The decline in biological diversity is real, rapid and serious, but a balance of fears, real and imagined, needs to be achieved.

A man looks to nature as a wild place where the mind can unwind. He enjoys that fierce battle, competing with the elements – the sea, the wind howling, the storm, the fires of hell, the safe haven to which he eventually wins through. To him nature is red in tooth and claw, but to her it is a green and harmonious place where the mind can find the balm of peace. Thus men and women find two natures in nature: one sees a tough, competitive wilderness that might be tamed, the other finds a holistic garden of innocence; and each is a metaphor for its finder's own nature. They are different natures, different views of the original state of nature, but they are not necessarily antagonistic. He may see the wilderness as a survival course and adventure playground, while she sees it as a reservoir of organic wholeness, but both can agree that the rivers should be unpolluted and the rainforests protected. The sadness is that too much of the green movement blames him for environmental damage, and perceives in every new road or green-field factory site a male-inspired threat to all creation. 'He who defends everything', Frederick the Great taught, 'defends nothing.' The male nature is part of nature itself, as much a part of the environment as the spotted owl or the snail darter, and to wish away human competitiveness, as the greens want, is merely to surrender our species to other predators.

CHAPTER NINE

Sex

His drive and her drive

Western wind, when will thou blow
The small rain down can rain?
Christ, if my love were in my arms
And I in my bed again!

It is a fair bet that the anonymous poet of that 16th-century quatrain was a man, for men, on average, have 400% more erotic fantasies than women. Men dream of women, they daydream of women, they fantasize about women, and they do not fantasize about having cosy little chats beside the fire. His fantasies are about sex, hers are about emotional involvement. Sex is where men and women approach each other most closely, and are driven by motives that are far apart.

He is sexually aroused far more easily than she is, and, as in the rest of his life, he craves novelty. He often finds that novelty in artificial stimuli, which is why he likes pin-ups, pornography and peepshows.[1] Is it insulting or degrading to her that he substitutes the perfect for the imperfect?

'Perhaps,' Anne says, 'he substitutes the available imperfect for the rarely available perfect?'
'Perhaps he does, perfect one. Can we proceed?'

In ancient Greece the most revered cult statue was a nude Aphrodite which was of such stimulating beauty that it bore the stains of semen.[2] Men have always sought such erotic objects, and frequently found them in art. Whether it is the Renoir model, the steamy odalisques of Ingres' Turkish baths, the gynaecological close-ups of Courbet's *Origin of the World*, or Rodin's and Picasso's sculptures of the pudenda, the female icons of the age are meant for the male gaze. These erotica were frequently disguised as religious or classical paintings; the story of Susannah bathing naked under the Peeping Tom gaze of the elders occurs in the Apocrypha, but that was close enough to the Old Testament to justify Tintoretto and the many other artists who painted the scene. It was not erotica, of *course* not: it was *scripture*. Titian's bedroom paintings of big nudes could be mistaken for classical allegories, but are really pin-ups commissioned by the Duke of Urbino and Cardinal Farnese for their erotic impact.

The model's eyes are frequently hidden, as in Gerome's *Phryne before the Areopagus*, presumably so that the male might indulge the voyeuristic pleasure of looking at a naked woman who is unaware of his gaze. The girl's averted eyes help give her a coy innocence (in 1840 a Scottish surgeon averred that one could identify prostitutes simply by 'the wild and impertinent glance of their eyes'). Some of the models seem rapt in self-regard; if she is so entranced by her own beauty, why should the onlooker feel any guilt at enjoying it? Later painters dropped the coyness, allowing the model to be splayed and displayed for the male's viewing pleasure. Manet's *Olympia* stares from the canvas with unmistakeable erotic challenge, while Degas' bathing nudes, the prancing, independent Dianas and Bathshebas, are painted as if the viewer were looking through a keyhole and lusting for what is for ever out of touch and, most often, out of sight.

'What about a Mapplethorpe exhibit?'
'Like,' says Anne, 'that photo of a guy sitting on a barrel, doubled up, with his bare buttocks spread over a crucifix?'
'Ugh!'
'Does it make you insecure, anxious – ?'

'Repelled, more like,' says Bill. 'Straights – 19 out of 20 guys – find gay imagery an affront to their natural eroticism.'
'Might it deprave or corrupt?'
'Only art critics who, in the postmodern manner, have a confused sense of the erotic.'

The dividing line between art and artful porn is often blurred. Richard Nixon, a man uncorrupted by artistic pretensions, said that if dirty pictures had no lasting effect on character, then great paintings and books had no ennobling effect either. 'Centuries of civilization and ten minutes of common sense tell us otherwise,' he asserted. Presumably he averted his eyes from all those curvaceous nudes in the Louvre. Or perhaps what keeps great art from being pornographic is an apprehension that the model is beyond male art, that she does not need it. There is a playful sense of the seductive, a tantalization, but with an air of control. In pornography she is there to be had, to be spattered like Aphrodite.

This is dead boring to most women. But men, remember, have four times as many erotic fantasies as women and, not surprisingly, it is the male hormones that spark those daydreams, so those women who were exposed to high levels of male hormones in the womb also have more sexual fantasies than women who did not experience such abnormal exposure. High levels of dopamine in the brain also increase the male's sexual interest (and his ability to perform), while serotonin inhibits such indulgences. It is time to leave the art gallery and look at the science of sex.

THE SCIENCE OF SEX

The sexual drive in both women and men is fuelled by testosterone; and men have 1,000% more.[3] The higher a person's testosterone, the stronger the sexual urge; in women testosterone peaks during the menstrual cycle just as the egg is produced, and the higher a woman's testosterone level is during that peak, the higher her sexual motivation throughout her cycle.[4] Women with a higher base level of testosterone are more sexually motivated than their sisters: and the higher a woman's T levels, the greater will be her number of sexual partners. Low T level females usually have only one partner in their lifetime, while high T level females average five.[5] The same is true of men, but the numbers are greater. His sexual activity, like hers, is directly related to testosterone levels,[6] and like hers those levels rise and fall, but in a male the fluctuations are on a daily and seasonal basis.[7] His T levels are highest in the morning and lowest in the evening. The level rises in the summer, peaks in the autumn and falls in the spring (so much for Tennyson's claim that 'in the Spring a young man's fancy lightly turns to thoughts of love'.) Sexual intercourse and masturbation increase during the high seasons.[8]

Testosterone and sexual aggression are also linked.[9] Sexual assaults by males peak at 17–25 years, but decline thereafter as the testosterone declines with age.[10] There are more sexual assaults in the autumn when the male's testosterone peaks.[11] Violent rape is associated with higher T levels, though the non-violent rapist generally has an average level.[12] (It will be argued, passionately, that there is no such thing as non-violent rape, but here the phrase is intended to describe an assault not accompanied by a physical beating that can often end with horrific injuries, quite apart from the sexual and emotional damage inflicted by the rapist.) It has become common to treat sexually aggressive men with drugs that block the production of testosterone and other androgens,[13] which makes the widespread use of anabolic steroids a worrying trend. Anabolic steroids are masculine hormones that can be even more potent than the androgens manufactured naturally, and one author is concerned that their consumption is increasing sexual violence. It is estimated that as many as 500,000 teenage boys use steroids in the USA, usually in an effort to increase musculature. 'This has become a national problem not only because of the personal health hazards. Individuals taking exogenous steroids appear to be more reactive to stimuli that elicit violent behaviour. While there is no proof at this time, it may be expected that a significant proportion of date rapes and other rapes may be from steroid self medication.'[14]

It is not just the adult hormones that drive sexual behaviour. Exposure to high levels of foetal androgens, especially testosterone, also tilt the sexual behaviour in certain directions. The brain's hypothalamic-limbic structure regulates most emotions, including the sex drive and, as we saw in Chapter One, men and women show marked differences in their hypothalami, differences forged by exposure to high levels of male hormones in the womb. What these differences mean in terms of general sexual behaviour has mostly been derived from studying animals, showing that high levels of testosterone increase the male's erotically assertive behaviour.[15] He is driven to sex in a way that females are not.

Exposure to high levels of testosterone also increases the probability of 'hypersexuality and extreme possessiveness'.[16] So maybe even jealousy is part of the hormone story, and certainly jealousy as extreme as that which drove Othello to violence is far more common among males than females.[17]

Even newer research suggests that the sexual arousal sites are different in males and females, and that the circuitry for both sexual and aggressive behaviour are the same in the male.[18] This is an area of science that is only now coming under the scrutiny of researchers, so we trespass on the very frontiers of science and must stress that much of the work has only been done on animals. We are learning, for example, that the male's sexual drive is not wholly fuelled by testosterone, but also by dopamine. A male mouse deprived of dopamine ceases to search for females.[19] But give Mickey back his dopamine and he is off on Minnie's trail again. The female mouse's sexual interest has nothing to do with this neurotransmitter, and some confirmation that this is also true for humans is emerging from new treatments offered for Parkinson's disease. It is now known that one of the causes of Parkinson's (once known as the shaking palsy) is a lack of dopamine in the brain. Patients given L-dopa show a significant improvement in their condition, but in male patients there are unwanted side-effects: spontaneous erections and increased sexual interest.[20] Women patients show no such increase in sexual desire.

The story does not end with dopamine. Vasopressin and oxytocin are neurotransmitters found in the crucial hypothalamus, and each plays a key role in the sexual and social behaviours of higher mammals. Vasopressin is present at a higher level in males and mediates sexual persistence (courtship, territorial marking, and inter-male aggression), while oxytocin (which is far more abundant in females) affects socialization, sexual responsiveness, and maternal nurturing.[21] More of that maternal instinct later. The male's vasopressin is found in the neurons of the amygdala and anterior hypothalamus; destroy that area of a male rat's brain and his sexual aggression is severely depleted; destroy the same area in the brain of a female rat and it has no effect on her sexual behaviour. The leading researcher in the field suggests that 'the coincidence of sexual and aggression control circuits in the male brain should also lead us to pause and wonder about that anatomical relationship'.[22]

So a male's sexuality is biologically linked with his aggressiveness. If a male animal is castrated then both his sexual ardour and his pugnacity gradually diminish, as do his levels of vasopressin. Sexual activity can continue without vasopressin, but it is sluggish and lacks the high level of persistence that is a characteristic of sexually aroused males. A male secretes vasopressin during foreplay, so this neurotransmitter appears to be more important to a male's sexual craving than it is to a female's. Indeed, if vasopressin is artificially increased in a female the reverse effect occurs: her sexual receptivity plummets. Oxytocin also affects the male's love-making. He possesses far less than she does, but it appears to have a different effect on him. In him it promotes erectile capacity and is also released in large amounts at orgasm. Oxytocin provides pleasure and it may well be a key ingredient in his orgasmic experience. In a woman, oxytocin mainly promotes caring, nurturing behaviour.

So what does this mean? Only that, once again, men and women do things differently. Expecting him to behave like her, or her like him, is unreal. They have different equipment. Perhaps the orgasmic drench of oxytocin is the nearest a man can ever get to the experience of Tiresias, the Theban seer, who was said to have lived both as a man and as a woman (he claimed women enjoyed sex more). This burst of oxytocin makes the male feel affectionate towards his partner and is responsible for that sexual afterglow of drowsy well-being. Professor Panksepp remarks of this difference that 'there is a certain beauty in the fact that oxytocin, a pre-dominantly female neuromodulator, is an especially important player in the terminal orgasmic components of male sexual behaviour. In that role it may allow the sexes to better understand each other. Indeed, sexual activity can invigorate this chemical system in the male brain and thereby help promote his nurturant behaviours.'[23]

SNIFFING OUT LOVE

'Phew!' says Anne. 'Get a whiff of that 5 alpha-16-androsten-3 alpha-ol!'
'It's nothing compared to that short chain fatty acid she's trailing,' says Bill.

The brain's neurotransmitters might modulate our sex behaviour, and the eye, at least to the male, might be the beholder of erotic delights, but the nose?

Pheromones such as 16-androstens are the unseen substances we secrete as a signal to others of our species. We trail an invisible cloud of scented pheromones that serve as a sexual signal. Androstenol comes from the sweat in men's armpits. (It is also, more romantically, found in truffles, the gourmet fungi, and its odour attracts truffle-hounds or snuffling pigs.) At University College London, 38 female student volunteers were exposed overnight to the vapour of 16-andostrene. They did not know they had been so exposed, but next morning 'resulted in significantly higher scores of exchanges with males'.[24] Research does not show any similar response in the male.Men's underarm sweat wafts its scent trail as a primitive form of communication, and it turns the female on.

So what biological weapon can she use in the sex-war? New research from Austria reveals that men have heightened testosterone levels (and consequent heightening of sexual readiness) when in the presence of ovulating women. The cause? Fatty acids that are found in the vaginal fluids, acids that change their composition during the menstrual cycle. The research was done by Astrid Jutte at the Ludwig Boltzmann Institute for Urban Ethology in Vienna, who carried out her tests on 106 men who were divided into four groups. One of the groups inhaled a vapour of the fatty acid (produced synthetically) secreted during ovulation, the second an acid from menstruation, the third from a period in between, while the fourth group were only exposed to water vapour. The *New Scientist* reported that: 'Jutte found that testosterone levels in the saliva of those men exposed to the scent of ovulation increased by half, while levels in those sniffing only water dropped by half. Levels in the two other groups increased slightly'.[25] Ovulation may be 'hidden' from men but, says Jutte, 'the effect on testosterone levels changes the picture completely.' Women respond to armits, men to ovulating women.

Human pheromones, the natural and most effective sexual attractants, are the secret weapons of the perfume industry. A woman wearing perfume leaves a sex-trail behind her, what the French call her *sillage*, and a vast, secretive industry works to capture the very expression of feminity, to bottle the zeitgeist, the *odor di femina*. The women's fragrance market is expected to amount to world sales worth $22 billion by the year 2000, while the total market for the two leading male scents is less than 1 per cent of this.[26] In the sophisticated world of perfumes, though perfumiers are reluctant to admit it, pheromones are big bucks.

Trsor is Lancome's block-busting global new 'old-fashioned' floral fragrance. As a classic perfume it is built around top, middle and base notes: hints of rose, apricot and peach skin, with more of the last-named. Top perfumier Sophia Grojsman created Trsor's sherbety smell and she says it is built around the odour of cleavage, the scent of a young girl's *décolletage*.[27] Every man leans closer – eyes shut, says Grojsman. 'Sorbet … surely that's that peach sorbet I smell?'

'Escaping the pressures and feeling more whole are what women want and they are saying as much in hundreds of focus groups,' says Ann Gottlieb, freelance 'nose' for Revlon, Esté Lauder, Unilever and Chanel.[28] 'The message is powerful – they don't want to be dictated to,' she says. 'They want to make their own decisions. Fragrance has become feminist.' Has it?

Allure is Chanel's perfume for the year 2000. A perfume and eau de toilette, it is composed of six equal notes, none dominating. One of those notes, also evident in Guerlain's Shalimar of 1925, is vanillin ethyl, which is nearly identical to the pheromone secreted by the glands of the aureola that surround a woman's nipple. And what of the traditional note of civet? That mossy, spicy evocation of a woman's sex – long a Guerlain favourite – comes from the yellow, buttery substance scraped from the anal scent glands of the Ethiopian cat. The message of such scents is very powerful. Allure, says the resident Chanel 'nose', Jacques Polge, began as a dream. He dreamt of someone who was 'more than just a woman. She is the very essence of woman, the woman who attracts all eyes, makes all hearts beat faster, the kind of woman one never forgets.'[29] Dream or PR exercise, the message is one of seduction, and the male is led by the nose.

There is, however, one fragrance that strongly proclaims the postmodernist message by blurring the difference between the genders. Unilever's unisex blockbuster scent cK one by Calvin Klein made its debut in 1994. In its advertisements the sexes are all but indistinguishable; the models are dressed in an androgynous uniform that minimizes the gender divide. Female faces in the adverts look like freshly scrubbed 1950s West Point cadets, while the males resemble slightly better-than-usual-looking ex-East German female gymnasts. 'It happened in fashion, so the next logical step was to capture the mood in a fragrance,' said Ann Gottlieb, the independent 'fragrance art director' who worked on the Calvin Klein image.[30] So gender-bending men are splashing on a hint of the feminine, and women a dash of masculinity. A special report in *Women's Wear Daily*, the fashion industry's newspaper, finds that 'generation X isn't as obsessed by conquest – sexual, business or otherwise – as previous generations were.'[31] Defined by a light, modern, herbal green-tea note, cK one is a perfume for a generation whose members do not know who they are or, worse, what.

Most women, we suspect, would rather wear *odor di femina* than green-tea. And why? Because they want to attract. Which leads to a somewhat obvious question.

WHAT DO MEN WANT?

When you ask men what they want in a woman they most frequently cite physical beauty. A study in the US which examined mating preferences over fifty years (1939–89) found that 'in all cases, men rate physical attractiveness and good looks as more important and desirable in a potential mate than do women.'[32] Studies of lonelyhearts advertisements show the same wishes: men want beauty and women want financial security.[33] So men are encouraged to compete and women are encouraged to enhance their looks. Superman meets trophy wife, and plastic surgeons become rich as women compete to conform to the image. In 1996 a survey of 13 countries showed that men share sexual prefer-ences. They like a woman to have firm, symmetrical breasts, full lips, large eyes, a small nose and her waist to be 60% of the circum-ference of her hips.[34] And, contrary to the adage that a woman can never be too thin, most men prefer the well-covered shape.[35]

There are exceptions; men of the Azande tribe of Eastern Sudan and of the Ganda of Uganda find long, pendulous breasts more attractive.[36] They would hardly be satisfied customers at the Crazy Horse Saloon in Paris, where Molly Molloy, choreographer of one of the world's most valuable collection of dancing nudes, looks for 'small breasts; otherwise it would be easy to fall into vulgarity'. The Crazy Horse's owner, Didier Bernardin, says that 'even feminists are fascinated by the idea of sublime women who dominate men as our dancers do.'[37] Be that as it may, Bernardin adds that his sublime women 'must be medium-sized with real bums, distinctive jaws, eyes, and small ears'. Hollywood has its ideas too. Louis B. Mayer once remarked to Hedy Lamarr, 'We have an obligation to the audience ... we make clean pictures ... you have a bigger chest than I thought! You'd be surprised how tits figure in a girl's career.'[38]

It is, of course, common to decry the male's desire for female beauty as a form of tyranny. Why should she conform to his desires? She does not want to be treated as a sex object, nor does she identify with his image of pneumatic bliss, and why should she? It is his dream, not hers. She wants to be loved for what she is; and perfect she is not. But in his fantasies he creates something that is not real; a sex symbol. All men do. But nor are men unrealistic fools. They know the woman of fantasy, the 'living doll', is not the person they will meet at the altar. They dream because their biology makes them dream, so why not let him indulge in the fictions? But no. These days she would have him attend that new institution of American university campuses, the sensitivity seminar. She would make him like her.

What men also want, of course, is lots of women, and for most that desire is only in their dreams. Most men, given the amount of nubile wenching that pervades their waking thoughts, are restrained in real life (six in ten American men never commit adultery). Men fantasize and women resent it, but in the mind we always experience more than life gives us. He scores, he hits the winning run, he scales the heights, he runs for President, he makes a billion, he wipes out the machine gun nest, he rescues Kim

Basinger, but it's all in his mind. That's his waking fiction; she reads a romantic novel. He does not feel cheated that life falls short of fantasy, for he knows it is not for real. Is she betrayed when he imagines success in another field? When he imagines scoring the winning goal? Sex in the mind, to paraphrase Clausewitz, is the gratification of passion by other means. Men often have sex on the brain, and often it is a better place to have it.

Even the happiest married man is not averse to the charms of women other than his wife, but it is an addiction to be heroically resisted, a bit like Dracula managing a blood bank. He may want to see himself as a Don Juan, but he will tell himself that his resolution not to stray is a noble, selfless act. In denying himself sex outside marriage he makes a biological sacrifice comparable to her having the children.

'Is infidelity so immoral?' asks Anne.
'If to cause grief is wrong,' says Bill.

PORNOGRAPHY

The domain of the pornographer used to be the seedy bookstore, sticky cinema or side-street strip-show. Today it is an online, virtual reality, cybersex industry with robo-bimbos, coitus artificialis, and tele-dildonics allowing the sex-surfer to pass from conquest to conquest with Pentium™ speed. The computer, once feared as big brother, has become the sex slave, a source of endless websites offering compliant women. In the cyberworld the female never rejects; she is conquered with a mouse, grasped without contact and possessed without a chase. No competition. No entanglement. No sweat. It is a low-arousal world of nerds locked, not in the bathroom, but to the screen. A survey of the Internet discovered that half the web-searches are aimed at locating pornography. Around 80% of Internet users are men, and 50% of them use it to seek for pornography.[39]

The worldwide sex industry, including prostitution, is estimated to be worth $20 billion a year.[40] It is probably higher. The pornographic market has become so strong that 5,000 American porn films were released each year in the mid-90s in the United States alone,[41] a business worth $2.5 billion dollars a year, while such films account for a quarter of all the videos rented or sold in American stores.[42] These figures do not include 'soft porn', which is the major, perhaps *the* major, sector of the male magazine market. A lot of people are making a lot of money providing customers with women who are available, pliant and uncomplaining. Those customers, of course, are men.

Women do not like this. A poll carried out in 1996 revealed that only 10% of women thought pornography was purely harmless, a further 45% thought it wrong but harmless, while 41% believed that it should be made a criminal offence.[43] Their allies in the fight against porn are the religious fundamentalists, strange bedfellows, for whom the sexually explicit is plain harmful. To the religious, pornography is sinful, while feminist divines preach that it leads to sex crimes, and paedophilia is often cited as a consequence of pornography. Research does not support the contention. 'Explicit child pornography was uncommon. However, sex offenders also generated their own erotic materials from relatively innocuous sources such as television advertisements, clothing catalogues featuring children modeling underwear, and similar sources. In no case did exposure to pornography precede offending-related behavior in childhood.'[44] The link is complicated by the finding that paedophilia is the result of specific and measurable abnormalities in the brain, specifically in the area that controls sexuality, the hypothalamus.[45] That abnormality drives men to crime, as well as to pictures of the crime, but do the pictures cause the offence? Or does pornography sublimate the desire? And if so, would a lack of pornography drive potential paedophiles to the real thing?

Studies of sexual sadists, overwhelmingly but not exclusively men, again indicate a brain and hormonal abnormality,[46] and again such abnormalities incline the men towards the crime as well as towards pornography. That correlation has led some researchers to claim that there is a link between pornography and sexual violence.[47] But it is only a correlation. Rates of train breakdown in India parallel an increased consumption of ice-cream. Correlations are not proof, and if one looks at the broad picture then sexual violence is more strongly related to biological factors such as brain abnormalities or unusually high testosterone levels.[48] The strongest argument against pornography is that its abolition will lead to a diminution of sexual criminality, but the evidence does not support the contention. The causes of sexual criminality are a great deal more complicated than the simplistic argument that 'pornography drove him to it'.[49]

Which is not to condone pornography, and it is certainly no defence of the wilder shores of the trade which caters to what most of us would consider to be perversions: paedophilia, say, or sadism. Pornography is distasteful (if it's tasteful, it is probably called 'art') and it is frequently disgusting, but the vast majority of pornography is heterosexual and adult, and it feeds unstoppable male desires. Men dream, they crave visual fantasies. Male desires may not coincide with the desires of women, but then, as Baudelaire noted, women are complicated machines designed to make men dream. (While we're quoting Frenchmen, Balzac once said that watching men fondle their wives made him think of orang-utans playing violins.) Banning pornography would be like the prohibition of alcohol in America; it would criminalize the trade without stopping it, especially now that nerds are making robo-bimbos available on the internet.

Pornography is also condemned because it 'objectifies' women. It denies her essential humanity, turning her into a sex-slave, or what Otto Preminger called Marilyn Monroe, 'a vacuum with nipples'. But it is precisely because he is *not* the object of her desire that he will create *himself* as the object of her desire. He worships the woman who sees *him* as a sex object. It is the male dreamland in which he can have all he wants, without jealousy, effort, or risk. It is a fantasy (not a fancy) woman that is the object of his adoration. And that fantasy is deliberately fed as much by real women as by their cyber-sisters.

LEADING HIM ON

He likes stretch jeans, low necklines, and perfume. She provides them. He likes a degree of sexual provocation, and she knows that, but she also knows that the challenge to his self-control is part of life, part of the delight in the game. He can, and nearly always does, resist.

In Botticelli's *Birth of Venus*, the goddess shields her breasts, convincingly curvaceous, by a not quite innocent hand, and tresses of long hair cover her pudenda. Today's bikini likewise celebrates the female sex: it focuses the male gaze, points to the sensual (or essentials) – the bum, pube and boobs. It is similar to the biblical figleaf on the original Eve, to the leather bikini on the walls of old Knossos, or to the displays of femininity on the beach of today. The mystery is as often found not in unrestricted nudity, but in a fragmentary – very masculine – view of the female body.

'The glimpse of the forbidden,' says Anne.
'Grrr.'

Objectification! Some women object. Women are being pressured into wearing revealing clothes. If left to themselves, the argument suggests, they would dress in shapeless bags. One doubts it very much, but perhaps, to quell men's lust, the modern woman might adopt the Islamic custom and hide her physical self in an all-enveloping black *chador*. Yet the veiled woman only encourages the male's fantasy life. The intimate is hidden, prompting visions of the unclad houri in Paradise. In the dark he finds the firm body that is always young, for ever shapely, sensual, and smooth. It is a vision of immaculate perfection, a divination of beauty that never fades, and the *chador*, above all garments, is worn as a response to male pressure. Men are denying other men a glimpse of their own women, it bespeaks possessiveness, just as it hints at forbidden mysteries. 'Love looks not with the eyes, but with the mind; And therefore is wing'd Cupid painted blind.'

So perhaps, if enshrouding mystery does not work, why not let it all hang out? In July 1991 a Canadian student, Gwen Jacob, decided to go topless on a hot day. She was charged with indecency and fined $75. Jacob's lawyer, Margaret Buist, appealed to the Ontario provincial Court of Appeal and in July 1996 won a reversal of the conviction, thus setting a precedent that women were to be allowed the same public exposure as men. Margaret Buist commented on her victory that, 'fundamentally, what Gwen's case was about was stopping the exploitation of women and changing the way women's bodies are perceived so they are no longer objectified by men'.[50]

'That's asking rather a lot of men,' suggests Bill.
'It's your chance to mature and accept the female body as a mundane thing,' says Anne.
'Just give me the chance. Please.'

UNSAFE SEX

The male courts excitement and danger. He needs a challenge. Part of the challenge is to avoid the traps, including the straitjacket that would bind him in her image. But a larger part of the challenge is taking risks. He is neurochemically addicted to novelty, and he needs variety to stimulate pleasures lost through familiarity. He is more impulsive than she is, and impulsiveness is linked with an inability to be still.[51] The extreme-sensation seeker is usually a male, and he is much more likely to seek sexual variety and to lack sexual inhibitions.[52] He receives a high from the sexual pursuit, and an even larger high if he succeeds. The pursuit of women is, to men, like going into a sporting competition. His testosterone rises in anticipation of the contest. Risky or illicit sex gives him a high just like the one he gets when he risks all in business or destroys a sporting opponent. 'A standing prick,' said Sir John Harington, Elizabeth I's courtier, 'hath no conscience.'

Men are by nature adventurous and high-sensation seekers tend to engage in a greater variety of sexual behaviours and with a greater number of partners than low-sensation seekers.[53] And high testosterone levels do not make for cosy and intimate relations. 'High sensation seekers seem to be more likely to divorce, and divorced men rank higher on sensation-seeking than the younger singles as well as married men. Among women, both single and divorced subjects were higher on sensation seeking than married women.'[54]

Then there is the novelty factor; he needs variety to keep his sexual interest high. It is a well-known phenomenon in animals. The male's sexual performance declines once he is familiar with his mate, but add a new mate to the scene and he becomes much more sexually active again.[55] An erotic film watched more than once loses its power to arouse. A study that measured penile arousal found that even on the second viewing his interest was much diminished, but a new movie immediately restored the interest.[56] And, as always, he is at the extremes; the autoerotic and dangerous sexual games are the male ones. The fatal victim of autoerotic asphyxia (a complex form of masturbation relying on the claim that near strangulation increases the intensity of orgasm) is typically a single male aged 15 to 29 years.[57]

The world of sex is an adventure playground to men, though most of the adventure takes place in the mind. But some men, a few, love the risks of the game, and if accidents happen, that is the price of the adventure.

But it is not a one-sided game. Women are not passive victims, even though one extreme feminist mantra claims that love is the victim's response to her rapist. Love is what binds us, and it is mutual, but sex is what attracts us, and she plays the game with the same zest as he. She initiates and he responds. This is *her* reversal of the old order, and it is not done by 'chatting up' or by languorous looks, but by degrees of undress. She plays on the male sexual fantasies. He responds, but he must always know that it is hands off till she says otherwise. Why should the new woman not expose herself? 'She's liberated, she's confident … she's herself,' says Mandy Courtney, account director of an advertising firm with a lingerie interest. 'A woman can take pleasure in her own sensuality, as opposed to worrying about how men perceive her.' She is the object of her own fantasy.[58]

> 'I once wrote that *exhibitionism among women is virtually non-existent*,'[59] says Anne.
> 'Stretch jeans on a nubile wench?' says Bill.
> 'So I was wrong.'

The new season's look for 1998 was titillatingly described in *The Times* by Jane Shilling, 'style correspondent': 'Sultry Latin babes in kitsch ruffles, flounces, mega-sexy briefs and crotch-skimming skirts … see-through plastic, governess blouses, with blood red seaming over the breasts.'[60] Pretty, sheer and flirty, it brings a lurch to the heart, says the liberating Shilling. Next day, Grace Bradberry, the style editor of the same staid newspaper, admired Stella McCartney's collection at Chloe: 'little drawstring tops that only just held strong across gaping cleavages'.[61] Who's harassing who? Or are we expected to believe that the new woman does not equate sensuality with sexuality? When it comes to sexual harassment only the male is usually assumed guilty should he make a pass, even verbally. With harassment there is little equality in practice.

> 'Never chat her up?' Bill asks.
> 'Certainly not in the workplace,' says Anne. 'A man should keep his hands and innuendoes to himself.'
> 'Would a social invitation to a colleague be construed as harassment?'

'And if the relationship sours? Think of subpoenas, the revenge, the publicity!'

'A peck on the cheek, then?' suggests Bill. 'As a friendly greeting?'

'Depends. If she's Dutch you might go three pecks. But nothing libidinous.'

'Suppose I compliment her? Tell her she looks great?'

'Depends again,' says Anne. 'The postmodern women might interpret this as *an evaluative practice that puts her at a situational disadvantage.*'

'You joke. Can I engage a female workmate in conversation?'

'Only with caution aforethought.'

Yet, sexual harassment cases notwithstanding, the dance will go on. 'The fact remains,' writes one sensible woman, 'that to most people, sexual chemistry between men and women – with or without the prospect of actual intimacy – is one of life's pleasures and ... the new feminists show no sign of recognizing this, or of trying to distinguish true sexual harassment from positive or ambiguous sexual dynamics.'[62]

LIVING TOGETHER

It is tough for a man and a woman to live together but, more often, it is harder for them to live apart. He is more impatient, demanding and impulsive, and he does not want a cloying togetherness. Living closely together is about separate development within a common space. It is about enabling the other. It is about providing trust and space. The private space we give to our partner is the measure of our trust and of our power.

His mistake was to seek power over her. Her mistake is to seek power over him.

She wants him to be like her

She would make him more like herself, to be more 'caring', more thoughtful, and she says she wants this because she cares for him. Does she? She would make him a clone of herself, and that is not understanding him. It is to lack imagination, sympathy and empathy. It is self-absorbed *Ms*understanding. It is to lack knowledge of what a man is. And if women remain unaware of male sexual imagery then they are guilty of something more than innocence. In the end it is the difference in the brain that constitutes the last intimate taboo: not the physical form or the lustful act of sex, but the other dimension – the eternal wondrous feminine difference – of mind.

He knows how much she does not understand him, but finds it hard to tell her.

He can help her, but in his own way. He will not be as good as she is on many fronts, but the sexism of the age is to insist on a sexual sameness: a genderless equality. It has never been easy to work out the problems of living together in harmony, but it becomes much more difficult when we fail to recognize the differences between the sexes.

He does not want her to be like him

He seeks a partner, not a rival. Getting along is not about seeking a balance of power: that leads to warfare. What he looks for is a different mind, the mystery that is always there – the person that is beyond conquest. Her mind, not her body, is always distant, strange and somehow unsafe. This is what he wants. Women remain unknown to men. Hollywood knows this (or used to). In films such as *Now Voyager*, *Letter from an Unknown Woman* or *Gaslight*, the woman was shown as isolated and inaccessible to men; and that very unknowingness was the trigger for heterosexual romance.[63] In love he does not seek a woman to compete with him. A man seeks the woman who completes him.

We began this chapter by talking about men's fantasies, but the fantasies quickly fade. He sees how vulnerable she is (not least to the likes of himself). He knows the world that is, and he sees her for what she is: reassuringly there – a comfort, a partner, a lover. He would be that to her, too. The dynamic chemistry between men and women is one of life's pleasures, and there is much more involved than the physical. She is essentially and perfectly other than he. She is every woman in a Vermeer painting: never to be understood, never to be possessed and never to be mastered – the wondrous enigma in the here and now.

Which sounds splendid. But isn't it time he helped her about the house? Time he took an equal share of parenting? Time for a new chapter.

SUMMARY
- Men have more vasopressin, the neurotransmitter that creates a persistent drive to find a mate.
- Testosterone fuels the sex drive in both men and women, but he has over ten times more of it.
- He has less oxytocin, the neurotransmitter that promotes affectionate nurturing.
- The male sex drive and aggression brain circuits are linked.

FUTURE TRENDS
- It seems unlikely that the male's need for visual stimulation or pornography will go away since it is part of his biological needs. It's clear that some people will never accept this and would seek to ban even the 'soft' type. That would be a nonsense, demonstrating an inability to recognize that he is not seeking to degrade but enjoying a fantasy of perfection.

DESIRABLE AIMS
- We would do well to understand that sex and aggression are closely linked in the male. Most men learn to control that biological link, but it must be learned. The boy turning into a

man will experience surges of sexual desire and aggression; if he understands his own biology then he will be more likely to learn to disconnect the two feelings. Biology is not destiny – it sets the sails but we soon learn that the rudder leads in the right direction.

- A man is not possessed of the same warm, friendly neuro-transmitter circuits as a woman is. He is an emotionally colder animal. But cool is also emotional. Understanding this will make living with him that much easier.

CHAPTER TEN

The Real New Man
Home truths

The New Man is reportedly a good guy and an example to all men. Once home from work he plays his full part in parenting and doing the household chores – he's a true partner. He cares. He shares. How can this portrait of epicene domesticity not appeal? Here is the preferred male of the future: the new and improved house spouse. This rosy view of the New Man is, if not media driven, media fed, for the New Man is news (the appendage 'new' helps make him *news*). Much of what makes for a good feature story in journalism is what goes against common sense, against common belief and against the common grain. The New Man fits that prescription because he is what most men are not. He cleans. He cooks. He minds the kids. He irons! The only problem is that reported sightings of the New Man do not tally with the population on the ground.

The number of single parent families in Britain increased by 27% in the five years from 1990 to 1995, according to the Office of National Statistics: in 1995 one in five children were living in a single parent household.[1]

94 per cent of lone-parent families with dependent children were headed by women in 1991.[2]

Most fathers spend less than five minutes a day with their children.[3]

The New Man's most salient characteristic is his rarity. If he had feathers he would be an endangered species. So how to recognize him?

THE NEW MAN SHOULD TAKE ON AN EQUAL SHARE IN PARENTING

This mantra is repeated so often that it has become dogma, yet experience and statistics show that men do not share the load of raising children. The opposite seems to be happening: men are opting out of their responsibilities. How did this happen?

On the surface a woman gained great freedom in the last generation of the 20th century. She can choose to work or not to work; she can choose when to have children, and how many, or not to have children. She has been given the power to be independent of men. For the first time in history she is, in theory, free of male domination. She has been put down for so long, but now she can reject him. There has been a revolution of expectations; not only of equal opportunity, but the promise of equal results in all things. Yet ...

The very things that were meant to free women, the pill, the chance to work, the expanding welfare state, bound her, and her alone, to subsidized housing, subsistence work and the children she bore. The downside of her 'liberation' was the breakdown of the family in the lower reaches of society:

> a six-fold increase in never-married single mothers (up from one in 20 to six in 20 in the UK)[4]
> a tripling of the divorce rate in a single generation
> a spiralling of young male crime with the failure of discipline and the absence of the adult male in the family

How did this affect the male?

It turns out that women's greater freedom was also his freedom to live without women – or, at least, to live without feeling responsible for his offspring. Accidental births or unwanted (on his part) children were her fault. The availability of the pill and easy access to abortion put the responsibility on her. The onus to get married no longer existed, and he felt less need to provide for her.

Why should he? She could work, or go on welfare – *on the social* – and that left him free. Women's lib freed men of responsibility.

Fathers too often evade their responsibilities, which is why there are so many mother-only one-parent families. This bodes ill for the future, for research reveals that children of one-parent families have higher rates of mortality and illness, are more at risk of abuse, are more likely to become delinquent or go into care, and are more likely to become involved in crime.[5] The unisex belief that mothers and fathers are interchangeable, and that one or other is dispensable, will only increase the likelihood of future un-happiness and delinquency.

Even where men do feel responsible for their families, the women, despite their vaunted liberation, are still the primary caregivers. Scandinavian countries are renowned for their liberal attitudes and progressive social policies. Equality between the sexes is not a mere aspiration in those countries, it's expected, and equal opportunity has been promoted longer and more actively than in any other society. In Sweden, for example, over 80% of women now have jobs outside the home, practically the same proportion as men, helped by excellent day-care facilities and other state-provided family support systems; yet, according to official Swedish government reports, 'women still bear primary responsibility for work in the home and with children'.[6]

Men's withdrawal from parenting responsibilities may also be due to some confusion in their roles. In the past fathers were expected to be men. They provided discipline and coached their sons in life's rough and tumble, but the new orthodoxy expects fathers to be mothers. Some of the pressure comes from wives who, because they have jobs, need more help than in the past, and still more pressure comes from so-called 'parenting' experts. In 1992 Jim Van Horn, Family Life Educator at Penn State University, devised a quiz to determine whether men were good fathers.[7] The man was expected to know 1) what size shoes his children wore, 2) when their next dental appointment was due and 3) whether their inoculations were up to date. It is a fair bet that most fathers would fail that test, which, in Van Horn's words, made them 'technically present, but functionally absent'. The test illustrates the feminization of the father's role and it is hardly a surprise that men shy away from such redefined responsibilities. At London's Heathrow Airport there are 'baby changing stations' in the men's toilets, something which is common enough in America and now, evidently, spreading in Britain. The folding tables seem somewhat forlorn, expressions of hope rather than of actuality, for most men would rather the baby stayed filthy than be seen using a baby changing station. Fathers are not mothers.

Yet still the pressure to change fathers into mothers continues. Soon after taking office the Hillary and Bill Clinton team proposed legislation to make sure that states and local governments adopted 'gender-equitable and multicultural materials' so that no American child could be raised without exposure to gender-bending cultural pressure. We get a preview of this desired New World of gender equality from a speech that President Clinton's Secretary of Health and Human Services, Donna Shalala, delivered in 1991 when she was Chancellor of the University of Wisconsin. Shalala invited us to imagine a little girl named Renata, and what her life would be like in the year 2004. After school, Shalala tells us, little Renata goes to a city-run day care centre where 'sometimes, she and her best friend, Josh, play trucks, sometimes they play mommy and daddy, and Josh always puts the baby to bed and changes the diapers, just like his own dad does at home'.[8]

Already, in north America, boys and girls are given parenting classes at school. Sometimes this involves eleven-year-olds being made to carry dolls, or even raw eggs, for two or three days so that they will learn 'responsibility'. Presumably the boy who doesn't drop the egg graduates, but all the boys are expected to grow up as caring, nappy-changing, New Fathers, and implicit in the classes is the expectation that both sexes will participate equally in child-rearing. But what is honoured in social theory doesn't pan out in practice. A study by the European Commission finds that the house-husband is a mythical creature, with less than one per cent of men aged 25 to 59 staying at home full time.[9] Boys, simply, will be boys. Josh, whatever Donna Shalala wishes, will not readily change nappies, no matter how many eggs his teachers force him to cradle. Dr Sebastian Kraemer of the Tavistock Clinic in London, and a prophet of the New Man, recognizes the failure of men to be women and, of course, it is all the male's fault: 'What is so pathetic about the plight of many young men is that they want to be loving towards their children, but don't dare,' says Kraemer. 'There is a taboo on tenderness due in part to the intensity of emotion created by being in close contact with your own baby and in part to the powerful social pressure on men not to behave like women.'[10]

We have seen that men are not made like women. Their aptitudes and skills are different. Not worse, not better, just different. A good father does not need retraining by the state to raise his children, he must just do what is right by his beliefs, and if society expects men to be surrogate mothers then it will be disappointed. Many men desperately want to be good fathers, but feel inadequate and confused because they fail to do what women want. They escape from the home because they feel that their own skills and nature are not valued; nor, perhaps, needed?

THE NEW MAN SHOULD DO HIS FULL SHARE OF HOUSEWORK

There is a common belief that men do nothing about the house. They slump in front of the television, maybe deigning to raise their legs to let the vacuum cleaner go beneath their feet. In fact he does just as much work about the house as she does. The difference is that his work is mostly houshold (DIY) or car maintenance, while she does most (70–90%) of the cooking, shopping and housework.[11]

The constant whingeing about men not carrying their share of the domestic burden seems particularly unfair when the statistics demonstrate that men work harder overall than women. In 1996 he averaged a working week of nearly 46 hours, six more than she did, while enjoying one day less holiday per year.[12] In paid work he works twice as many hours as she does. Though men travel twice as far to work they tend to get there five minutes earlier than women (37 as against 33 minutes). Professor Colin Pooley of the University of Lancaster has shown that women not only use slower forms of transport but also use the time to shop and take the children to school.[13] Most men do work hard, only to be told that they do not work hard enough and that they should be cleaning the carpets when they get home.

Endless bickering about who does what is destructive to a marriage, yet it is encouraged. Two-thirds of women say their men do not pitch in as much as they should.[14] According to the magazine *Top Sant*, in a survey of 5,000 women, men help out equally in only one in ten households.[15] Over half of women (53%) have sole responsibility for cleaning the house.[16] Eight in ten of the women in the *Top Sant* survey said they are expected to perform too many roles (except for one: most of the women said they were too exhausted by life to think about sex). Washing and *ironing* is done by only 2% of married men.[17] Yet there is a hidden bias in the surveys. Her vacuuming is work, but his raking of leaves is not? One survey maintained that housework (what the woman usually does) is 'essential' work, while car maintenance (100% male activity) and lawn-mowing (95% male) were deemed 'unessential' chores.[18] That survey was surely designed by a woman, and one can only hope that her car is now permanently broken down and her garden choked with long grass. Such conclusions, that traditional male chores are 'unessential', also ignore that in most western economies twice as many men as women work full time. In Britain 55% of the workforce is male, 45% female. That might make it seem that there is a near parity of work between the sexes, but dig a little deeper and it is discovered that nine in ten of those men (91%) work full time, but only just over half of the women (55%). That is, half of the full-time workforce is male, only a quarter is female.[19]

Yet men, working harder outside the home, are also expected to work harder inside it as well? In Britain women spend 150 minutes a day doing unpaid domestic work; men, 40 minutes a day.[20] That is, women in general spend 13 hours more a week doing these chores than men. Working wives spend 120 minutes a day doing unpaid work at home, or 9 hours 20 minutes a week. Their husbands spend 23 minutes a day, or 2 hours 10 minutes a week on the chores. Professor Jonathan Gershunny, author of this survey of over 10,000 people, concludes that the women are hard done by: 'Their husbands have, in effect, one job where they have two'.[21] The professor would seem to be ignoring the longer time that men spend at paid work.

How much work do women do outside the workplace? A British survey by the Office for National Statistics[22] found that women do more work in the home than men – 60% compared with 40%; though men conpensate by doing more hours in paid employment. In this survey shopping was defined as unpaid work. Shopping and driving the car and entertaining friends are all calculated in the hours *worked* at home. All preparation of food is classed as toil; sometimes it is, but not always. It seems that spending money and giving pleasure is to be equated with earning money when it comes to work. As a corrective it is suggested that women be paid to shop (though a sensible few might imagine that they are already).

'Aren't most statistics nonsense?' asks Anne.
'Isn't that a statistic?' asks Bill.
'I mean, aren't we being a little unfair to working women and the hours they work …'
'Don't most women exaggerate how little work men do?'
'Yes.'
'Finding that men do more work paints a fuller picture.'

Male laziness is, typically, less of a problem on the domestic front than the failure to get a grip on a mind unlike his own. The traditional Tyrannosaurus rex or Neanderthal Man is still very much with us. But the failure is not just the male's. Women's view of men remains that he fails to grow up; especially that he remains Eros, the boy-child of Aphrodite. Each sex finds comfort in treating the other as an appendage of its own.

'We know that the peak period for couples to quarrel is when they have young children,' says Ann Oakley, a feminist sociologist at the University of London Institute of Education. 'Then they become very unequal. Women ought to be able to make the same kinds of choices as men.'[23] Here is the sociology of failed expectations; the mean-spirited totting up of chores instead of the giving of little pleasures; the cringing idea that *I am the victim*. To which Professor Oakley adds: 'Women are almost as oppressed now as they were in the late Sixties.'

Female expectations of equity at work and in the home are in many cases unreal. There are inevitable disappointments, and the male is the obvious scapegoat.

This gender rancour gets full support from American academic psychologist Virginia Valian, in her book *Why So Slow? The Advancement of Women*. Valian is distressed that men *plainly* do less housework and child-raising than women: that the men are 'slackers' – freeloaders who dupe their womenfolk. Her aim is the revolt of the housewife, in the name of Equality. 'Egalitarian parents,' concludes Valian, can 'bring up their children so that both girls and boys play with dolls and trucks, help care for younger children, are active in sports, learn self-defence ...' We leave her in puzzlement: 'Why doesn't the man *want* to do his share?'[24]

Most couples who share in the breadwinning and the housework revert to traditional spousal roles after having a baby, new research shows. According to psychologists Gill Cappuccini and Ray Cochrane from Birmingham University, a husband's job often assumes more importance than the woman's, while the wife does more of the domestic chores. In a study of 100 married couples it was found that two-thirds were living together in equal partnership, both having jobs and sharing the chores. 'In nearly all cases,' says Ms Cappuccini, in an address to the British Psychological Society Conference at Strathclyde University, 'the man's career becomes more important after the birth.'[25] In a majority of cases people were quite happy with the new arrangement and marital satisfaction remained high.

The *Independent* newspaper soundly concluded nine months later, 'On sexual equality, we should agree to differ':

When a researcher reports to the British Psychological Society that working fathers do not behave like new men (rare nappy changes, not a lot of cooking, comes home late, doesn't look after the kids when they're ill) you can see all the women in the audience groaning, 'yeah, tell me something I don't know already.' But are men and women profoundly, ineluctably different? ... The probability [is] that there is a genetic predisposition in women to be more adept at communicating and co-operating, while there is a converse predisposition among men to drive for lone achievement. Technology now enables us to scan brains in ways that may identify a wide range of 'soft-wired' differences, including intelligence, social and sexual differences. But there is a great reluctance to report such research in the open; it is largely hidden from view, for fear that it will upset our cherished presumptions.

What are we scared of? First, just suppose, purely for the sake of argument, that women do indeed have a genetic predisposition to be more co-operative in their social relations than men, and that men, conversely, are more likely to adopt aggressive postures. Why is the one propensity necessarily 'better' than the other? Surely there are obvious situations in which the male propensity to go solo and compete is more useful than the female propensity to compromise, just as the reverse of this is true.[26]

That male-female relations are often unequal, that their roles differ, does not mean that this inequality is demonstrably unjust.

249

Men do not share domestic chores equally. And there are many instances of unfair distribution of the chores (though, as we show, not the significant difference overall that is commonly alleged). It is not so much in sharing chores – and certainly not in the making of lists as to who has done what – as in the shouldering of different tasks that makes for the small pleasantnesses that bind.

In work, home, school, or play, there is, and will remain, a sexual divide. This divide, this difference in understanding, is based on the different experience of the sexes: the experience of the external world – the social world; and the experience of the world within – the biological world. The distance between the understandings makes for mystery. It is part of understanding to strive to close the distance. The desire to possess, to control, means that each sex wants to interpret the other as the self. The desire for a sexual sameness – imposing one's own image upon the other – is at the root of sexual imperialism. To look out for what is distinct between the sexes is to appreciate others for what they are. To miss what is different or distinct is to subtract from the whole understanding of human nature.

Overall, women with jobs do 9 hours 20 minutes more unpaid domestic work a week than men with jobs, but men, overall, work 20 hours more a week at their paid jobs than women do. Adam delves hard, Eve spins hard, and it is ridiculous to say that just because she spins at home she is the more valuable.

'So why the grand female whinge?' says Bill.

'It's me, me, me,' says Anne. 'But let's not paint too black a pic. I read somewhere that six out of seven mothers think their male partners do a good or very good job as parents.'[27]

'But they still think men don't pull their weight at home?'

'Some men do behave badly. Think of all those traditional males who expect the meal on the table and slippers by the easy chair the moment they walk in the door, even when she does work full time.'

'Sure, but you can't use exceptions to prove the rule.'

So what is to be done? Feminist mother Melissa Benn has the answer. She suggests that a father's commitment to work might one day be interpreted as 'a form of parental irresponsibility'.[28] Work outside the home, which pays the bills, is bad, while work inside the home is good.

Most men and women do both, and try to balance their lives as best they can. Professor Kermit Daniel, of the University of Pennsylvania, suggests that the division of labour within the home is good for both men and women. Professor Daniel's research found that marriage raised productivity by allowing specialization of labour within the family.[29] That makes sense. The man, after all, would much rather repair the car, put up a shelf or clean out the garden shed than clean, iron or do the washing-up. Received wisdom says this is all social conditioning, that women were brainwashed as small girls into thinking they should do the housework. The traditional man, the unreconstructed 'old' male, certainly believes that housework is woman's work, while the New Man, that rare creature, believes that all work should be equally shared. But neither is correct. There are biological reasons for the sex differences in the home.

So why don't men iron? Women do 93% of washing and ironing. There seems no obvious reason why men don't press shirts and skirts. After all, they have excellent spatial imagery and all the necessary technical skills. But take note: it is 'don't', not 'can't'. The army-trained male is totally expert and obsessional about his perfect ironing; indeed, many a male living on his own is very good at it. But put a man and a woman together and he doesn't and she does, and the reason is in his biology.

Remember that a man needs more stimulation than a woman to motivate his brain, and this means that it is much harder for the male to cope with the mundane and the repetitive. Men get bored more easily. His biology has equipped him with sensation-seeking qualities that build empires and take him to the moon, but also make him shy away from dull tasks. The low serotonin and high dopamine addiction that is so useful at his work can be a disaster in the home because he simply cannot concentrate as well as she does. Domestic chores are simply not exciting enough a challenge to turn on his frontal cortex, and so he is liable to burn the shirt as his mind strays in search of something to relieve his boredom. He is the same with any repetitive task except those that stimulate his interest like the maintenance of a car or a boat.

Men also have a lower sensitivity to detail, which means he simply does not notice the dust as she does. She has better peripheral vision, she sees more of the detail. Many studies have shown that there is a marked difference in how well men and women register and remember details,[30] and to a man dust on a shelf or a scum ring around a bath are just that – details. Even if he does notice them, he may simply not accord them the importance that a woman does. To her dirt is offensive, to him it is part of the natural world. From very early in childhood males have a greater tolerance for, and even liking for, dirt:[31] What a man perceives as 'clean' a woman might find dirty, and what he finds merely 'dirty' she might find utterly disgusting. His sense of smell is different, too; the stale socks and sweaty shirt don't bother him because they are among the pheromone-related smells that women are acutely aware of but men simply do not detect.

So a woman might well be annoyed that a man does not help keep the house clean, but in all probability he has not even noticed that it is dirty. He is oblivious to dust, dirt, and even to mould on a mug. His observational powers are simply not as acute as hers. He is not her and it's not because he's mean, unhelpful or does not care, its simply because these things do not register on his mind.

And can he even do the job as well as her? The organization of a man's brain makes running the home more difficult for him. The focused nature of his thinking makes it difficult for him to do many things at once. His brain is designed to go step by step, to concentrate on one job, to do it well and then go on to the next. The very nature of a home filled with the competing demands of children, laundry and cleaning makes it imperative that several jobs are all running at the same time. The kids want things, the breakfast must be made, the phone rings and messages must be taken, someone has lost their keys and the dog wants feeding. All at once. To a man it is sheer chaos, but a woman's networked brain makes it easier for her to do several things at once.

This sounds like special pleading: men are simply unfitted to be good housekeepers; but there have been a number of laboratory tests that indicate how his more focused brain makes it difficult for him to do several things at once. One such experiment[32] is the mirror tracing test in which the subject simply has to draw a line around the outline of a shape; the snag being that the subject does not see the outline-shape and pencil directly, but in a mirror so that left becomes right and right left. Even so it sounds a simple challenge, but most right-handed men find it almost impossible. His brain is in compartments, with the verbal on the left side and spatial processing on the right, and his problem is that the right hand is controlled by the left side of the brain. When he tries to trace the mirror image, he needs to rotate it in his mind's eye for the correct brain signal to be given to the right hand, and he cannot do it. He freezes, his hand will not move because his left brain, lacking visual spatial processing, is confused and does not know which way to direct the right hand. It is impressive to watch, especially because the man is shocked and cannot believe that his hand just won't move, and it won't move for some time until his left brain has consulted his right brain. The male using his left hand to do the very same tracing problem has no difficulty; the right brain instantly sorts out the reverse image in the mirror and directs the left hand to trace correctly.

A woman has no such problems. Verbal and spatial problems are dealt with in both the left and right sides of her brain and she finds no difficulty in tracing the mirrored shape with either hand. Another test,[33] the finger-tapping test, shows similar results. A man is asked to read a story aloud and, at the same time, to tap a finger on the tabletop, and the rate of tapping is recorded. When the male taps with his left hand, which is controlled by the right side of his brain, the tapping remains at a constant speed, but ask him to tap with his right hand and the rate immediately slows. What is happening is that both the finger tapping and the reading are being controlled by the left side of the brain, and the one activity interferes with the other. Women have verbal skills on both sides of the brain so they tap with either hand at a constant speed. Male musicians find it much harder to play a tune with the right hand and talk at the same time. It's easier if they transfer the melody to their left hand.[34]

Tapping a table or tracing a reflected image are not, of course, proof that a male is less suited than a woman to the complex demands of running a house when many jobs may need doing at once. Nevertheless the tests do show how men find it difficult to do more than one thing at a time. As part of our television series we set out to demonstrate this, though we had to be content with a manageable number of volunteers. If we had wanted to run a properly scientific test we would have needed some 100 carefully selected subjects from all walks of life, but budget constraints kept us to twelve. A recruitment agency found us six female and six male volunteers and we then tested them on their ability to do a series of tasks in a very limited time. They had to wash up, brew coffee, make toast and scrambled eggs, iron a shirt and take a phone message that listed various items which needed to be sorted and put into a briefcase. They had ten minutes to do all this; not impossible, but certainly not easy either. Each step towards completing a task earned them points; thus breaking the eggs, one point, whisking them another and so on, though they lost a point if the scrambled eggs were inedible. Altogether they could each earn a maximum of forty points if they successfully completed the tasks inside the allotted ten minutes.

The result was a walkover for the women. One man did well, the other five brought up the rear of the field. The numbers involved were too small for the results to be significant, but they are a pointer towards the fact that women are simply better at performing several tasks at once. We then used a simple indirect method to test the brain organization of our volunteers. It is called dichotic listening, and it works by having two different sounds transmitted at once, one to the right ear and one to the left. The subject is then asked to repeat what they heard – remember, the sound coming into the right ear is relayed to the left side of the brain and vice versa, so a person whose verbal skills are located in the left brain will only report the sounds that are fed into the right ear. Sure enough, the men usually only reported that sound, while the women reported both sounds – since they have verbal skills on both sides of the brain. And the one man who scored high in the multi-task, restricted-time test? When we gave him the dichotic listening test he showed a female-organized brain. The other males, all low-scorers, had typical male brains.[35]

The tests and studies all indicate that men are simply not very good at doing more than one thing at a time. His more compart-mentalized brain makes him, literally, more single-minded and so he needs to focus on one thing at a time. Talking, walking and chewing gum simultaneously is not his strongest point. His lower serotonin level also makes it difficult for him to persevere with a boring chore, because his reward circuitry is not switched on by this sort of tedious activity. He gets no pleasure out of doing housework. She may not enjoy doing it either, but she does get the reward of a satisfying high when she sees the result.

None of this means that a man should not help about the house, but expecting him to be as assiduous at cleaning as a woman is to expect the unnatural. The very nature of household chores seems to play to a woman's strengths and a man's weaknesses. That's why he doesn't iron.

THE NEW MAN SHOULD BE IN TOUCH WITH HIS EMOTIONS

'She doesn't understand me,' the traditional male says. To which today's feminist replies: 'Have you tried to make yourself understood? Have you tried to understand her?' He is being asked to open up, an oyster in an oyster bar. The gap in understanding is made real in the moment of its denial. He is about to be prised open and eaten alive.

Instead of understanding he gets a dumbing down of the emotions ... a smug one-dimensional, self-centred, *be-as-me* imitation of life as it exists in an Aussi soap. Her aim is an enveloping intimacy. This disparages what science finds typically male; degrades his cool, enterprising self.

It has become received wisdom in the last few years that the world would be a better place if only men could get in touch with their emotions. One (female) letter-writer to the *Financial Times* summed up the claim: 'if more men got in touch with their emotions the world would be a calmer, much calmer place.'[36] It is a beguiling vision; the world would be at peace, bereft of hostility, if men could only be a bit more touchy-feely, if they could weep openly, if they could be warmer, if they could simply become more like, well, women?

'Your heart on your sleeve, eh?' asks Bill.
'You're so strong and silent.'

The demand that a man get in touch with his emotions is sheer psychobabble for, unless he is dead, a man is already in complete touch with them. It just so happens that his emotions are not hers. What that letter-writer was really saying was that if only men could be gentle, caring, considerate, forgiving, soft-hearted and compassionate, and, just as importantly, could express those virtues in soothing tones, then she would find the world a more congenial place. And doubtless she might, but would the world really be a better place if men's emotions were feminized? When danger lurks do we really want him to respond with empathy? His emotions are not hers, and because his can be far more explosive they require more rigorous controls.

'Women weep buckets,' says Bill.
'And men just boil over mindlessly.'

Compared to women, men have an emotional short circuit. Strong signals, whether of anger, fear or lust, avoid the rational controls of his upper brain and flash straight to his limbic system. His vastly different hormonal environment, particularly his testosterone-driven need to compete and his surge of adrenal rage or fear, means that the fires of his feelings can burst into instant and even terrifying flame. 'Why are some emotions – the warm and comforting ones – to be trusted, while anger and lust are not?' asks a University of London sociologist, Mary Ann Elston. 'To say that the first are women's and the second men's only begs the question, quite apart from being self-evidently untrue.'[37] Mary Ann Elston is warning us not to draw too sharp a distinction here. Women do feel lust and anger, while men can feel the gentler emotions, but our common experience tells us that, on the whole, men are more suspicious and hostile, and women are warmer.

> 'Emotion isn't just a female thing, you know,' says Bill. 'He too broods, boils over, has rages …'
> '… and lusts,' says Anne. 'Perhaps his emotions are closer to that ancient word *passion* – those rather male eruptions that upset the mental calm.'
> 'So women are creatures of emotion and men of passion?'
> 'Hmm … let's have passion fruit for dessert.'

But if men are capable of feeling the warm and comfortable emotions, why can't they express them more often? Why do they shy away from connecting with their inner world? Why can't a man just sit down and have a heart-to-heart talk about his feelings? One might as well ask why he cannot give birth to a baby. A man is not a woman, his emotional processes are not like hers, and a man's inner world has been shaped by profound biological forces that are quite different from those that shape a woman's emotional outlook.

A man is certainly more disposed to anger and lust. We saw in the previous chapter how he has some 400% more visual (and lust-provoking) fantasies about her than she has about him, and the culprit for that rich sexual fantasy life is his high level of male hormones (ten times higher than hers). The same hormones are an integral part of the risk and rage cycle that we met in Chapter Four. Unlike a woman, a man achieves an emotional high out of taking risks, so when he rides a motor-cycle too fast or climbs an impossibly sheer cliff-face he is getting in touch with his emotions. But those emotions, plainly, are not hers.

Science is illustrating the difference. PET scans reveal that even when a man is resting he continues to show a high level of activity in those parts of his brain that control movement and aggression. He might be slumped in the armchair, but his brain is still primed for ambush.

What the scientists are studying[38] when they scan the resting brain is the limbic area, the primitive part of the brain which is the seat of our emotional responses, and which can be divided into two parts. The 'old' limbic system, as its label suggests, is the more primitive and it governs action. A caveman attacking a mammoth was relying on his old limbic system. What he was not using was his cingulate gyrus, the 'new' limbic system which processes communication through such means as facial expressions, body language and speech. The old limbic system drives action, the new facilitates communication, and researchers have discovered that even in a resting male brain the old limbic area is still flickering with activity. The resting female brain shows no such signs in the old limbic system, instead it is her cingulate gyrus that is lit up. This has consequences; think of the two parts of the limbic system as running motors, out of gear. Present the man with an emergency and it is his activity motor that is engaged, while in a woman it is the communicating engine that kicks in. If they have a row then he is much more likely to strike out. In the USA 96% of road-rage drivers are men.[39]

His resting brain is oriented towards action, which is why he will often relax by watching sport. The constant motion, the aggression and the competition complement his old limbic system. His strong reactions to the game, whether of delight at a goal scored or derision at a referee's decision, may not make it appear that he is relaxing, but the emotional engagement with the game's progress suits his restless brain. 'Restless' may seem an odd word to apply to a couch potato watching television sport, but men's lower levels of serotonin make them far more prone to boredom. Her higher serotonin levels, and the fact that she has a greater number of serotonin receptors in her frontal brain,[40] make her more able to keep the irrational limbic system under the control of her thinking cortex. He finds such control harder and so he needs more stimulation, and the constant challenges, victories and disappointments of the sports field satisfy the primitive needs of his limbic emotional system. Men need challenges and, lacking mammoths to kill, he will satisfy himself with the exploits of Manchester United or the Green Bay Packers.

The differences do not stop there. We saw, in the discussion of how boys and girls learn in different ways, that the female brain is networked for verbal skills.[41] It is also networked to allow ample communication between the verbal and emotional areas of her brain. We have seen how the splenium (part of the corpus callosum that links the brain's two hemispheres) is almost a fifth larger in women, and as a result she has more connections between her feelings and her verbal expressions. She thus finds it much easier to express her emotions because she can verbalize them. He finds that difficult, for the male brain is more compart-mentalized than the female. He possesses one compartment for emotional feeling, but it is not linked with the compartment that deals with words. When she feels something she wants to say it. When he feels a similar emotion it will register on his conscious-ness, but he won't feel the urge to express it.

That emotional silence frequently persuades women that men are insensitive, and in many ways they are quite right. Men are genuinely less sensitive than women. She literally sees more than he does; she has superior peripheral vision because she has more rods in the eye, and it is these that pick up the detail. She sees better than he does in the dark. His vision is superior in the bright daylight and he has greater visual acuity and a better ability to judge the speed and position of objects, but a woman's more subtle vision sees obscure things that he never registers. This includes colour, for her ability to distinguish colours is far superior to his; indeed, the far red end of the spectrum is a mystery to half the male population because they cannot see it at all, but she can.[42]

She also hears better than he does. He does not hear high-frequency sounds nearly as well as she does,[43] and he hears even less as he gets older. He finds it difficult to pick up individual sounds when there is a lot of background noise.[44] Talk to him while you are doing the dishes and he cannot distinguish the higher-pitched female voice from the other sounds. That is why men like the car radio turned up higher than women do, because a man cannot hear it above the general noise. At 85–90 decibels (which is a very soft sound) women hear about twice as well as men: thus a small persistent sound like a dripping tap will annoy her and he will not even notice it. He is also incapable of picking up slight inflections of voice level and intensity, signals which form emotional flags to women. He is simply deaf to these things and so is accused of being insensitive, but in truth he is merely less well equipped to pick up nuances from his surroundings.

'You talk to me from two rooms away and expect me to hear you,' says Bill.
'Lots of women do that. They assume their husbands have women's hearing.'

Men are also less sensitive to pain and to touch.[45] The sex difference in touch-sensitivity is so great that there is little overlap between the sexes,[46] and this means that the gentle caress, which is so meaningful to a woman, leaves him unmoved; indeed, he probably won't even notice it. His memory for detail is not as good as hers. He is four times less likely to remember a tune than she is (and six times less likely to sing it in tune if he does).[47] Women perform better than men on simple memory tests, so is it surprising that he cannot remember what dress she wore on a special occasion? Or even that she is wearing a new outfit? When he fails to compliment a woman on a new dress it is not because he is being deliberately crass, but probably because he has not even noticed. All clothes look much the same to him – unless, of course, they are provocatively revealing, in which case they do register strongly on his regrettably male mind. So his apparent carelessness towards the woman he ostensibly loves is not a personal failing but a biological one. He simply cannot help it.

He sees, hears and remembers far less than she does, while the details of social encounters hardly even register on his brain. Those details are expressed by nuance and gesture, things that women note effortlessly, but which pass him by. Various studies[48] show that men are bad at reading delicate social situations. An awkward subject crops up at a dinner party, someone stiffens, the wife notices, but the husband blunders on in hob-nailed boots until she kicks him beneath the table. She wonders how he could possibly have missed the reaction shown by the embarrassed guest, but his blunt senses are simply not sensitive enough to detect subtle signals. And what does get through to his brain is stored in compartments without being cross-referenced or integrated. He lacks what one scientist has termed social cognition, or what some call intuition. A recent paper in *Nature* suggested there may be a gene that triggers the cascade of genes that code for this particular trait and that in most men it is switched off.[49] If that is true then nature has simply denied men the ability to feel the empathy that most women feel. The paper suggests that autism is the extreme end of the male's emotional blindness, and autism is five times more common in males than in females, while the less extreme form of autism, Asperger's syndrome, is almost exclusively male.

Autism is characterized by a profound failure to develop social relationships. Autistic people are unaware of other people's feelings – indeed, in its extreme form, they may be unaware that other people have any feelings at all. This, naturally, inhibits the formation of meaningful relationships, whether with friends or lovers. Autism is an extreme emotional dysfunction, of course, but still a reflection of the less sociable male. To women, most men are partially autistic. They put less value on family relationships and friends, they care less about social relations and they are more selfish.

Why is he like this? Again his brain was forged and moulded by a past in which the ability to empathize would have been a distinct disadvantage. If the invader is storming ashore with spears and shields then it is not very productive to empathize with the attacker's feelings or try to engage him in meaningful discussions. What was needed from the male was the limbic brain's swift and primitive response. The male brain was forged over hundreds of thousands of years to engage in action, in attack and defence, and it was not equipped to be as sensitive as a woman's brain to the feelings of others.

To which a woman might well answer 'so what?' Just because a man once needed to be quick with a spear does not mean he should now be slow with a compliment, but this is to disregard how well his brain can serve him. If he were as easily distracted as she is, if he were to be given pause by every small gesture of hurt feelings, then he would not be as good at competing in the corporate jungle. Wishing he were other than he is, is simply trying to feminize him and denying the importance of his way of seeing the world.

Nevertheless, in the day-to-day business of living together, there is small doubt that it is men's emotional bluntness that most irritates women. The opposite is also true, of course, and men can be thoroughly aggravated by what they see as women's extreme susceptibility to emotion, best lampooned by P. G. Wodehouse's Madeline Basset who thought the stars were God's daisy chain. There is truth in both prejudices.

He can be annoyingly dismissive of emotional considerations

He does not like 'confusing' issues with emotional factors, preferring a swift, concrete solution, while she will try to take everyone's feelings into consideration. We've all been there, done that. Faced with a problem a woman will often appear to talk around it, probing every angle, worrying about every consequence, while a man simply proposes a blunt solution. Perhaps the children are behaving foully, or the neighbours are being a nuisance. She wishes to explore the problem and deepen her awareness of what everyone in the situation is thinking, feeling, planning or wanting, and he just wants to fix it. This is natural; after all, his brain is not equipped to make links across the complex emotional field, and she reads emotional clues far better than he does (if he reads them at all). He, in turn, finds her views emotionally coloured ('sentimental rubbish!'). But her greater emotional sensitivity does not give her a privileged insight into his mind. To complain of a man's inability to get in touch with his emotions is to be out of touch with him.

He is too frequently cold

This is also true, for most men confronted with an emotional row will retreat behind a wall of silence. He uses silence to unnerve her, as a shield of scorn. She cries, but is unable to reach him or to tell him how hurt she is, because he shows nothing back. There is sadness in her face, and she thinks that must be obvious to him, but he seems oblivious. Most men do use silence as a means to attack a woman, yet, in fairness, he is less able to read that sadness in her expression.[50] He simply cannot pick up, as women do, those 'emotional flags', and even when he does he is likely to show less reaction. He is frequently accused of 'bottling up' his emotions, and it is even suggested that he is damaging his health and his relationships by this bottling process; but in truth there is no bottle and, even if there were, it is doubtful if he could fill it. When his emotional system short-circuits and explodes it is because his limbic system has taken control of his mind, not because his mind was filled with inexpressible emotions that were looking for an outlet. Women frequently suspect that men are hiding their emotions, and they do, but they also have much less emotion to hide. Women feel more deeply than men; they feel more joy and more sadness.[51]

A recent study examined this contrast by asking men and women to remember sad events.[52] Each memory triggered a burst of extra brain activity in the cortex, but the bursts were many times more intense in the women than in the men. This ability to feel more deeply may explain why bouts of depression severe enough to require medical treatment are three times more common in women than in men. He is colder than she is, for he does not feel as much as she does, nor does he react so acutely.

His coldness is often defined as being the antithesis of emotion, but this is surely wrong. To display an icy coldness is also to display an emotion, albeit not a fuzzy or comforting one, and that is the real complaint women have about men. Why can't they be warmer?

Biology provides the answer, and once again the culprit is testosterone. This is the hormone of maleness, the fuel of challenge, of attack and of domination, and its presence militates against his being a warm, touchy-feely, sensitive human being. Even the amount a man smiles is related to his testosterone levels; the higher his levels the less he smiles. Indeed, men with very high T levels are less likely to marry and less likely to establish long-term relationships with women than males with lower levels.[53] Of course some high T level males do marry, but they are 43% more likely to be divorced and 38% more likely to indulge in extramarital sex. 'Once married,' the report pointed out, 'this type of individual is more likely to leave home because he is having trouble getting along with his wife, more likely to have extramarital sex, more likely to report hitting or throwing things at his wife, and more likely to experience a lower quality of spousal interaction.'[54]

The conclusion seems obvious. You can have a man, but you cannot have a man who feels, touches, cares, and empathizes like a woman, not if you want him to stay a man. And if you really want him to be in touch with his feelings, take care, for those feelings might be explosive.

So how do men show their emotions? He is more likely to do it by actions than by words, so when he rebuilds the kitchen cabinets, perhaps he is really saying 'I love you' (or perhaps he was just nagged enough). But what he won't do, hates doing, is talking about his feelings. He detests being under the microscope and, rather than endure the scrutiny, he will become curt, he will back off or he will simply walk away. He does not want to talk about it; she thinks everything could be put right if only he would, so she pushes him and he reacts angrily.

He needs space (even in company)

A famous actor, known for his many love affairs, was once asked what he liked most about women. 'Proximity,' he answered, but the truth is that men are not much given to proximity except when sexually aroused. He lies on the edge of the double bed so that they do not touch, and he reads nothing into that fact though she might read a lot. Indeed, she might think he is keeping his distance because he has no interest in her, but in truth he is keeping his distance because that is natural behaviour for a man. She finds allure in emotional closeness, he does not, and that aspect of a man is one of the hardest things for a woman to understand.

The male's distrust of proximity again has its roots in biology. One of the strongest triggers for a hormonal surge is the invasion of a male's territory, and this is true for most species.[55] Any intruder, whether it is male or female, triggers a hormone-fuelled readiness to defend the territory. Men simply do not like being close to other people. Not all the time, of course, but for much of the time. They need their space, and invading it only irritates them.

He is good at feigning emotions

This is something that most of us learn; call it the Game of Getting Our Own Way, and men, on the whole, are better at games than women because they enjoy competing. But faking emotions is more than mere play; it is a familiar tactic at work, at home and in politics. Most men believe that an emotional display betrays vulnerability, so they learn to hide what they are thinking. She dislikes this, but he regards a successfully disguised emotion as a victory for self-control.

One of the best ways to disguise emotion is to use humour, and men employ humour far more broadly than women.[56] Women use humour to be sociable, they laugh with other people and use jokes as a way of making others feel comfortable, but this is not the man's way. He uses it as a weapon. The aggressive banter and joke-making that is typical of male-to-male discourse is his way of getting along with his testosterone-fuelled fellow men. One researcher claims he can find an element of aggression in every instance of male humour,[57] even the most innocuous, and women can find such humour very uncomfortable as a recent complaint by women MPs showed: they found their male colleagues' constant low-level joking offensive. But that is how men communicate. Insult, jest and innuendo are the common stuff of male discourse. A man expresses his friendship to another man by making a joke, not by revealing his soul. A man deflects antagonism with a jest, for if he can make his enemy laugh then he has defused the situation.

All this makes it sound as though the male spends much of his time hiding from his passions, and that is probably true. Remember how powerful the male emotional equipment is, and how ungoverned it is by the rational cortex. Adolescence is a terrifying experience for many males, for it is then that they receive their second drenching of male hormones and so experience for the first time the surges of rage and hostility that testosterone engenders. A recent study of normal adolescent boys found a clear relationship between T levels and aggression.[58] High levels of testosterone, the study reported, 'increase the probability that the boys will initiate aggressive destructive behaviour, by making them more impatient and irritable, so they have a lower frustration tolerance which increases their readiness to engage in aggressive behaviour of the unprovoked and destructive kind (start fights, say nasty things, without being provoked).'[59]

Testosterone engenders violent emotions, so violent that they scare men into learning to control them for fear of what would happen if they were allowed full expression. The adult male, if he is to survive in a civilized society, must discipline his raw emotions. Adolescent males find this hardest to do, which is why many of them sublimate their strong feelings in sporting contests. What else is education, but the taming of an animal? And most men are civilized, learning to express their rage or hostility through accepted social channels. But not all achieve this discipline, and women who complain that men are not in touch with their emotions should probably be grateful, for his emotions can be explosive, hurtful and savage. Most wife-beaters and rapists are all too firmly in touch with their emotions.

The wife-beater and rapist is not the norm, despite what proponents at the outer limits of the feminist movement preach. Instead such creatures are men who have never learned to control their strong feelings and who see atavistic violence as the only answer to their immediate problems. The rogue male who cannot control his temper or his lust is no more to be admired than the man who has never learned to control his bladder.

Control is the key to understanding a man's emotional life. He might swing between chilly detachment and over-heated responses, but most of the time he prefers to have things under control. This is why so many women believe men are emotionally cold, while the truth is that men simply fear their passions and so suppress them. Once more, those who deny that the male is distinct have a problem when they ask him to abandon the differences they deny.

THE NEW MAN IS EVERY BIT AS GOOD A PARENT AS A MOTHER

Adrienne Burgess, a research fellow at the Institute for Public Policy Research, argues that there is nothing in the nature of the male that disqualifies him from looking after his children in the manner of the female. Ms Burgess says that most fathers have been *conditioned* not to be as caring as mothers and that men have been *conditioned* out of 'fathering behaviour'. Men, she claims, have been brought up to believe it is unmanly to take too close an interest in their children and she believes that fathers should be given 'at least a dozen' parenting classes before the birth of their children. By such means we will achieve 'the primary caregiving father'.[60]

> 'Easier,' suggests Bill, 'just to give him a womb and breasts?'
> 'And all the hormones to go with them,' says Anne. 'But why don't men use baby changing stations?'
> 'For the same reason women don't change the car oil. Nature.'

Is it true, as Adrienne Burgess claims, that there is nothing in the nature of the male that disqualifies him from looking after his children in the manner of the female? By definition he has no maternal instincts, but the existence of those instincts is now denied by the postmodernists. To believe in the maternal instinct is a heresy, for if you think that women have a unique ability for looking after babies then that destroys the idea that there are no innate differences between men and women. The whole idea of

THE REAL NEW MAN

the New Man is predicated on his gentleness, sensitivity and willingness to use the baby changing stations in men's toilets.

The first obvious point to make is that women take far more interest in babies than men do, and the way a woman responds to a baby, her facial expressions and her gestures, are distinctly different.[61] Some people will protest that these differing reactions are merely the result of social conditioning. Women, they will say, are bound to take more interest in babies because they have been playing the role of mother almost since the day they were born. If small boys were encouraged to play with dolls, would they not grow up to be as fascinated by babies as women are?

Rats, rabbits, and indeed all mammalian mothers exhibit characteristic mothering behaviour.[62] Their brains are wired for this during foetal development, and indeed the female foetus must be exposed to the right balance of sex hormones if she is to exhibit maternal behaviour in adulthood.[63] The brains of all mammals, be they rats, monkeys or humans, need to be prepared to take a nurturing interest in their offspring. If the female is exposed to high levels of male hormones as a foetus then she shows no aptitude for 'nest-making' and no desire to nurture her young.[64]

Human females, of course, are subject to far more complex cultural influences than rabbits, but there is strong evidence that, in common with all other mammals, there are some features of human mothering behaviour that are wired into the brain.[65] For evidence of this we need to look again at those girls with congenital adrenal hyperplasia, or CAH, who were exposed to high levels of male hormone in the womb. Mary's story is a classic example.

As a young girl, Mary was a tomboy. She preferred the company of boys, she hated dolls and refused to wear a dress. Her mother thought she would grow out of it as she matured, but instead Mary's interests became even more masculine. At thirteen, when her few girl friends were preoccupied with makeup, clothes and the opposite sex, Mary was more interested in studying for her special maths exams.

When her elder sister had a baby, Mary was totally uninterested

269

and even rude, telling her sister that she was destined to be nothing more than a boring old hausfrau for the rest of her life. Her sister was upset and wanted Mary to take an interest in her child, but when she gave her the baby to hold, hoping to trigger some affection, Mary was awkward. She did not know how to hold the baby and soon it was bawling its head off, and she quickly thrust the child back into her sister's arms. From then on she took little notice of her niece.

She told her mother, 'Babies are boring, I'm never going to have kids. I want to make something of my life, and you can't if you're stuck with baby responsibilities.'

Mary is now 36 and has never married. 'I like men,' she says, 'but I'm just not interested in settling down. Besides, my career is so important to me that I just wouldn't have the time to be a good wife, let alone a mother.'

This case is classic and the pattern it reveals is consistent. In some fifteen international studies of girls who were exposed to the wrong sex hormones in the womb, the same story emerges: they have no maternal instinct. Their brains were wired in the male pattern, and CAH girls, at maturity, show a typically masculine obsession about their jobs and careers. Very few of them have babies, even though they are biologically equipped to do so. They have ovaries and all the normal female hormones, but they have no desire for motherhood.

Motherhood does not just depend on being properly wired in the womb, it also relies on some extraordinary biological changes that occur in the pregnant woman.[66] During pregnancy progesterone gradually rises to over 1,000 times its normal levels, and the expectant mother's oestrogen rises too, but the key change is in oxytocin, a neurochemical which is produced in large amounts during labour and appears to be the essential ingredient for the bonding that occurs between a mother and her offspring.[67]

In studies where the production of oxytocin is blocked,[68] the mother does not behave maternally towards her new offspring. She ignores them, indeed she does not even recognize them as her own. So what does this magical neurotransmitter do? Oxytocin is linked to the pleasure centres in the brain that produce natural opiates like endorphin, so in effect it gives the mother a pleasurable high. Having a baby, then, is a trip.

Obviously not all mothers have their oxytocin induced by labour. Plenty of women adopt children and are just as loving as natural mothers, but women, in general, have more of the oxytocinergic neural circuits in their brains than men.[69] It is this neural circuitry that makes women more sociable and more open to warm, friendly relationships. It also plays a key role in the relationship of a mother and her infant.

Dr Kerstin Unväs-Moberg, Professor of Physiology at the Karolinska Institute in Stockholm, is one of the few researchers in the world who studies oxytocin effects in humans.[70] She has found that oxytocin has a calming, almost sedative effect on mother and child. When a mother breastfeeds it stimulates her oxytocin secretion, and, significantly, it also stimulates the baby's oxytocin. So both mother and child experience pleasure. Women who breastfeed their babies have higher overall levels of oxytocin than women who bottle-feed, which is why they are more contented. However, the difference is not so great if the bottle-feeding mother cuddles and holds her baby while she feeds it. The reason? Because even the simple act of stroking an infant can cause a mutual rise in mother's and child's oxytocin levels.

This research shows why mothers can soothe a fractious baby with a cuddle; both mother and child are off on their endorphin trip. And the oxytocin also gives the mother a higher tolerance of monotony and helps her to be more affectionate.[71] It is a magical substance; having a child, especially a first child, ought to be a highly stressful experience fraught with anxiety, but a mother's biology helps her overcome the worries. One study examined what happened to new mothers in hospital when they were denied close proximity to their babies[72] and, not surprisingly, it was discovered that the mothers who spent more time cuddling their children were calmer and more affectionate than the mothers who were kept apart from their offspring. One group was oxytocin-rich, the other was not.

Men, even the New Men who have been put through a dozen parent-craft classes, are not endowed with the same quantity of oxytocinergic circuits and, even more significantly, his oxytocin is not triggered in the same way as hers.[73] She gets her high from cuddling her baby, but, as we saw in Chapter Nine, he gets his oxytocin high by achieving orgasm.[74]

The point hardly needs labouring, but it is surely significant that a man does not receive a neurochemical high from nurturing a child and a woman does. That has been demonstrated, yet there are still people who believe a man can look after a baby as well as a woman. Nature designed women for the task; it did not equip men nearly so well.

There is still more evidence for a maternal instinct. A woman's more acute senses make her better at reading her baby's cues. She can interpret those inarticulate murmurings and outbursts, and knows when her infant is hungry or in distress. Men are not nearly as sensitive to such non-verbal messages. She can recognize the cry of her own baby when it is only a few hours old.[75] He can't. She can even recognize her own baby by smell after a few days. He can't. Women are much lighter sleepers and are much more likely to wake at the sound of a baby crying, while men simply sleep on.[76]

Professor Panksepp has even related the impact of music to our differing oxytocin systems.[77] He believes music is experienced mainly in the lower, more primitive regions of the brain rather than in the higher, thinking areas where language is processed, and he deduces that music is thus an essentially primal experience linked to emotional brain mechanisms designed to make mammals and other animals respond to the needy cries of their offspring. The professor has been studying what he calls the 'chill': that reaction to certain musical sounds that can send a shiver down the spine. It can be measured by the physiological and brain-wave changes it produces. Chills are evoked more often by sad music than by happy music and women, on the whole, experience more musical chills than men.[78]

Professor Panksepp believes that the same mechanism that produces the 'chill' comes into play when a mother hears her baby's cries for help or attention. When the child cries a woman feels an emotional pain that a man does not, and this prompts her to go and comfort the baby.[79] Cuddling produces a soothing release of oxytocin and endorphin, and so promotes feelings of warmth. The mother feels good and the baby sleeps again. A man's oxytocin does not respond in the same way. He does not feel an emotional pain at the baby's distress, more likely he feels annoyance. That is, of course, if he wakes at all. In many marriages there is resentment that he sleeps on while she is dragged out of bed in the small hours, but that, sadly, is how nature designed him.

So even the New Man, splendid though he may be, is at a biological disadvantage when it comes to being the house-husband. Women, whether they like it or not (and nature tries to make sure they do), are left holding the baby.

Denying the existence of the New Man is not to validate the unreconstructed old male who believes that women are basically weaker versions of himself. But the new orthodoxy claims that men are basically the same as women, only without the self-evident female merits. The remedy being urged on him is that he should strive to be more like her. He is told to 'get in touch with his emotions' and encouraged to bridle his aggressiveness. He must become more feminine and train his thinking to be more female, but science is telling us that if we want a man's mind to become more like a woman's, then he will need to change it – literally – because the brains are different. Researchers can tell a male mind from a female mind simply by looking at a brain scan, and they are right 19 times out of 20. To imagine that he will become more like her, or she more like him, is part of a unisex ideal that depends on the belief that the genders have similar brains and similar ways of thinking. They don't.

THE AGE OF THE UNSEXED

The mediocre mind casts all in its own image, and rests on the soft pillows of cliché: 'Equal but different; different and, in that, the same'. Thus does a middling mind find an equality that otherwise would not be there. Such minds demand a comfortable mediocrity that pulls everyone down to the level that challenges no one.

Old-style sexism meant that a man stamped his view of the world upon women. New-style sexism means that women are imposing their view of the world upon men, and this is the prevailing sexism in the unisex age: the age of the unsexed. Differences – real, substantive and determinable – in the mental worlds of the sexes are denied. It is a genderless dream, a world without sexual conflict in which fathers are mothers. There was a time when men did not expect to be present at their baby's birth (they were down the pub handing out cigars), but today he is an integral part of the 'birthing experience' and is expected to go hand in hand with the mother through the rest of his child's infancy. Many men are made to feel guilty by their inability to feel the right emotions during this process, but that guilt is imposed on him by a feminine view. The home truth is that he is not going to rock the cradle, though he might well build it. The New Man is a biological fantasy, a fancy of the New Woman.

A man can move with the times. He will collect the non-chlorine-bleached Pampers from Mothercare in the four-wheel-drive pickup, and he will even do more. He will love his children, play with them, and enjoy their company, but it is useless and counter-productive to force him into a unisex frame that denies what he is and tries to make him what he cannot be. Fathers are not mothers. Men don't iron. And he has no need to be ashamed of that. He has his own virtues and, if he is thoughtful, he will not impose his world upon hers. The mature human – the real new man – is in touch with minds other than his own.

We do not denigrate masculine traits that do exist – that search for variety, action, competition, risks, in his hard-focused world. Nor do we ridicule her more caring, familial, connected, competent, security-conscious world. The easiest way for a mind, male or female, is to follow old courses. At the same time we do not look for radical change – a different sexual chemistry or aesthetic as proposed by the social reformers of the sexes. Only by pointing out the differences in the brains does science open up windows on reality.

SUMMARY
- Men's brains are organized to deal with one thing at time. They find it difficult to do lots of different things at once.
- He is neurologically designed to find housework more boring and less rewarding than she.
- His brain is built for action, hers for talking; he does, she communicates.
- His primitive brain is more active – he boils over more easily, then goes away to 'chill out'. Her communicative brain area is more active – she likes to consider the problems.
- Men are not equipped to read the social cues – they find it hard to gauge the emotional temperature. They do not feel the empathy with others' pain that she does.
- He is a creature of emotions – but his are not hers. He has a passion that can explode – a passion that is better under control.

FUTURE TRENDS
- Legislation to enforce private domestic equality. Material equality and more housework for men is to replace the 'old feminism'.[80]
- Pre-nuptial contracts – which may cover not only division of assets, but what is expected of role-sharing within a marriage – are on the cards. In England the Prime Minister's family policy group endorses the principle of such contracts, and is working out the legislation on the issue.[81]

DESIRABLE AIMS
- Demands like those we have described are doomed to failure. He

is not equipped to do the home-making jobs as well as she is. The sexes would be happier together if they were more generous about each other's virtues – he has many.

- We can continue to pretend that he has all the capacities to be like her, but it will only lead to disillusionment and resentment. He cannot be what society deems the 1990s man should be. The way to a good relationship lies in understanding the differences in the male and female mind. Learning to try and see things from his and her mind's eye. That way leads to peace –contentment – the other to strife.

- The idea that men lack emotions or are not in touch with them is one of the most destructive of the myths. It has led to an assumption that if men were in touch with their emotions, men and women would live together in more harmony. There has been an expectation that he could and would change – but he has failed to do so. She is angry with him and gives up. He is angry with her and, unable to fulfil her dreams, he gives up. Yet men have strong emotions – or passions. He is a wise man who recognizes that and learns not to be too much in touch with them – for they are his dark side.

References

Introduction

1 Shown on ITV; *The Times*, 31 Jan. 1996, 43.
2 Roseanne Barr, *Ruby Wax Meets*, BBC 1, 11 Feb. 1996.
3 *New Yorker* Special Edition, *Women*, 1996.
4 MacLeod, A., *The Changeling*, Macmillan, London (1996).
5 Haraway, D., 'Primatology is Politics by Other Means', *Feminist Approaches to Science*, ed. R. Bleier, Pergamon Press, Oxford (1986), 85.
6 Koertge, N., 'How Feminism is Now Alienating Women from Science', *Skeptical Inquirer* (March/April, 1995), 42–3.
7 Gross, P., Levitt, N., 'Knocking Science for Fun and Profit', *Skeptical Inquirer* (March/April, 1995), 41.
8 Braidotti, R., 'Feminism and Modernity', *Free Inquiry* (Spring, 1995), 23–9.
9 Segal, L., 'Feminism and the Family', in *Gender, Power and Relationships*, ed. C. Burck and B. Speed, Routledge, London (1995), 248–9.
10 *Daily Telegraph*, 19 Nov. 1997, 14.
11 Segal, op. cit., 248.

1 He's Not Part One, Part Another

1 GMP Publishers London, *Homosexuality, Which Homosexuality?* International Conference on Gay and Lesbian Studies (1989), 23.
2 Patel, S., *et al.*, 'Personality and Emotional Correlates of Self-Reported Antigay Behaviours', *Journal of Interpersonal Violence* (Sept. 1995), Vol. 10 (3), 354–66.

3 Booghard, H. van den, 'On Anti-homosexual Violence: its nature and the needs of the victims?', *Homosexuality, Which Homosexuality?*, 48.

4 Herek, G. M., 'The Social Psychology of Homophobia: toward a practical theory', *New York University Review of Law and Social Change* (1986), 923.

5 Herek, G. M., 'Stigma, Prejudice and Violence Against Lesbians and Gay Men', *Homosexuality Research Implications for Public Policy*, ed. J. C. Gonsiorek and J. D. Weinrich, Sage Publications, London (1991), 62.

6 Wolfe, A., *One Nation, After All*, Viking, New York (1998).

7 Patel, op. cit., 360.

8 Sigelman, C. K., *et al.*, 'Courtesy Stigma: the social implications of associating with a gay person', *Journal of Social Psychology* (Feb. 1991), Vol. 131 (1), 49.

9 Wolfe, A., *One Nation, After All*, quoted in *New York Times Magazine*, 8 Feb. 1998, 46.

10 Herek, G M., 'Stigma, Prejudice, and Violence Against Lesbians and Gay Men', 60.

11 Schwanberg, S. L., 'Attitudes Towards Gay Men and Lesbian Women: instrumentation issues', *J Homosexuality* (1993), Vol.26 (1), 107.

12 Wainwright, C., *Homosexual Behavior Among Males*, Hawthorn Books, New York (1967).

13 LeVay, S., *Queer Science*, MIT Press (1996), 49.

14 Jones, J., *Alfred C. Kinsey, A Public/Private Life*, Norton, New York (1997).

15 Peterman, T., 'Can We Get People To Participate In a Study of Sexual Behaviour?', *Sexually Transmitted Diseases* (May/June 1995), Vol.22 (30), 164–8.

16 Diamond, M., 'Homosexuality and Bisexuality in Different Populations', *Archives of Sexual Behaviour* (1993), Vol.22 (4), 291–310.

17 *Ibid.*, 229.

18 *Ibid.*, 304.

19 *Ibid.*, 300.

20 Ellis, L., *Theories of Homosexuality, The Lives of Lesbians, Gays and Bisexuals*, Harcourt Brace College, New York (1996).

21 Diamond, op. cit., 305.
22 Remafedi, G., *et al.*, 'Demography of Sexual Orientation in Adolescents', *Paediatrics* (April 1992), Vol.89 (4 Pt.2), 714–21.
23 Seidman, S. N., *et al.*, 'A Review of Sexual Behaviour in the United States', *American Journal of Psychiatry* (April 1992), Vol.151 (3), 330–41.
24 Hamer, D., *et al.*, *The Science of Desire*, Simon & Schuster, New York (1994), 66; Burr, C. I., *A Separate Creation*, Bantam Press, London, New York (1996), 167–77; LeVay, S., op. cit., 49–51.
25 LeVay, op. cit., 52.
26 *Ibid.*, 2–9.
27 Kirsch, J., *et al.*, 'Homosexuality, Nature, and Biology: Is homosexuality natural? Does it matter?', *Homosexuality Research Implications for Public Policy*, 15.
28 *The Times*, 20 Feb. 1997, 21.
29 Burr, op. cit., 168.
30 Whitam, F.L., 'Culturally Invariable Properties of Male Homosexuality: Tentative conclusions from cross-cultural research', *Archives of Sexual Behavior* (1983), Vol.12 (3), 215.
31 *Ibid.*, 224.
32 Davis, A., *et al.*, 'Handedness as a Function of Twinning, Age and Sex', *Cortex* (1994), Vol.30, 105–111; Corballis, M. C., *et al.*, 'Location of the Handedness Gene on the X and Y Chromosomes', *American Journal of Medical Genetics (Neuropsychiatric Genetics)* (1996), Vol.67, 50–2; McManus, I. C., 'The Inheritance of Left-handedness', *Biological Asymmetry and Handedness* (1991), Vol.162, 251–81.
33 Hamer, D. H., *et al.*, 'A Linkage Between DNA Markers on the X Chromosome and Male Sexual Orientation', *Science* (1993), Vol.261, 321–27.
34 Bone, J., 'Investigation Stirs Doubt on "Gay Gene" Claim', *The Times*, 10 July 1995; D'Alessio, V., 'Born to be GAY?', *New Scientist*, 28 Sept. 1996.
35 Tatchell, P., '"Gay Genes" and Selective Abortion', Letter to *The Times*, 20 Feb. 1997, 21.
36 Friedman, R.C., *et al.*, 'Neurobiology and Sexual Orientation: current relationships', *Journal of Neuropsychiatry and Clinical Neurosciences* (1993), Vol.5 (1331–153).

37 Ellis, L., *et al.*, 'Sexual orientation of human offspring may be altered by severe maternal stress during pregnancy', *Journal of Sex Research* (Feb. 1988), Vol.25 (1), 152.

38 Gorski, R. A., 'Gonadal Hormones and the Organization of Brain Structure and Function', *The Lifespan Development of Individuals, Behavioral, Neurobiological and Psychosocial Perspectives*, ed. D. Magnuson, Cambridge University Press (1996), 317–21.

39 Gorski, R. A., 'Sexual Differentiation of the Endocrine Brain and its Control', *Brain Endocrinology*, 2nd edn, Vol.1 (1991), 80–83.

40 Hadley, M. E., *Endocrinology*, 4th edn, Prentice Hall International Editions (1996), 380.

41 Turkenburg, J. L., *et al.*, 'Effects of Lesions of the Sexually Dimorphic Nucleus on Sexual Behaviour of Testosterone-Treated Female Wistare Rats', *Brain Research Bulletin* (1989), Vol.21, 162.

42 Rhees, R. W., *et al.*, 'Onset of the Hormone-Sensitive Perinatal Period for Sexual Differentiation of the Sexually Dimorphic Nucleus of the Preoptic Area in Female Rats', *J Neurobiology* (United States), (July 1990), Vol. 21 (5), 781–6.

43 Hoyenga, K., Hoyenga, K.T., *Gender-Related Differences*, Allyn & Bacon (1993), 161–6.

44 LeVay, op. cit., 199.

45 Allen, L. S., *et al.*, 'Two Sexually Dimorphic Cell Groups in the Human Brain', *J Neuroscience* (Feb. 1989), Vol.9 (2), 497–506.

46 LeVay, S. A., 'A Difference in Hypothalamic Structure Between Heterosexual and Homosexual Men', *Science* (30 Aug. 1991), Vol.253 (5023), 1034–7.

47 LeVay, S., 'Evidence for a Biological Influence in Male Homosexuality', *Scientific American* (May 1994), Vol.270 (5), 44–9.

48 Swaab, D. F., *et al.*, 'Brain Research, Gender and Sexual Orientation', *Homosex* (1995), Vol.28 (3–4), 283–301; Swaab, D. F., 'Development of the Human Hypothalamus', *Neurochem Research* (United States), (May 1995), Vol.20 (5), 509–19.

49 Allen, L. S., *et al.*, 'Sexual Dimorphism of the Anterior Commissure and Massa Intermedia of the Human Brain', *Complete Neurobiology* (1 Oct. 1991), Vol.312 (1), 97–104; Allen, L. S., 'Sexual Orientation and the Size of the Anterior Commissure in the Human Brain', *Proceedings of National Academy of Science USA* (1 Aug. 1992), Vol.89 (15), 7199–202.

50 Hoyenga, op. cit., *Instructor's Manual*, 69–87; Friedman, op. cit., 131–53.

51 Hoyenga, op. cit., *Instructor's Manual*, 82.

52 Dittmann, K. W., *et al.*, 'Sexual Behaviour in Adolescent and Adult Females with Congenital Adrenal Hyperplasia', *Psychoneuroendocrinology* (May, July 1992), Vol.17 (2–3), 153–70.

53 Reinisch, J. M., *et al.*, 'Hormonal Contributions to Sexually Dimorphic Behavioral Development in Humans', *Psychoneuroendocrinology* (1991), Vol.16, 213–78.

54 Friedman, op. cit., 131–53.

55 *Ibid.*, 139.

56 Hall, J. A. Y., 'Sexual Orientation and Performance on Sexually Dimorphic Motor Tasks', *Archives of Sexual Behavior* (1995), Vol.24 (4), 395–407.

57 Kimura, D., 'Sex, Sexual Orientation and Sex Hormones Influence Human Cognitive Function', *Current Opinion in Neurobiology* (1996), 6259–63.

58 Hall, J. A. Y., 'Dermatoglyphic Asymmetry and Sexual Orientation in Men', *Behavioral Neuroscience* (1994), Vol.108 (6), 1203–6; Kimura, D., *et al.*, 'Dermatoglyphic Asymmetry: relation to sex, handedness and cognitive pattern', *Pergamon* (1995), Vol.19 (4), 471–8; 'Lesbians and the Inner Ear Source', *The Economist*, 7 March 1998, 124–5.

59 Diamond, op. cit.; Remafedi, op. cit.

2 Foodsex I

1 *Independent*, 3 Feb. 1993, 10.

2 *Financial Times*, 6 Nov. 1996, 4.

3 Peterkin, B. P., *et al.*, 'Diets of American Women: looking back nearly a decade', *National Food Review* (Summer 1986), Vol.34, 12–15.

4 Gallup Survey, *The Times*, 3 April 1990, 3.

5 Wild, E. L., *et al.*, 'Matriarchal Model for Cardiovascular Prevention', *Obstetric Gynecological Survey* (Feb. 1994), Vol.49 (2), 147–52.

6 Costain, L., The British Diabetic Association, personal communication, 10 Nov. 1996.

7 Gleim, G. W., 'Exercise is not an Effective Weight Loss Modality in

Women', *Journal of the American College of Nutrition* (Aug. 1993), Vol.12 (4), 363–7.

8 Meijer, G. A., *et al.*, 'The Effect of a 5 Month Endurance Training Programme on Physical Activity: Evidence for a sex-difference in the metabolic response to exercise', *European Journal of Applied Physiology* (1991), Vol.62 (1), 11–17.

9 Wardle, M. G., *et al.*, 'Response Differences', *Sex Differences in Human Performance*, ed. M. A. Baker, John Wiley & Sons (1987), 110.

10 Levenstein, H., *Paradox of Plenty: A Social History of Eating in Modern America*, Oxford University Press (1994), 244.

11 *Cosmopolitan* (March 1993).

12 *Diagnostic and Statistical Manual of Mental Disorders*: DSM–IV, American Psychiatric Association, Washington DC, 4th edn (1994), 548.

13 Ferraro, R., *et al.*, 'Lower Sedentary Metabolic Rate in Women Compared with Men', *Journal of Clinical Investigation* (Sept. 1992), Vol.90, 780–4.

14 *Wissenchaftliche Tabeller, Geigy, Körperflüssigkeiten*, ed. Ciba-Geigy, Basel, Vol.8 (March 1981), 225; Fisher, R., *Science* (March 1989), Vol.243, 1536.

15 Wells, J. C., *et al.*, 'The Effect of Diet and Sex on Sleeping Metabolic Rate In 12 Week Old Infants', *European Journal of Clinical Nutrition* (May 1995), Vol.49 (5), 329–35.

16 Washburn, R. A., *et al.*, 'Leisure Time Physical Activity: Are there black/white differences?', *Preventive Medicine* (Jan. 1992), Vol.21 (1), 127–35.

17 Phillips, S. M., *et al.*, 'Gender Differences In Leucine Kinetics and Nitrogen Balance In Endurance Athletes', *Journal of Applied Physiology* (Nov. 1993), Vol.75 (5), 2134–41.

18 Lemon, P. W., 'Effect of Exercise on Protein Requirements', *Journal of Sports Science* (Summer 1991), Vol.9, 53–70.

19 Pannemans, D. L., *et al.*, 'Whole Body Protein Turnover in Elderly Men and Women: Responses to two protein intakes', *American Journal of Clinical Nutrition* (Jan. 1995), Vol.61, 33–8.

20 Chernoff, R., 'Effects of Age on Nutrient Requirements', *Clinical Geriatric Medicine* (Nov, 1995), Vol.11 (4), 641–51.

21 Morley, J., 'Nutrition and the Older Female', *Journal American*

Nutrition (Aug. 1993), Vol.12 (4), 337.

22 Campbell, W. W., *et al.*, 'Increased Protein Requirements in Elderly People: New data and retrospective reassessments', *American Journal of Clinical Nutrition* (1994), Vol.60, 460–9.

23 Garrow, J. S., James, W. P. T. (eds.), *Human Nutrition and Dietetics*, Vol.79, Churchill Livingstone, 9th edn (1994), 309; *Davidson's Principles and Practice of Medicine*, Churchill Livingstone, 17th edn (1995), 553; Yoshimura, N. N., *et al.*, 'Protein Quality, Amino Acid Balance, Utilization and Evaluation of Diets Containing Amino Acids as Therapeutic Agents', *Neutricion* (Sept/Oct. 1993), Vol.9 (5), 460–9.

24 Southgate, D. A. T., 'Meat, Fish, Eggs and Novel Proteins', *Human Nutrition and Dietetics*, Vol.309, 314.

25 Wurtman, R. J., *et al.*, 'Precursor Control of Neurotransmitter Synthesis', *Pharmacological Review* (1981), Vol.32, 315–35.

26 Lehnert, H., *et al.*, 'Amino Acid control of Neurotransmitter Synthesis and Release: physiological and clinical implications', *Psychotherapy Psychosomatics* (1993), Vol.60, 18–32; Alfieri, A., *et al.*, '2 Effects of Inhibition of Serotonin Synthesis on 5-Hydroxyindoleacetic Acid Excretion, in Healthy Subjects', *Journal of Clinical Pharmacology*, Vol.34 (2), 153–7; Spring, B. J., *et al.*, 'Effects of Protein and Carbohydrate Meals on Mood and Performance: interactions with sex and age', *Journal of Psychiatric Research* (1983), Vol.17, 144–67.

27 Smith, A. P., *et al.*, 'Effects of Breakfast and Caffeine on Performance and Mood in the Late Morning and After Lunch', *Neuropsychobiology* (1992), Vol.26 (4), 198–204; Smith, B. D., *et al.*, 'Effects of Caffeine and Gender on Physiology and Performance', *Physiology and Behaviour* (1993), Vol.54, 415–22.

28 Blum, I., *et al.*, 'The Influence of Meal Composition on Plasma Serotonin and Norepinephrine Concentrations', *Metabolism* (Feb. 1992), Vol.41 (2), 137–40.

29 Conrad, M. E., *et al.*, 'Ironic Catastrophes: One's food – another's poison', *American Journal of Medical Science* (June 1994), Vol.307 (6), 434–7.

30 Reunanen, A., *et al.*, 'Body Iron Stores, Dietary Iron Intake and Coronary Heart Disease Mortality', *Journal of Internal Medicine* (Sept. 1995), Vol.238 (3), 223–30.

31 Halleberg, L., *et al.*, 'Iron, Zinc and Other Trace Elements', *Human Nutrition and Dietetics*, 176.

32 *Ibid.*, 183.

33 Alexander, D., *et al.*, 'Nutrient Intake and Haematological Status of Vegetarians and Age-Sex Matched Omnivores', *European Journal of Clinical Nutrition* (Aug. 1994), Vol.48 (8), 538–546.

34 Stuttaford, T., *The Times*, 30 April 1996, 4.

35 Halleberg, op. cit., 178.

36 Dollahite, J., *et al.*, 'Problems Encountered in Meeting the Recommended Dietary Allowances for Menus Designed According to the Dietary Guidelines for Americans', *Journal of the American Dietetic Association* (March 1995), 341–7.

37 Westermarch, E. A., 'Diet in Relation to the Nervous System', *Human Nutrition and Dietetics*, 663.

38 Hambridge, M. K., *et al.*, 'Zinc and Chromium in Human Nutrition', *Journal of Human Nutrition* (1985), Vol.1, 306.

39 Gibson, P. D. S., *et al.*, 'A Growth-Limiting, Mild Zinc-Deficiency Syndrome in some Southern Ontario Boys with Low Height Percentiles', *American Journal of Clinical Nutrition* (1989), Vol.49, 1266.

40 Dollahite, op. cit., 344.

41 *Ibid.*, 341

42 Retzlaff, B. M., *et al.*, 'Changes in Vitamin and Mineral Intakes and Serum Concentrations Among Free-Living Men on Cholesterol-Lowering Diets', *American Journal of Clinical Nutrition* (1991), Vol.53, 890–8; Baghurst, K. I., 'Demographic and Dietary Profiles of High and Low Fat Consumers in Australia', *Journal of Epidemiology Community Health* (1994), Vol.48, 26–32; Kies, C. V., 'Mineral Utilization of Vegetarians: impact of variation in fat intake', *American Journal of Clinical Nutrition* (1988), Vol.48, 884–7.

43 Halsted, C. H., 'Water-Soluble Vitamins', *Human Nutrition and Dietetics*, 254.

44 Rappoport, G. R., *et al.*, 'Gender and Age Differences in Food Cognition', *Appetite* (1993), Vol.20, 33–52.

45 Dollahite, op. cit., 344, 347.

46 Mattes, R. D., 'Sensory Influences on Food Intake and Utilization in Humans', *Human Nutrition: Applied Nutrition* (1987), Vol.41A, 91.

47 Dollahite,op. cit., 342.
48 Sandström, B., 'Considerations in Estimates of Requirements and Critical Intake of Zinc, Adaption, Availability and Interactions', *Analyst* (March 1995), Vol.120, 913–15.
49 Benton, D., *Food For Thought: How What You Eat Affects Your Mood, Memory and Thinking*, Penguin Books, London (1996), 149.
50 Ryan, A. S., *et al.*, 'Nutrient Intakes and Dietary Patterns of Older Americans: A national study', *Journal of Gerontology* (Sept. 1992), Vol.47 (5), 145–50.
51 de Pee, S., *et al.*, 'Lack of Improvement in Vitamin A Status with Increased Consumption of Dark-Green Leafy Vegetables', *Lancet* (8 July 1995), Vol.346 (8967), 75–81.
52 Sandström, op. cit., 913.
53 Lee, D. Y., *et al.*, 'Homeostasis of Zinc in Marginal Human Zinc Deficiency', *Journal Laboratory Clinical Medicine* (Nov. 1993), Vol.122 (5), 549–56.
54 Prasad, A. S., 'Discovery of Human Zinc Deficiency and Studies in an Experimental Human Model', *American Journal of Clinical Nutrition* (Feb. 1991), Vol.53 (2), 403–12.
55 Sandström, op. cit., 913.
56 Favier, A. E., 'Hormonal Effects of Zinc on Growth in Children', *Biological Trace Element Research* (Jan/March 1992), Vol.32, 383–98.
57 Halleberg, op. cit., 191.
58 *Ibid.*, 192–4.
59 McGee, H., *On Food and Cooking: The Science and Lore of the Kitchen*, Allen & Unwin, London (1984), 233.
60 *Ibid.*, 282–4.
61 Abel, T., *et al.*, 'Patterns of Unhealthy Eating Behaviours in a Middle Aged Scottish Population', *Scottish Medical Journal* (1992), Vol.37, 170–4.
62 Rosado, J.L., *et al.*, 'Bioavailability of Energy, Nitrogen, Fat, Zinc, Iron and Calcium from Rural and Urban Mexican Diets', *British Journal of Nutrition* (July 1992), Vol.68, 45–58.
63 Black, A. K., *et al.*, 'Iron, Vitamin B-12 and Folate Status in Mexico', *Journal of Nutrition* (Aug. 1994), Vol.124 (8), 1179–88.
64 Johnson, J. M., *et al.*, 'Zinc and Iron Utilization in Young Women Consuming a Beef-Based Diet', *Journal of American Dietetic*

Association (Dec. 1992), Vol.92 (12), 1474–8.

65 Halleberg, op. cit., 178.

66 *The Times*, 9 Sept. 1996, 4.

67 Boyle, P., 'Nutritional Factors and Cancer', *Human Nutrition and Dietetics*, 705.

68 Torre, M., *et al.*, 'Effects of Dietary Fibre and Phytic Acid on Mineral Availability', *Critical Review Food Science Nutrition* (1991).

69 *The British Medical Association Complete Family Health Enclyclopedia*, Dorling Kindersley, London, 2nd edn (1995), 603.

70 Lucey, M. R., *et al.*, 'Is Bran Efficacious in Irritable Bowel Syndrome? A double blind placebo controlled crossover study', *Gut* (Feb. 1987), Vol.28 (2), 221–5.

71 Lampe, J. W., *et al.*, 'Sex Differences in Colonic Function: A randomised trial', *Gut* (April 1993), Vol.34 (4), 531–6.

72 Stephen, A. M., *et al.*, 'The Effect of Age, Sex and Level of Intake of Dietary Fibre from Wheat on Large-Bowel Function in Thirty Healthy Subjects', *British Journal of Nutrition* (Sept. 1986), Vol.56 (2), 349–61.

73 Sharpe, R. M., *et al.*, 'Are Oestrogens Involved in Falling Sperm Counts and Disorders of the Male Reproductive Tract?', *Lancet* (29 May 1993), 341.

74 *Financial Times*, 7 Oct. 1996, 41.

75 Maitland, A., 'Against the Grain', *Financial Times*, 15 Oct. 1996, 13.

76 Nuttall, N., 'Stores Lose Fight Over "Superbean" Labelling', *The Times*, 10 Oct. 1996, 11.

77 Ballantyne, A., 'Why Our Men Are Getting Less Fertile', *The Times*, 29 Aug. 1995.

78 *The Times*, 9 March 1998, 9.

79 *The Times*, 15 Sept. 1997, 5.

80 *The Times*, 22 Jan. 1998, 24.

3 Foodsex II

1 *The Times*, 21 Nov. 1997, 20.

2 Leiobwitz, S.F., *et al.*, 'Developmental Patterns of Macronutrient Intake in Female and Male Rats from Weaning to Maturity', *Physiological Behaviour* (Dec. 1991), Vol.50 (6), 1167–74.

3 Lieux, E., *et al.*, 'Evening Meals Selected By College Students:

Impact of the food service system', *Journal of American Dietetic Association* (May 1992), Vol.92, 560–66.

4 Putman, J. J., 'Food Consumption, Prices and Expenditure: 1966–87', *U.S. Department of Agriculture Bulletin* (1989), Vol.773.

5 Press Office, Meat and Livestock Commission, Milton Keynes, 2 Oct. 1996.

6 McIntosh, W. A., *et al.*, 'Factors Associated With Sources of Influence/Information in Reducing Red Meat by Elderly Subjects', *Appetite* (June 1995), Vol.24 (3), 219–30.

7 'Deaths from Selected Infectious Diseases, 1984–1994', Office for National Statistics, London, Series MB2 No.21, Table 1b (1996), 3.

8 *The British Medical Association Complete Family Health Encyclopedia*, 19.

9 Kankelovich and Skelly, *The Consumer Climate for Meat Products*, New York, (1985).

10 O'Keefe, C. J., *et al.*, 'Insights into the Pathogenesis and Prevention of Coronary Artery Disease', *Mayo Clinic Proceedings* (Jan.1995), Vol.70 (1), 69–79.

11 *The Times*, 17 July 1997, 16.

12 Ravnskov, U., 'Cholesterol Lowering Trials in Coronary Disease: Frequency of citation and outcome', *British Medical Journal* (1992), Vol.305, 15–19.

13 Pedersen, T. R., 'Baseline Serum Cholesterol and Treatment Effect in the Scandinavian Simvastin Survival Study (4S)', *Lancet* (20 May 1995), Vol.345, 1274–5.

14 Law, M. R., *et al.*, 'Assessing Possible Hazards of Reducing Serum Cholesterol', *British Medical Journal*, (5 Feb. 1994), Vol.308, 373–9; 'Commentary: Having Too Much Evidence (Depression, Suicide and Low Serum Cholesterol)', *British Medical Journal* (1996), Vol.313, 651–2.

15 Dunnigan, M. G., 'The Problem with Cholesterol', *British Medical Journal* (22 May 1993), Vol.306, 1355–6.

16 Barker, D. J. P., 'The Fetal Origins of Adult Disease', The Wellcome Foundation Lecture, 1994, *Proc. Royal Society* (1995), Vol.262, 37–43; 'Intrauterine Programming of Adult Disease', *Molecular Medicine Today* (1995), 418–23.

17 Scott, L. W., *et al.*, 'Effects of a Lean Beef Diet and of a Chicken and Fish Diet on Lipoprotein Profiles', *Nutrition, Metabolism and*

Cardiovascular Diseases (1991), Vol.1., 25–30.

18 Gonen, B., *et al.*, 'The Effects of Short-Term Feeding of a High Carbohydrate Diet on HDL Subclasses in Normal Subjects', *Metabolism* (1981), Vol.30, 1125–9; Knuiman, J. T., *et al.*, 'Total Cholesterol and High Density Lipoprotein Cholesterol Levels in Populations Differing in Fat and Carbohydrate Intake', *Arteriosclerlosis* (1987), Vol.7, 612–19; Mensink, R. P., *et al.*, 'Effects of Monounsaturated Fatty Acids Versus Complex Carbohydrates on High-Density Lipoproteins in Healthy Men and Women', *Lancet* (1987), 122–5.

19 *The Times*, 13 Jan. 1998, 4.

20 *The Times*, 11 Feb. 1998, 1; 9 March 1996, 17.

21 *The Times*, 29 May 1997, 18.

22 Felton, C. V., *et al.*, 'Dietary Polyunsaturated Fatty Acids and Composition of Human Aortic Plaques', *Lancet* (29 Oct. 1994), Vol.344, 1195–6.

23 *The Times*, 24 Dec. 1997, 5.

24 *Manual of Nutrition*, HMSO, London (1995), 16.

25 Southgate, D. A. T., 'Meat, Fish, Eggs and Novel Proteins', *Human Nutrition and Dietetics* (1994), 310.

26 *The British Medical Association Complete Family Health Encyclopedia*, 741.

27 *Ibid*.

28 Widdowson and McCance, *Composition of Foods*, The Royal Society of Chemistry, Cambridge, 5th edn (1994).

29 *The Times*, 7 Jan. 1997, 13.

30 Widdowson and McCance, op. cit., 551, 235.

31 National Food Survey: Table 4.37, Ministry of Agriculture Fisheries and Food, HMSO, London (1994).

32 Widdowson and McCance, op. cit.

33 *Financial Times*, 26 Oct. 1997, 16.

34 *The Times*, 24 April 1996, 9.

35 'Healthy Choice', *M&S Magazine* (Spring 1996), 71.

36 'Easy Ways to Cut Down on Fat', J. Sainsbury plc, London (1996).

37 'Your Top 10 Diet Questions and Answers', *Best*, 12 Sept. 1995, 34.

38 Social Trends, HMSO, London, Report No 425 (Jan. 1996), 26.

39 *The Times*, 20 Oct. 1995, 5.

40 Conway, M., *No Man's Land: A History of Spitsbergen*, Oslo (1995).

41 Gurr, M., 'Fats', *Human Nutrition and Dietetics*, 77.
42 Folsom, A. R., *et al.*, 'Nutrient Intake in a Metropolitan Area, 1973–74 vs 1980–82: The Minnesota Heart Survey', *American Journal of Clinical Nutrition* (June 1987), Vol.45 (6), 1533–44.
43 Baghurst, K. I., *et al.*, 'Demographic and Dietary Profiles of High and Low Fat Consumers In Australia', *Journal of Epidemiology and Community Health* (1994), Vol.48, 26–32.
44 Putler, D., *et al.*, 'Diet/Health Concerns About Fat Intake', *Food Review* (Jan/March 1991), 16–20.
45 *Ibid.*, 20.
46 Rappoport, L., *et al.*, 'Gender and Age Differences in Food Cognition', *Appetite* (1993), Vol.20, 33–52.
47 *The Times*, 7 Nov. 1996, 10.
48 Visser, M., *Much Depends on Dinner*, Penguin Books, London, (1989), 151–3.
49 Bourdieu, P., *Distinction*, Harvard University Press, Boston (1984), 190–1.
50 Phillips, L., 'Meatless and Fancy Free in Paris', *Financial Times*, 11 May 1996, 7.
51 Rappoport, op. cit., 37.
52 Drewnowski, A., 'Sensory Preferences and Fat Consumption in Obesity and Eating Disorders', *Dietary Fats*, ed. D. J. Mela, Elsevier Science Publishers, Barking (1992), 71.
53 Musaiger, A. O., *et al.*, 'Dietary Habits of School Children in Bahrain', *Journal of the Royal Society of Health* (Aug. 1992), Vol.112 (4), 159–62.
54 'U.K. Value Added Meat and Poultry Products Report', *Financial Times*, 24 June 1991.
55 Rappoport, op. cit., 33–52.
56 'The European Lunchtime Report', *The Times*, 20 Aug. 1992.
57 Aris, P., 'Mad About the Tapas', *Financial Times*, 20 Aug. 1996.
58 Frank, R. A., 'The Contribution of Chemosensory Factors to Individual Differences in Reported Food Preferences', *Appetite* (1994), Vol.22, 101–23.
59 Chamberlain, L., 'A Spoonful of Dr Liebig's Beef Extract', *Times Literary Supplement*, 9 Aug. 1996, 15.
60 Rifkin, J., *Beyond Beef*, HarperCollins, London (1993), 236–44.
61 Knox, B., *et al.*, 'Food Preferences During Human Pregnancy: A

review', *Food Quality and Preference* (1990), Vol.2, 131–54.

62 Gerard, F., *Sausage & Small Goods Production*, Leonard Hill Books, London (1969), 126–7.

63 Knox, op. cit., 131–54.

64 'Healthwatch', *Maclean's Magazine*, 16 Oct. 1995, 66.

65 Hargreaves, D., *et al.*, *Financial Times*, 30 Dec. 1993.

66 Harvey, V., Presentation and displays specialist at the UK Meat and Livestock Commission, personal communication, 29 Oct. 1996.

67 Landale, J., 'Iron Lady Turned Squeamish Over Painted Scenes of Bloodshed', *The Times*, 18 Sept. 1996, 5.

68 Putler, op. cit., 19.

69 Gallup Survey for the *Daily Telegraph*, Aug. 1995.

70 *Financial Times*, 4/5 Sept. 1995.

71 'Young Adults; Health and Lifestyles: Diet', MORI Poll for the Health Education Authority, Nov. 1996.

72 *The Times*, 7 Oct. 1996.

73 'Changing Attitudes to Meat Consumption', The Realeat Survey, (1984–1995).

74 Dwyer, J. T., *et al.*, 'The New Vegetarians', *Journal of the American Dietetic Association* (1974), Vol.65, 529–33.

75 Willetts, A., *The Times*, 13 Sept. 1995, 6.

76 Mennell, S., *All Manners of Food: Eating and Taste in England and France from the Middle Ages to the Present*, Blackwell, Oxford (1985), 103–8.

77 Douglas, A., *The Feminization of American Culture*, Papermac, London (1996).

78 *Financial Times*, 15/16 June 1996), IV.

79 Davenport, P., *Financial Times*, 13 Jan. 1991.

80 Bissel, F., *The Times*, 5 Sept. 1992, 6.

81 'If He Did More In The Kitchen', *Good Housekeeping* (Nov. 1995), 123–6.

82 Brown, L., *Tough Choices*, Worldwatch Institute, Washington DC (1996).

83 *The Times*, 10 March 1998, 11.

4 Brainsex I

1 Diamond, M., 'Sex Reassignment at Birth, Long-Term Review and

Clinical Implications', *Archives Paediatric Adolescence* (March 1997), Vol.151, 298–304.

2 *Time* magazine, 8 Jan. 1973.

3 Diamond, op. cit.

4 Maccoby, E. E., 'Gender and Relationships', *American Psychologist* (April 1990), Vol.45 (4), 513–20.

5 McGuinness, D., 'Behavioral Tempo in Pre-School Boys and Girls', *Learning and Individual Difference* (1990), Vol.2 (3), 315–25.

6 *Ibid.*, 321.

7 *The Times*, 5 Jan. 1998, 9.

8 Hoyenga, K. B., Hoyenga, K. T., *Gender-Related Differences*, Allyn & Bacon (1993), 343–5.

9 *Ibid., Instructor's Manual*, 115.

10 Maccoby, op. cit., 516.

11 Hoyenga, *Instructor's Manual*, 142.

12 *Ibid.*, 79–82.

13 Reseach interviews with parents and CAH girls, for documentary series 'Why Men Don't Iron', Channnel 4, June 1998.

14 Reinisch, J. M., *et al.*, 'Effects of Prenatal Exposure to Diethylstilbestrol (DES) on Hemispheric Laterality and Spatial Ability in Human Males', *Hormonal Behaviour* (March 1992), Vol.26 (1), 62–75; Reinisch, J. M., *et al.*, 'Hormonal Contributions to Sexually Dimorphic Behavioral Development in Humans', *Psychoneuroendocrinology*, Vol.16 (1–3), 213–78.

15 Imperato-McGinley, J., *et al.*, 'Cluster of Male Pseudo-hermaphrodites with 5 Alpha-Reductase Deficiency in Papua New Guinea', *Clinical Endocrinology* (Oxford, England), (April 1991), Vol.34 (4), 293–8; Imperato-McGinley, J., '5 Alpha-Reductase Deficiency', *Current Therapy Endocrinology Metabolism* (1994), Vol.5, 351–4.

16 Udry, R., 'The Nature of Gender', *Demography* (1991), Vol.31, 561–73; Udry, R., Morris, N.M., *et al.*, 'Androgen Effects on Women's Gendered Behaviour', *Journal of Biosociology and Science* (1995), Vol.27, 359–68.

17 *Financial Times*, 21 June 1996, 12.

18 *The Times*, 4 April 1997, 40.

19 *Independent* (Education Supplement), 3 April 1997.

20 Maccoby, op. cit., 513–20.

21 *The Times*, 6 March 1996.

22 *Financial Times*, 5 Jan. 1998, 8.

23 Hoyenga, op cit., 321–2; Mann, V., *et al.*, 'Sex Differences in Cognitive Abilities: A cross-cultural perspective', *Neuropsychologia* (1990), Vol.28, 1063–77.

24 Bray, R., *et al.*, 'Can Boys Do Better?', Secondary Heads Association, (April 1997); Charter, D., 'Schoolboys Need Help to Catch Up with the Girls', *The Times*, 11 July 1996; Williams, L. P., *et al.*, NAEP 1994 'Reading: A first look' (October 1995); Mullis, I. V. S., *et al.*, NAEP 1992 'Trends in Academic Progress Achievement of U.S. Students in Science', Vol.23–TRO1 (July 1994).

25 Bray, op. cit.

26 Hoyenga, op. cit., *Instructor's Manual*, 162–6.

27 Bray, op. cit.; Charter, op. cit.; Mullis, op. cit.

28 Halpern, D. F., *Sex Differences in Cognitive Abilities*, Lawrence Erlbaum Associates (1992), 66–7; Barrs, M., *Reading the Difference*, Centre for Language in Primary Education,, UK (1993).

29 Watson, N. V., 'Nontrivial Sex Differences in Throwing and Intercepting: Relation to psychometrically-defined spatial functions', *Person and Individual Differences* (1991), Vol.12, 375–85; Kimura, D., 'Sex, Sexual Orientation and Sex Hormones Influence Human Cognitive Function', *Current Opinion in Neurobiology* (1996), 259.

30 Govier, E., 'Brainsex and Occupation', *Gender and Choice in Education and Occupation*, ed. J. Radford, 1998, 3–5; Halpern, op. cit., 59–78.

31 Hoyenga, op. cit., 321–2; Mann, op. cit., 1063–77.

32 O'Boyle, M. W., 'Enhanced Right Hemisphere Involvement During Cognitive Processing May Relate to Intellectual Precocity', *Neuropsychologia* (1990), Vol.28 (2), 211–16; 'Intelligence, Learning and Associated Characteristics', *Developmental Neuropsychology* (1995), Vol.11 (4), 373; Haier, R. J., Benbow, C. P., 'Sex Differences and Lateralization in Temporal Lobe Glucose Metabolism During Mathematical Reasoning', *Developmental Neuropsychology* (1995), Vol.11 (4), 405.

33 Halpern, op. cit.

34 Hoyenga, op. cit., *Instructor's Manual*, 189–190; Bachevalier, J., Hagger, C., 'Sex Differences in the Development of Learning

Abilities in Primates', *Psychoneuroendocrinology* (1991), Vol.16 (1–3), 177–88.

35 Kimura, D., 'Sex Differences in the Brain', *Scientific American* (Sept. 1992), 119.

36 Halpern, op. cit., Preface, xi.

37 Kimura, D., 'Sex, Sexual Orientation and Sex Hormones Influence Human Cognitive Function', *Current Opinion in Neurobiology* (1996), 259.

38 Lubinski, D., Benbow, C. P., *The Study of Mathematically Precocious Youth: The First Three Decades of a Planned 50 Year Study of Intellectual Talent*, Ablex Publishing Corporation (1994); Lubinski, D. A., Schmidt, D. B., *et al.*, 'A 20 Year Stability Analysis of the Study of Values for Intellectually Gifted Individuals from Adolescence to Adulthood', *Journal of Applied Psychology* (1996), Vol.81 (4), 443–51.

39 Lubinski, D., Benbow, C. P., 'Reconceptualizing Gender Differences in Achievement among the Gifted'. International Handbook for Research on Giftedness and Talent, ed Heller K. A., Pergamon Press, Oxford, (1993)

40 Lubinski, D., Benbow, C. P., *et al.*,'Stability of Vocational Interests Among the Intellectually Gifted From Adolescence to Adulthood: A 15 Year Longitudinal Study', *Journal of Applied Psychology* (1995), Vol.80 (1), 196–200.

41 Munro, P., Govier, E., 'Dynamic Gender-Related Differences in Dichotic Listening Performance', *Neuropsychologia* (1993), Vol.31 (40), 347–53.

42 Shaywitz, B. A., Shaywitz, S. E., *et al.*, 'Sex Differences in the Functional Organization of the Brain for Language', *Nature* (16 Feb. 1995), Vol.373, 607.

43 *Ibid.*, 609.

44 Azari, N., Pettigrew, K. D., *et al.*, 'Sex Differences in Patterns of Hemispheric Cerebral Metabolism: A multiple regression/discriminant analysis of positron emission tomographic data', *International Journal of Neuroscience* (March 1995), Vol.81, 1–20; Hoyenga, op. cit.

45 Harasty, K. L., *et al.*, 'Language Associated Cortical Regions are Proportionally Larger in the Female Brain', *Archives of Neurology* (1007), Vol.54, 171–6.

46 O'Boyle, M. W., interview in documentary series 'Why Men Don't Iron'.

47 O'Boyle, op. cit., 211–16.

48 Allen, L. S., et al., 'Sex Differences in the Corpus Callosum of the Living Human Being', *Journal of Neuroscience* (April 1991), Vol.11 (4), 933–42.

49 Hines, M., et al., 'Cognition and the Corpus Callosum: Verbal fluency, visuospatial ability, and language lateralization related to midsagittal surface areas of callosal subregions', *Behavioural Neuroscience* (1992), Vol.106 (1), 11.

50 Insel, R. T., 'The Development of Brain and Behavior', *Psychopharmacology: The Fourth Generation of Progress*, ed. F. E. Bloom and D. J. Kupfer, Raven Press, New York (1995), 683–93.

51 *Ibid.*, 690.

52 Hoyenga, op. cit., 168–175; Hoyenga, op. cit., *Instructor's Manual*, 69–87; Hampson, E., 'Spatial Cognition in Humans: possible modulation by androgens and estrogens', *Journal of Psychiatry Neuroscience* (1995), Vol.20 (5), 397–405.

53 Hampson, E., 'Spatial Reasoning in Children with Congenital Adrenal Hyperplasia Due to 21-Hydroxylase Deficiency', *Developmental Neuropsychology* (1998), Vol.14 (2), 299–320.

54 Hoyenga, op. cit., *Instructor's Manual*, 189–93.

55 Grimshaw, G. M., Sitarenios, G., et al., 'Mental Rotation at 7 Years: Relations with prenatal testosterone levels and spatial play experiences', *Brain and Cognition* (1995), Vol.29, 85–100; Grimshaw, G. M., Bryden, M. P., et al., 'Relations Between Prenatal Testosterone and Cerebral Lateralization in Children', *Neuropsychology* (1995), Vol.9 (1), 68–79; Grimshaw, G. M., interview for documentary series 'Why Men Don't Iron'.

56 Kimura, op. cit. (1992), 119.

57 Moffat, S. D., Hampson, E., 'A Curvilinear Relationship Between Testosterone and Spatial Cognition In Humans: Possible influence of hand preference', *Psychoneuroendocrinology* (1996), Vol.21 (3), 323–37; Kimura, D., 'Estrogen Replacement Therapy May Protect Against Intellectual Decline in Postmenopausal Woman', *Hormones and Behavior* (1995), Vol.29, 312–21; Hampson, E., 'Estrogen-Related Variations In Human Spatial and Articulatory-Motor Skills', *Psychoneuroendocrinology* (1990), Vol.15 (2), 97–111.

58 Moffat, op. cit., 323–37; Kimura, D., op. cit. (1992), 312–21; Hampson, op. cit. (1990), 97–111.
59 Court, G. et al, *The IES Annual Graduate Review*, Institute For Employment Studies (1995–6).

5 Brainsex II

1 *The Times*, 28 March 1996, 1; 21 Nov. 1996, 6.
2 Bray, op. cit., 35.
3 *Ibid.*
4 *The Times*, 21 Nov. 1996, 6.
5 Comings, D. E., Comings, B. G., 'SIDS and Tourette Syndrome: Is there an etiologic relationship?', *Journal of Developmental and Physical Disabilities* (1993), Vol.5 (3), 265–279.
6 Raine, A., *The Psychopathology Of Crime: Criminal Behaviour as a Clinical Disorder*, Academic Press, New York (1993).
7 Salford-Jacquinet, M., 'Sleeping Tablet Consumption, Self-Reported Quality of Sleep and Working Conditions', *Journal of Epidemiol. Community Health* (Feb. 1993), Vol.47 (1), 64–8; Yarcheski, A., 'A Study of Sleep During Adolescence', *Journal of Pediatric Nursing* (Dec. 1994), Vol.9 (6), 357–67; Coren, S., 'The Prevalence of Self-Reported Sleep Disturbances in Young Adults', *International Journal of Neuroscience* (Nov. 1994), Vol.79 (1–2), 67–73.
8 Lee, E, *et al.*, 'Androgens, Brain Functioning, and Criminality: The neurohormonal foundations of antisociality', *Crime in Biological, Social and Moral Contexts*, ed. H. Hoffman, Praeger, New York (1991), 162–93; Satterfield, J. H., *et al.*, 'Preferential Neural Processing of Attended Stimuli in Attention-Deficit Hyperactivity Disorder and Normal Boys', *Psychophysiology* (1994), Vol.31, 1–10.
9 *Diagnostic and Statistical Manual of Mental Disorders, Fourth Edition* DSM–IVO, American Psychiatric Association (1995), 82.
10 Reilly, J. S. *et al.*, 'Consumer Product Aspiration and Ingestion in Children: Analysis of emergency room reports to the national electronic injury surveillance system', *Annals, Otology, Rhinology and Laryngology* (9 Sept. 1992), Vol.101 (9), 739–41; Kotch, J., 'Child Day Care and Home Injuries Involving Playground Equipment', *Journal Paediatrics Child Health* (June 1993), Vol.29

(3), 222–7; Towneer, E. M. L., *et al.*, 'Measuring Exposure to Injury Risk in Schoolchildren Aged 11–14', *British Medical Journal* (12 Feb. 1994), Vol.308, 449; Centres for Disease Control and Prevention, 'Morbidity and Mortality Weekly Report: Youth risk behavior surveillance – United States', *CDC Surveillance Summaries* (27 Sept. 1996), Vol.45 (No. SS-4).

11 *Trends in Alcohol-Related Traffic Fatalities, by Sex – United States, 1982–1990*, Centre for Disease Control, Atlanta.

12 McCrum, N. G., 'The Academic Gender Deficit at Oxford and Cambridge', *Oxford Review of Education* (1994), Vol.20 (1), 3–26.

13 Hoyenga, K. T., Hoyenga, K. B., *Gender-Related Differences*, Allyn & Bacon (1993), 180–224.

14 Olweus, D., *et al.*, 'Circulating Testosterone Levels and Aggression in Adolescent Males: A causal analysis', *Psychosomatic Medicine* (1988), Vol.50, 261–72.

15 Department for Education and Employment, 'GCSE and GCE A/AS Examination Results 1994/95', *Statistical Bulletin*, Issue 6/96 (May 1996), 4.

16 'Men Take a Higher Proportion of First Class Degrees Nationally', *The Times*, 3 May 1994.

17 McCrum, op. cit.

18 *Diagnostic and Statistical Manual of Mental Disorders*, 82.

19 *Ibid.*; *Drug and Therapeutics Bulletin* (Aug. 1995), Vol.33 (8), 57–60.

20 *Diagnostic and Statistical Manual of Mental Disorders*, 68.

21 *Ibid.*, 64.

22 *Ibid.*, 49.

23 *Ibid.*, 45.

24 *Ibid.*, 102.

25 Comings, D. E., *Tourette Syndrome and Human Behavior*, Hope Press (1994); 'Tourette's Syndrome: A behavioral spectrum disorder', *Advances Neurology* (1995), Vol.65, 293–303.

26 Comings, op. cit. (1995).

27 Hughes, S., *What Makes Ryan Tick?*, Hope Press (1996).

28 *Ibid*, 269.

29 *Diagnostic and Statistical Manual of Mental Disorders*, 78.

30 *Ibid.*, 79.

31 Taylor, E., 'Treating Hyperkinetic Disorders in Children', *British Medical Journal* (24 June 1995), Vol.310 (24), 1617.

32 *Diagnostic and Statistical Manual of Mental Disorders*, 82.

33 Zachary, G. P., 'Boys Used To Be Boys, But Do Some Now See Boyhood as a Malady?', *Wall Street Journal*, 2 May 1997, 1–6.

34 McGuinness, D., 'Behavioral Tempo in Pre-School Boys and Girls', *Learning and Individual Difference* (1990), Vol.2 (3), 315–25.

35 Forbes, 'An Agreeable Affliction', *Staying Healthy* (12 Aug. 1996), 150.

36 *Independent on Sunday*, 27 Oct. 1996, 12–16.

37 *Diagnostic and Statistical Manual of Mental Disorders*, 82.

38 McGuinness, D., 'How Schools Discriminate Against Boys', *Human Nature* (Feb. 1979), 82–8; 'Stimulants and Children', *Mothering* (Summer 1991), 108–13.

39 Satterfield, op. cit.; Levy, F., 'Neurometrics, Dynamic Brain Imaging and Attention Deficit Hyperactivity Disorder', *Journal Paediatric Child Health* (1995), Vol.31, 279–83.

40 Faigel, H. C., *et al.*, 'Attention Deficit Disorder During Adolescence: a review', *Journal Adolescence Health* (March 1995), Vol.16 (3), 174–184.

41 Lewis, C., *et al.*, 'The Prevalence of Specific Arithmetic Difficulties and Specific Reading Difficulties in 9 to 10 Year Old Boys and Girls', *Journal Child Psychological Psychiatry* (1994), Vol.35 (2), 283–92.

42 Bray, op. cit.

43 Trembath, R. C., 'Genetic Mechanisms and Mental Retardation', *Journal Royal College of Physicians* (March/April 1994), Vol.28 (2), 121–5; Pennington, B., 'Genetics of Learning Difficulties', *Journal Child Neurology* (Jan. 1995), Vol.10 (Supp.1), 69–77; Hechtman, L., 'Genetic and Neurobiological Aspects of Attention Deficit Hyperative Disorder: A review', *Journal Psychiatry Neuroscience* (May 1994), Vol.19 (3), 193–201; Hynd, G. W., 'Attention Deficit-Hyperactivity Disorder and Asymmetry of the Caudate Nucleus', *Journal Child Neurology* (1993), Vol.8, 339–47; Anderson, K., 'Developmental Language Disorders: Evidence for Basal processing deficit', *Current Opinion Neurology Neurosurgery* (Feb. 1993), Vol.6, 98–-106.

44 Laxova, R., 'Fragile X Syndrome', *Advances In Pediatrics* (1994), Vol.41, 305–42.

45 Tallal, P., 'Hormonal Influences in Developmental Learning

Disabilities', *Psychoneuroendocrinology* (1991), Vol.16 (1–3), 203–11.

46 Inglis, J., 'Sex Differences in the Effects of Unilateral Brain Damage on Intelligence', *Science* (1981), Vol.212, 693–5.

47 *Boston Globe*, 26 Oct. 1997, F1.

48 *Ibid.*

49 Morris, J., *The Times*, 7 May 1996, 6.

50 MacMillan, B., *The Times*, 4 April 1994, 40.

51 *Ibid.*

52 *The Times*, 9 Sept. 1997, 3.

53 Grundy, F., *The Times*, 20 March 1996, 5.

54 Bozionelos, N., 'Gender Differences in Attitudes Towards Computers with Organizational and Workplace Implications', *Occupational Psychologist* (26 Aug. 1995), 3–5; Bozionelos, N., 'Computer Anxiety and Negative Attitudes Towards Computers: Issues of no concern for the future', *BPS Annual Conference* (1996), 1–5.

55 *Financial Times* (Education Supplement), 1 July 1996.

56 *Independent* Special Edition, 3 April 1997.

57 *The Times*, 31 July 1996, 7.

58 *Ibid.*

59 *Ibid.*

60 *The Times*, 9 Sept. 1997, 43.

61 *The Times*, 14 July 1997.

62 *Financial Times*, 22 Aug. 1997, 7.

63 *Financial Times*, 15 July 1996, 16.

64 *Ibid.*

65 *Independent* Special Edition, 3 April 1997.

66 *Weekly Telegraph*, 12–18 Nov. 1997, Issue 329.

67 Bray, op. cit., 9.

6 Brainsex III

1 Cooper, C., University of Manchester Institute of Science and Technology, *Financial Times*, 6 Oct. 1995, 10.

2 Brown, G. L., *et al.*, 'CSF Serotonin Metabolite (5-HIAA) Studies in Depression, Impulsivity and Violence', *Journal Clinical Psychiatry* (April 1990), Vol.51 (4), 31–41; Bourgeois, M.,

'Serotonin, Impulsivity and Suicide', *Human Psychopharmacology* (1991), Vol.6, 531–6;. Virkkunen, M., *et al.*,'Brain Serotonin and Violent Behaviour', *Journal of Forensic Psychiatry* (1992), 10–13; Virkkunen, M., *et al.*, 'Serotonin in Alcoholic Violent Offenders', *Ciba Found. Symptoms* (1996), Vol.194, 168–77; Coccaro, E. F., 'Neurotranmitter Correlates of Impulsive Aggression In Humans', *New York Academy of Science* (20 Sept. 1996), Issn 0077-8923.(794), 82–9.

3   Roy, A., *et al.*, 'Acting Out Hostility in Normal Volunteers: Negative correlation with levels of 5H1AA in cerebrospinal fluid', *Psychiatric Research* (1988), Vol.24, 187–94; Hoyenga, K. T., Hoyenga, K.B., *Gender-Related Differences*, Allyn & Bacon (1993), 368–9; *Ibid.*, *Instructor's Manual*, 153–6.

4   Linnoila, M., *et al.*, 'Serotonin, Violent Behavior and Alcohol', *Laboratories of Clinical Studies and Neurogenetics*, Vol.23 (41), 156; Von Knorring, L. L., *et al.*, 'Personality Traits Related to Monamine Oxidase Activity in Platelets', *Psychiatry Research* (1984), Vol.12, 11–26.

5   Ellis, L., 'Monoamine Oxidase and Criminality: Identifying an apparent biological marker for antisocial behavior', *Journal of Research in Crime and Delinquency* (1991), Vol.28 (2), 227–51.

6   Arato, M., 'Serotonergic Interhemispheric Asymmetry; Gender difference in the orbital cortex', *Acta Psychiatrica Scandinavica* (July 1991), Vol.84 (1), 110–111.

7   *Ibid.*

8   Andreason, P.J., *et al.*, 'Gender Related Differences in Regional Cerebral Glucose Metabolism in Normal Volunteers', *Psychiatry Research* (1993), Vol.51, 175–83.

9   Nishizawa, S., *et al.*, 'Differences Between Males and Females in Rates of Serotonin Synthesis in the Human Brain', *Proceedings of the National Academy of Sciences* (1997), Vol.94, 5308–15.

10   Mann, J. J., 'Violence and Aggression', *Psychopharmacology; The Fourth Generation of Progress*, ed. F. E. Bloom and D. J. Kupfer, Raven Press, New York (1995).

11   Bloom, F. E., *Brain, Mind, and Behaviour*, W. H. Freeman and Co (1985, 1988), 208–17, 227–28.

12   *Ibid.*, 214; Zuckerman, M., *Behavioural Expressions and Biosocial Bases of Sensation Seeking*, Cambridge University Press, 1994, 22–4,

301–4.

13 *Ibid.*, 295–305.

14 Zuckerman, M., 'The Psychobiological Model for Impulsive Unsocialized Sensation Seeking: A comparative approach', *Neuropsychobiology* (1996), Vol.34, 125–9; *Behavioural Expressions* ..., 309–11.

15 Zuckerman, *Behavioural Expressions* ..., 298; Ellis, op. cit., 227–51; Bridge, T. P., *et al.*, 'Platelet Monoamine Oxidase Activity: Demographiic characteristics contribution to enzyme activity variability', *Journals of Gerontology* (1995), Vol.40, 23–8.

16 Zuckerman, *Behavioural Expressions* ..., 125–9.

17 *Ibid.*, 297.

18 *Ibid.*

19 *Ibid.*

20 Kruesi, M. J. P. *et al.*, 'Cerebrospinal Fluid Monoamine Metabolite, Aggression, and Impulsivity in Disruptive Behavior Disorders of Children and Adolescents', *Archives General Psychiatry* (May 1990), Vol.47, 419–26; Kruesi, M. J. P., Hibbs, E. D., *et al.*, 'Child Behaviour Disorders/CF/DI', *Archives General Psychiatry* (June 1992), Vol.49 (6), 429–35.

21 Zuckerman, M., interview, documentary series 'Why Men Don't Iron'.

22 Zuckerman, *Behavioural Expressions* ..., 27.

23 *Ibid.*, 100–1.

24 *Ibid.*, 314.

25 Hoyenga, op, cit., 178–9.

26 Zuckerman, *Behavioural Expressions* ..., 375–6.

27 Harlow, W. V., Brown, K. C, *The Role of Risk Tolerance in the Asset Allocation Process: A New Perspective*, Research Foundation of The Institute of Chartered Financial Analysts (1990).

28 Zuckerman, *Behavioural Expressions* ..., 149.

29 *The Times*, 20 Oct. 1997, 45.

30 Mann, op. cit.

31 Hoyenga, op. cit., *Instructor's Manual*, 162–4.

32 Virkkunen, op. cit.(both); Goldman, op. cit.; Brown, op. cit.

33 Whipp, B. J., *et al.*, 'Will Women Soon Outrun Men?', *Nature* (2 Jan. 1992), Vol.355, 25.

34 Wells, C. L., *Women, Sport and Performance: A Physiological*

Perspective, Human Kinetics Books, Ilinois (1991); Overfield, T., *Biologic Variation In Health and Illness, Race, Age and Sex Differences*, CRC Press, 2nd edn (1995), 73–7.

35 Hoyenga, op. cit., 178–9.

36 Overfield, op. cit., 73–7; Holmes, B., 'Titter Ye Not', *New Scientist*, 27 April 1996, 2–3.

37 *The Times*, 30 June 1997, 11.

38 *Ibid..*

39 *The Times*, 16 Feb. 1996.

40 Hoyenga, op. cit., 178–9.

41 Booth, A., *et al.*, 'Testosterone and Winning and Losing Human Competition', *Hormones and Behaviour* (1989), Vol.23, 556–71; Mazur, A., Booth, A., *et al.*, 'Testosterone and Chess Competition', *Social Psychology Quarterly* (1992), Vol.55 (1), 70–7.

42 Dabbs, J. M., 'Age and Seasonal Variation In Serum Testosterone Concentration Among Men', *Chronobiology International* (1990), Vol.7 (3), 245–9.

43 Dabbs, J. M., *et al.*, 'Testosterone, Crime and Misbehavior Among 692 Male Prison Inmates', *Pergamon* (1995), Vol.18 (5), 627–33; Dabbs, J. M., 'Testosterone, Aggression and Delinquency', Second International Androgen Workshop (18–20 Feb. 1995); Booth, A., *et al.*, 'The Influence of Testosterone on Deviance in Adulthood: Assessing and explaining the relationship', *Criminology* (1 Nov. 1993), Vol.31 (1), 93–117.

44 Dabbs, J. M., *et al.*, 'Testosterone and Occupational Choice: Actors, ministers and other men', *Journal of Personality and Social Psychology* (1990), Vol.59 (6), 1261–5.

45 Coccaro, E. F., *et al.*, 'Heritability of Aggression and Irritability: A twin study of the Buss-Durke aggression scales in adult male subjects', *Biological Psychiatry* (1 Feb. 1997), Vol.41 (3), 273–84.

46 Reiss, A. J., *et al.*, *Understanding and Preventing Violence*, National Academy Press, Washington DC (1994), 21–50.

47 Zuckerman, M., interview, documentary series 'Why Men Don't Iron'; Booth, op. cit.; Mazur, op. cit.

48 Booth, op. cit.; Mazur, op. cit.

49 Booth, op. cit.; Mazur, op. cit.; Booth, A., 'Cortisol, Testosterone and Competition Among Women: Hormones in women competitors', In Press.

50 Booth, A., op. cit. 49; Mazur, op. cit..
51 Zuckerman, *Behavioural Expressions* ..., 314–15.
52 Searamella, T., *et al.*, 'Serum Testosterone and Aggressiveness in Hockey Players', *Psychology Medical*, Vol.40, 262–5.
53 TV and Sports, BARB, Jan–Oct. 1996.
54 *The Times*, 14 Jan. 1996.
55 Gur, R. C., *et al.*, 'Sex Differences in Regional Cerebral Glucose Metabolism During a Resting State', *Science* (United States) (27 Jan. 1995, Vol.267 (5197), 528–31.
56 Hoyenga, op cit., 319.
57 Frankenhaeuser, M., 'Psychoneuroendocrine Sex Differences in Adaptation to the Psychosocial Environment', *Clinical Psychoneuroendocrinology in Reproduction*, Academy Press, London, Vol.22 (1978), 215–23; 'Sex Differences in Psychoneuro-endocrine Reactions to Examination Stress', *Psychosomatic Medicine* (June 1978), Vol.40 (4), 334–43; Schmeelk, K. H., Rosenberg, D., *et al.*, 'Gender-Differences in Cognitive-Behavioral Correlates of Adrenocortical Reactivity to Social Challenge', Department of Biobehavioral Health (March 1997); Lundberg, U., 'Sex Differences in Behaviour Pattern and Catecholamine and Cortisol Excretion in 3–6 Year Old Day-Care Children', *Biological Psychology* (1983), Vol.16, 109–117.
58 Hoyenga, op. cit., 319.

7 Extremes Are Not Rules

1 *The Times*, 20 Jan. 1998, 50.
2 Warren W. W., Cole, N. S., 'Gender and Fair Assessment', Lawrence Erlbaum Associates (March/April 1995).
3 British Chess Federation (1998).
4 *Financial Times*, 17 May 1996, 17.
5 *Financial Times*, 29 May 1996, 15.
6 *Ibid.*
7 *Financial Times*, 7 May 1998, 12.
8 'National Earnings Table', from the Office for National Statistics, *Financial Times*, 26 Sept. 1997.
9 *Financial Times*, 18 March 1998, 26.
10 *Financial Times*, 7 May 1998, 12.

11 *The Times*, 19 Nov. 1997, 39.
12 *Globe and Mail*, 16 July 1991, A8.
13 *Financial Times*, 16 Oct. 1997, 13.
14 'Women: Setting New Priorities', Whirlpool Foundation (Jan. 1996).
15 *Financial Times*, 28 Jan. 1997, 10.
16 *Independent*, 12 Oct. 1989.
17 *Ibid.*
18 *Financial Times*, 29/30 Jan. 1997, 7.
19 *Ibid.*
20 *Financial Times*, 29 Jan. 1998), 12.
21 'Equal Opportunities Commission Report', *Financial Times*, 21 Oct. 1997.
22 *Financial Times*, 17 June 1997, 20.
23 *The Quality of Working Life*, Institute of Management and The University of Manchester Institute of Science and Technology, London, (1997).
24 *Financial Times*, 30 April, 1996, 18.
25 'Labour Force Survey', Office for National Statistics (Dec. 1997).
26 Govier, E., 'Sex and Occupation as Markers for Task Performance in a Dichotic Measure of Brain Asymmetry', *International Journal of Psychophysiology* (Dec. 1994), Vol.18 (3), 7–10; Govier, E., 'Brainsex and Occupation', *Gender and Choice in Education and Occupation*, ed. J. Radford, Routledge, London and New York (1998).
27 *Financial Times*, 13 Feb. 1997, 13.
28 *Financial Times*, 22 Oct. 1995, 12.
29 'The Role of the Non-Executive Director', MORI Survey (Oct. 1997).
30 *Financial Times*, 3 June 1997, 16.
31 *Financial Times*, 7/8 June 1997, 4.
32 *Independent* Tabloid, 30 May 1997, 8.
33 *Independent*, 16 June 1997.
34 *Independent* Tabloid, 12 June 1997, 11.
35 'Company and Markets', *Financial Times*, 24/30 June 1977.
36 *Breaking Through the Glass Ceiling: Women in Management*, International Labour Organisation, London (Dec. 1997).
37 *Ibid.*

38 *Financial Times*, 10 Aug. 1996, 8.
39 'Catalyst', *Financial Times*, 15 Sept. 1997, 16.
40 *Financial Times*, 30 March 1995, 12.
41 *The Times*, 20 July 1996, 7.
42 *World's Women: Trends and Statistics*, United Nations (1970–1990).
43 Press release, Dun & Bradstreet, 16 June 1997.
44 *Financial Times*, 16 June, 1997; *Independent*, 16 June 1997; *Independent on Sunday*, 22 June 1997.
45 *Breaking Through the Glass Ceiling*.
46 *Financial Times*, 15 Sept. 1997, 16.
47 'Women as Directors Workshop: Programme Overview', Cranfield University School of Management (Aug. 1997).
48 *Financial Times*, 2/3 Nov. 1996, XI.
49 *The Times*, 6 Oct. 1997, 8.
50 *Financial Times*, 9 Feb. 1998, 14.
51 McGinn C., *Times Literary Supplement*, 20 March 1998, 13.
52 *Financial Times*, 21 Jan. 1998, 8.

8 Painting Him Green

1 Zimmerman, M., *Contesting Earth's Future*, 1996.
2 Warren, K. J. (ed.), *Ecological Feminist Philosophies* (Indiana University Press, 1996), 24.
3 *Ibid.*, 26.
4 Adams, C. J., 'Ecofeminism and the Eating of Animals', *Ibid.*, 115.
5 Curtin, D., 'Toward an Ecological Ethic of Care', 76–7.
6 Sessions, R., 'Deep Ecology versus Ecofeminism', *Ibid.*, 142.
7 *Ibid.*
8 Kimbrell, A., *The Masculine Mystique: The Politics of Masculinity*, Ballantine Books, New York, 1995.
9 *Ibid.*, 31, 75, 304, 306, 313, 318.
10 *Financial Times*, 3 May 1996, 29.
11 *Prima* (Sept. 1995), 19–20.
12 Henry Doubleday Association leaflet, 1994.
13 *Garden News*, 24 April 1996, 30.
14 *Financial Times*, 9 Oct. 1990.
15 *Financial Times*, 20 Sept. 1997, 11.
16 *Financial Times*, 25 Jan. 1991, 28.

17 Adiscott, T. M., Whitmore, A. P., Powlson, D. S., *Farming, Fertilisers and Nitrate Problems*, CAB International (1992).

18 *Financial Times*, 10 April 1996.

19 *The Times*, 25 Aug. 1993, 3.

20 *Financial Times*, 11 Aug. 1994.

21 Maitland, A., 'The Wheat from the Chaff', *Financial Times*, 17 Oct. 1996, 19.

22 Tallis, R., *Neutron's Sleep*, Macmillan, London (1995).

23 Prola, M., letter to *The Times*, 30 Dec. 1997.

24 *The Times*, survey on complementary medicine, 5 July 1995, 20.

25 Adams, J., *Risk*, UCL Press, London (1995).

26 Blacke-Lee Harwood, Press Officer for Friends of the Earth, 6 Nov. 1996.

27 *Financial Times*, 21 Oct. 1996, 40.

28 *The Times*, 18 Oct. 1996, 17.

29 *The Times*, 19 Sept. 1991.

9 Sex

1 Buss, D. M., *The Evolution of Desire: Strategies of Human Mating*, HarperCollins, London (1994), 84–5.

2 Spivey, N., *Understanding Greek Sculpture*, Thames & Hudson, London, (1996).

3 Hoyenga, K. B., Hoyenga, K. T., *Gender-Related Differences*, Allyn & Bacon (1993), 387.

4 *Ibid., Instructor's Manual*, 187.

5 *Ibid.*

6 *Ibid.*, 188.

7 *Ibid.*, 387; Dabbs, J. M., 'Age and Seasonal Variation In Serum Testosterone Concentration Among Men', *Chronobiology International* (1990), Vol.7 (3), 245–9.

8 Hoyenga, op. cit., *Instructor's Manual*, 188.

9 Thiessen, D., 'Hormonal Correlates of Sexual Aggression', *Crime in Biological, Social and Moral Contexts*, ed. L. Ellis and H. Hoffman, Praeger, New York (1991), 153–61.

10 Dabbs, op. cit.

11 Hoyenga, op. cit., *Instructor's Manual*, 18.

12 Thiessen, op. cit., 154; Hoyenga, op. cit., 188.

13 Thiessen, op. cit., 156–8.

14 *Ibid.*, 155; Ellis, L., 'Monoamine Oxidase and Criminality: Identifying an apparent biological marker for antisocial behavior', *Journal of Research in Crime and Delinquency* (1991), Vol.28 (2), 227–51; Hoffman, op. cit., 155.

15 Ellis, L., 'Evidence of Neuroandrogenic Etiology of Sex Roles from a Combined Analysis of Human, Nonhuman Primate and Nonprimate Mammalian Studies', *Personal and Individual Differences* (1986), Vol.7 (4), 525.

16 *Ibid.*, 536.

17 Daly, M. *et al.*, *Homeside*, Aldyne de Gruyler (1998), 196–205.

18 Panksepp, J., *The Foundations of Human and Animal Emotions*, Oxford University Press, New York: In Press.

19 Melis, M., 'Dopamine and Sexual Behaviour', *Neuroscience Biobehavioural Reviews* (1995), Vol.19 (1), 19.

20 *Ibid.*, 32.

21 Panksepp, op. cit.

22 *Ibid.*

23 *Ibid.*

24 Cowley, J. J., et al., 'Human Exposure to Putative Pheromones and Changes in Aspects of Social Behaviour', *Journal of Steroid Biochemistry and Molecular Biology* (Oct. 1991), Vol.39 (4B)., 647–59.

25 *New Scientist*, 7 Sept. 1996.

26 Irvine, S., *The World Market for Fragrances*, Euromonitor, London (1997).

27 *Ibid.*, 73–6.

28 Irvine, S., 'On The Scent of Liquid Gold', *Financial Times*, 26 Nov. 1995, 'How To Spend It', 66–8.

29 Van Der Post, L., 'The Sweet Smell of an Event', *Financial Times*, 4/5 May 1996, V.

30 Irvine, S., 'Fragrance is a Feminist Issue', *Financial Times*, 23 Nov. 1996, 'How To Spend It', 73–6.

31 *The Times*, 8 May 1996, 16.

32 Buss, op. cit., 60–1.

33 Hoyenga, op. cit., 378–80.

34 Survey by *Newsweek*, reported in *The Times*, 29 May 1996, 12.

35 Buss, op. cit., 57–9.

36 *Ibid.*, 58.
37 *Financial Times*, 14/15 Sept. 1996, III.
38 Latham, A., *Crazy Sundays*, Secker & Warburg, London (1975), 154.
39 *The Times*, 13 Sept. 1995, 6.
40 *Economist*, 14 Feb. 1998.
41 *The Times*, 15 March 1996, 9.
42 *Economist*, 14 Feb. 1998.
43 British Public Opinion MORI Poll (July 1996), 6.
44 Howitt, D., 'Pornography and the Paedophile: Is it criminogenic?', *British Journal of Medical Psychology* (March 1995), Vol.68 (1), 15–27.
45 Flor, H. P., *et al.*, 'Quantitative EEG Studies of Pedophilia', *International Journal Psychophysiology* (Jan. 1991), Vol.10 (3), 253–8.
46 Langevin, R., 'Sexual Sadism: Brain, Blood and Behavior', *Annals of the New York Academy of Sciences* (1988), Vol.528, 163–71.
47 Brannigan, A., 'Obscenity and Social Harm: A contested terrain', *International Journal Law Psychiatry* (1991), Vol.14 (1–2), 1–12; Cramer, E., *et al.*, 'Pornography and Abuse of Women', *Public Health Nursing* (Aug. 1994), Vol.11 (4), 268–72; Fukui, A., Westmore, B., 'To See or Not to See: The debate over pornography and its relationship to sexual aggression', *Australian & New Zealand Journal of Psychiatry* (Dec. 1994), Vol.28 (4), 600–6.
48 Raine, A., *The Psychopathology of Crime, Criminal Behavior as a Clinical Disorder*, Academic Press (1993).
49 Moir, A., Jessel, D., *A Mind To Crime*, Michael Joseph, London (1995).
50 *Maclean's*, 23 June 1997, 44.
51 Zuckerman, M., *Behavioural Expressions and Biosocial Bases of Sensation Seeking*, Cambridge University Press, 1994.
52 *Ibid.*, 186.
53 *Ibid.*, 144–45.
54 *Ibid.*, 122.
55 Symons, D., *The Evolution of Human Sexuality*, Oxford University Press (1979).
56 Koukounas, E., 'Habituation and Dishabituation of Male Sexual Arousal', *Behavioral Research Therapy* (July 1993), Vol.31 (6),

575–85.

57 Tough, S.C., *et al.*, 'Autoerotic Asphyxial Deaths: Analysis of nineteen fatalities in Alberta', *Journal Psychiatry* (April 1994), Vol.39 (3), 157–60.

58 *The Times*, 20 June 1996.

59 Moir, op. cit., 228.

60 *The Times*, 20 March 1998, 23.

61 *The Times*, 23 March 1998, 18.

62 Young, C., 'How Typical is Sally?', *Times Literary Supplement*, 29 May 1995.

63 Cabell, S., *Contesting Tears: The Hollywood Melodrama of the Unknown Woman*, University of Chicago Press (1997).

10 The Real New Man

1 *The Times*, 22 Jan. 1998, 2.

2 Wolf, M., *Financial Times*, 12 Sept. 1994.

3 UK Charity Survey, 'Care for the Family' (June 1995).

4 *Financial Times*, 14 Oct., 1997, 20.

5 Hoyenga, K. B., Hoyenga, K.T., *Gender-Related Differences*, Allyn & Bacon (1993), 298–307.

6 National Report by Government of Sweden, *Shared Power Responsibility* (1995), 12.

7 *Daily Mail*, 21 Oct. 1992.

8 Kimball, R., 'More Equal Than Others', *Times Literary Supplement*, 17 Jan. 1997, 24.

9 *Independent*, 30 May 1997.

10 *Independent*, 15 Jan. 1996, 2.

11 *Leisure Futures*, Vol.1. (1996), 25–6.

12 *Financial Times*, 30 Jan. 1996, 7.

13 Pooley, C., University of Lancaster, *The Times*, 8 Jan. 1998, 10.

14 Survey by Relate, *The Times*, 12 Feb. 1996, 9.

15 Survey by *Top Sant* in conjunction with BUPA, *The Times*, 10 Feb. 1998, 4.

16 'What Women Want in the 1990s', Nationwide Building Society for *Cosmopolitan* (Dec. 1989).

17 Survey of 10,000 people, Henley Centre for Forecasting (Feb. 1990).

18 *Leisure Futures* (1996), 25.

19 *Financial Times*, 29 Jan. 1998, 12.

20 Office of National Statistics, quoted in *Financial Times*, Jan. 1998.

21 Gershunny, J., 'The British Household Panel Survey', University of Essex for the Social Research Council, 1991–1995, *The Times*, 8 Sept. 1997, 12.

22 *Financial Times*, 7 Oct. 1997, 9.

23 *The Times*, 17 March 1998, 17.

24 Valian, V., 'Why So Slow?', *The Advancement of Women*, MIT Press, (1998).

25 Cappuccini, G., to the British Psychological Society Conference, Strathclyde University, *Independent*, 18 Nov. 1996.

26 'On Sexual Equality, We Should Agree to Differ', *Independent*, 2 July 1997, 19.

27 Survey by 'Catalyst', *Financial Times*, 13 June 1997, 12.

28 Benn, M., *Madonna and Child: Towards a New Politics of Motherhood*, Jonathan Cape, London (1998).

29 OPST, Eurostat (March 1996).

30 Silverman, E. M., 'The Hunter-Gatherer Theory of Spatial Sex Differences: Proximate Factors Mediating The Female Advantage In Recall of Object Arrays', *Ethology Sociobiology* (1994), Vol.15., 95–105; McGuinness. D., 'Sex Differences in Incidental Recall for Words and Pictures', *Learning and Individual Differences* (1990), Vol.2 (3), 263–85.

31 Hoyenga, K. B., Hoyenga, K.T., personal communication.

32 O'Boyle, W. M., *et al.*, 'Gender and Handedness Differences In Mirror-Tracing Random Forms', *Neuropsychologia* (1987), 1–6.

33 O'Boyle, W. M., documentary *Brainsex*, Discovery Channel, (Nov. 1991).

34 Lempert, H., *et al.*, 'The Effect of Visual Guidance and Hemispace on Lateralized Vocal-Manual Interference', *Neuropsychologia* (1985), Vol.23 (5), 691–5.

35 'Why Men Don't Iron', documentary series, Channel 4.

36 *Financial Times*, 10 August 196, 16.

37 'Women and Animals First', *New Scientist*, 24 Feb. 1996.

38 Gur, R. C., 'Sex Differences in Regional Cerebral Glucose Metabolism During a Resting State', *Science* (27 Jan. 1995), Vol.267, 528–31.

39 *The Times*, 29 May 1997, 15.

40 Arato, M., *et al.*, 'Serotonergin Interhemispheric Asymmetry: Gender difference in the orbital cortex', *Acta Psychiatrical Scandanavia* (July 1991), Vol.84 (1), 110–11.

41 Allen, L. S., *et al.*, 'Sexual Dimorphism of the Anterior Commissure and Massa Intermedia of the Human Brain', *Journal Complete Neurology* (1 Oct. 1991), Vol.312 (1), 97–104.

42 Baker, M. A.,'Sensory Functioning', *Differences in Human Performance*, ed. M. A. Baker, John Wiley & Sons (1987), 11–13; McGuiness, D., *When Children Don't Learn*, Basic Books, New York (1985), 157–62.

43 Baker, op. cit., 6–10; McGuinness, op. cit., 77–80.

44 McGuinness, op. cit., 80.

45 Baker, op. cit., 22–6.

46 *bid.*, 21–2.

47 McGuinness, op. cit., 90.

48 Noller, P., 'Sex Differences in Non Verbal Communication: Advantages lost or supremacy regained', *Australian Journal of Psychology* (1986), Vol.38, 23–32; Wagner, H. L., *et al.*, 'Communication of Specific Emotions: Gender differences in sending accuracy and communication measures', *Journal of Nonverbal Behaviour* (Spring 1993), Vol.17 (1), 29–53; Morgado, I. A., *et al.*, 'Accuracy of Decoding Facial Expresions in Those Engaged in People Oriented Activities vs Those Engaged in Non People Oriented Activities', *Studia Psychologica* (1993), Vol.35 (1), 73–80.

49 Skuse, D.H., *et al.*, "Evidence From Turner's Syndrome of an Imprinted X-Linked Locus Affecting Cognitive Function', *Nature* (12 June 1997), Vol.387, 705.

50 Erwin, R. J., *et al.*, 'Facial Emotion Discrimination: Task construction and behavioral findings in normal subjects', *Psychiatry Research, Ireland* (June 1992), Vol.42 (3), 231–40.

51 Wood, W., *et al.*, 'Sex Differences in Positive Well-being: A consideration of emotional style and marital status', *Psychological Bulletin* (1989), Vol.106, 249–64.

52 George, M. S., *et al.*, 'Gender Differences in Regional Cerebral Blood Flow During Transient Self-Induced Sadness or Happiness', *Society of Biological Psychiatry* (1996), 869–71.

53 Booth, A., Dabbs, J. M., 'Testosterone and Men's Marriages', *Social Forces* (Dec. 1993), Vol.72 (2), 463–77.

54 *Ibid.*, 472.

55 Ellis, L., 'Evidence of Neuroandrogenic Etiology of Sex Roles from a combined Analysis of Human, Nonhuman Primate and Nonprimate Mammalian Studies', *Personal and Individual Differences* (1986), Vol.7 (4), 519–52.

56 Holmes, B., 'Titter Ye Not', *New Scientist*, Supplement, 27 April 1996, 3–5.

57 *Ibid.*, 3.

58 Olweus, D., *et al.*, 'Circulating Testosterone Levels and Aggression in Adolescent Males: A causal analysis', *Psychosomatic Medicine* (1988), Vol.50, 269.

59 *Ibid.*, 270.

60 Burgess, A., *Fatherhood Reclaimed: The Making of the Modern Father*, Vermilion (1997).

61 Hoyenga, op. cit., *Instructors Manual*, 141; Larsson, K., 'The Psychobiology of Parenting in Mammals', *Scandinavian Journal of Psychology* (1994), Vol.35, 131.

62 Pederson, C. A., Caldwell, J. D., Jirikowki, G. F. Insel, T. R., *Oxytocin in Maternal, Sexual, and Social Behaviors*, New York Academy of Sciences, New York (1992); Krasnegor, N. A. (ed.), *Mammalian Parenting*, Oxford University Press (1990).

63 Rosenblatt, J. S., 'Landmarks in the Physiological Study of Maternal Behavior with Special Reference to the Rat', *Mammalian Parenting*, 40–60; Keverne, E. B., 'Psychopharmacology of Maternal Behaviour', *Journal of Psychopharmacology* (1996), Vol.10.(1), (1996), 16–62.

64 Panksepp, J., 'The Foundations of Human and Animal Emotions', Oxford University Press, New York, In Press.

65 Hoyenga, op. cit.; *Instructor's Manual*, 79–82.

66 Uvnäs-Moberg, K., 'Neuroendocrinology of the Mother-Child Interaction', *Trends in Endocrinology and Metabolism*, Vol.7 (4) (1996), 126–31.

67 Keverne, op. cit.

68 Pedersen, C. A., *et al.*, 'Oxytocin Activation of Maternal Behavior in the Rat', *Oxytocin in Maternal, Sexual and Social Behaviors*, 58; Larsson, op. cit., 107.

69 Panksepp, op. cit.
70 Uvnäs-Moberg, K., *et al.*, 'The Relationships Between Personality Traits and Plasma Gastrin, Cholecystokinin, Somatostatin, Insulin and Oxytocin Levels in Healthy Women', *Journal of Psychosomatic Research* (1993), Vol.37 (6), 581–8.
71 *Ibid.*; Uvnäs-Moberg, op. cit. (1996).
72 Widström, A.M., *et al.*, 'Short-Term Effects of Early Suckling and Touch of the Nipple on Maternal Behaviour', *Early Human Development* (1990), Vol.21, 153–63.
73 Panksepp, op. cit.
74 *Ibid.*
75 Larsson, op. cit., 123; Leon, M., 'The Neurobiology of Filial Learning', *Annual Review Psychology* (1992), Vol.43, 377–98.
76 See Chapter 5, note 7.
77 Motluk, A., 'The Big Chill', *New Scientist*, Supplement, 27 April 1996, 17–19.
78 *Ibid.*
79 *Ibid.*; Panksepp, J., 'Oxytocin Effects on Emotional Processes: Separation distress and social bonding, relationships to psychiatric disorders', *Annals of the Academy of Science* (1992), Vol.652, 243–52.
80 Waltors, N., *The New Feminism*, Little, Brown (1998).
81 *The Times*, 8 May 1998.

Index